Capitalism and Religion in World History

Purity condemns filth; piety disparages corruption. Amassing riches offered to a transcendental world, the priests of ancient faiths found themselves trapped in a contradiction. By loaning out their resources to merchants, they made themselves pariahs to true prophets. Before Islam squared the circle, bringing capital mobility and credit creation into coexistence with devotion, religion stymied merchant capitalism. Spread through trade, Islam's innovations in commerce soothed the path for the coexistence of credit and faith globally. Had a second form of capitalism—technological capitalism—not emerged, binding science to innovation, harmony between faith and capitalism would have prevailed. However, scientific advances depend on empirical evidence that is buttressed by critical debate, which is anathema to powerful elites in countries saturated with religious nationalism. Consequently, easy cooperation between capitalism and religion is blocked in these lands, and so their potential for economic progress withers. Thus, many of these states, trapped in the invidious stranglehold of religion, are condemned to sustained poverty.

Carl Mosk is Emeritus Professor at the University of Victoria, Canada.

T0382946

Routledge Studies in Modern History
https://www.routledge.com/history/series/MODHIST

Capitalism and Religion in World History

Purification and progress

Carl Mosk

Routledge
Taylor & Francis Group

LONDON AND NEW YORK

First published 2018 by Routledge

2 Park Square, Milton Park, Abingdon, Oxfordshire OX14 4RN
52 Vanderbilt Avenue, New York, NY 10017

Routledge is an imprint of the Taylor & Francis Group, an informa business

First issued in paperback 2019

British Library Cataloguing in Publication Data
A catalogue record for this book is available from the British Library

Library of Congress Cataloging in Publication Data
A catalog record for this book has been requested

ISBN: 978-1-138-30349-2 (hbk)
ISBN: 978-0-367-34895-3 (pbk)

Typeset in sabon
by Deanta Global Publishing Services, Chennai, India

For Asher, Lilya, and Torin

Contents

x   *Contents*

Figures

Tables

Preface

I have always believed taking risks is admirable. This book is a perfect example. It grapples with a vast topic; yet it is short, succinct, to the point.

Its tapestry encompasses a protracted sweep of human history going back as it does to the Neolithic revolution. It treats monotheistic, polytheistic, even godless religions as ideologies. It defines capitalism as a two-headed ideology that conflicted with ancient religions of all stripes. It explains why one Middle Eastern religion, Islam, pioneered faith consistent with one type of capitalism—merchant capitalism—spurring on a global spread in merchant capitalist ideology, demonstrating convincingly why religion and credit creation are not irreconcilable. It embraces paradox, pointing out that a second form of capitalism—technological capitalism—is less likely to be compatible with religion, particularly when it serves as a crucial pillar for modern nationalism.

In short, this volume invites controversy. Scholars specializing on ancient Confucianism, Greek philosophy, Judaism, medieval society, seventh-century natural philosophy, Marxism, neo-classical economics and contemporary nationalism may well take me to task for straying into their bailiwicks. All I ask, by way of defense, is for a chance to convince you to hear me out. Accept, reject, or consider me ill-advised if you wish, but please listen.

Ideologies are crucial to societies. One of the deficiencies within mainstream economics is its failure to incorporate ideology into analysis. Still, one of the truths of mainstream economics sometimes ignored by those overly impressed with the power of ideologies is heterogeneity, diversity of opinions and attitudes. Within an ideology are many mansions. A crucial facet of an ideology is its "big tent" character, housing as it does a variety of factions under its canopy. Mainstream economics also focuses on practical results: production and distribution of material goods and services. Ideologies are about ideas. However, to be viable as motivators of behavior, ideologies must provide avenues fitted with road signs guiding and channeling the messy practical world of humdrum human agency. Absent this, they are nothing more than theories. But abstruse theories primarily of interest to intellectual elites—philosophers, poets, antiquarians—offer little practical significance. The material world cannot be ignored. Emphasizing the interaction of materialism and idealism operating under the umbrella of a trenchant ideological framework is a major theme in this study.

Adding to the controversial nature of this volume are definitions. Consider religion. For the purposes of this study, religion is defined as purification buttressed by faith. Purification operates in three ways: it defines what is ritually acceptable and what is taboo; it guides attitudes towards right and wrong; it determines political status, defining who is considered the most and the least pure. Note that nothing is said about God or gods or heaven or hell or an afterlife with this definition. Monotheism and polytheism are both compatible with this definition. So is classical Confucianism with its emphasis on the Mandate of Heaven; equally compatible are certain forms of Buddhism viewed as atheistic by some. Ideal types are ruled out. Religious ideologies are treated as "big tent" phenomena. The common element running through all religions is belief in a transcendental reality, contact with that reality conferring purity. Armed with this definition it proves possible to grapple with the compatibility of religion and capitalism in a global context.

What about capitalism? I define it as capital mobility buttressed by credit creation. With this definition, it is possible to see Communism as State Capitalism; the market oriented American variety as capitalism with far less state intervention, for radical libertarians the less the better. In formulating this approach to analyzing capitalism I reject other commonly understood ways of understanding capitalism. For instance: I do not associate it with private property and profits; I do not associate it with individualism; I do not associate it with freedom from government interference in the affairs of the citizenry; I do not associate it with exploitation of workers; I do not associate it with Western values—an error made by Max Weber, whose writings nonetheless remain one of the pinnacles in the field; I do not find it surprising that capitalism is fully compatible with group oriented societies like Japan or China; or highly individualistic societies like the United States.

I argue capitalism comes in two distinct forms. Like Janus, it has two distinct faces, as it were. One is merchant capitalism, which emerged in the seventh century in Mecca and Medina. The second face is technological capitalism, which emerged in Western Europe. I argue that this latter form is tied up with science, patents, precision machinery, and an obsession with efficiency in the employment of resources, both human and material. Squandering energy in all forms is anathema. These two faces of capitalism are frequently at war with one another. Moreover, I believe some societies downplay technological capitalism while embracing merchant capitalism. Examples are societies in which religion serves as a major pillar for nationalism. These are two crucial points I attempt to drive home in this book.

To repeat: this is a short book on a vast topic. What justifies the approach I use here is my thesis, which motivates my choice of examples. It is the guidepost for the organization of this volume. Hence why this study reaches back to the ancient world and across a global landscape. This is the reason why the reader will find within it rich diversity. Without an overriding thesis the disparate topics treated here—ancient Greek theater; Roman military activity; Japanese feudalism; the struggle between Arian and Nicene schools of Christianity; the debates between the Newtonians and Cartesians; the surprising and wholly unintended impact of steam engine construction upon breakthroughs in scientific theory, namely upon the First Law of Thermodynamics; the constraints imposed upon the flourishing of modern capitalism by religious nationalism; the existence of religious traps hampering economic development and fomenting civil unrest—would be like so much flotsam adrift in the open seas.

Acknowledgements

I have benefitted from the criticisms and opinions of colleagues too numerous to adequately acknowledge in these pages. That said, I would like to draw attention to persons who have been unusually helpful.

In Victoria David Giles was kind enough to carry out econometric analysis that I make use of in this volume. Cornelius (Kees) van Kooten did yeoman service as a verbal critic, one who took seriously my research focus while disagreeing with my conclusions, peppering my seminar presentations with incisive dissent. As well Merwan Engineer enlivened the seminars that served as stepping stones to the writing of this book, offering trenchant observations and objections. Visiting from England where she teaches at Cambridge University, Sheilagh Ogilvie gave me valuable feedback both verbal and written.

At a distance transmitted through the wizardry of the internet, other scholars provided valuable comments. Stanley Engerman was kind enough to offer extensive and supportive written comments on several versions of this manuscript. Peter Lindert, Peter Temin, Deirdre McCloskey, and J. Mark Ramseyer commented on various papers that found their way into sections of the present text.

Lastly, I would like to acknowledge my two greatest debts. One is owed Robert Langham, editor at Routledge who has been incredibly generous toward me and my authoring endeavors. Rob and I met sixteen years ago in Victoria. It was with his encouragement that I joined the family of Routledge authors. The other—my greatest debt—is to my wife Donna: devoted wife; dearest friend; faithful companion.

Part I

Predation, purification, and prices

Prologue
Fire

Our humanity is deeply entrenched in fashioning and organizing symbols.[1]

Deriving these symbols from the animate and inanimate objects—from the desiderata—populating the material world we transform perceptions into mental concepts. We string concepts together, linking one symbol to another, creating ideas. Pushing through onto a path to growing complexity we arrive at ideal systems. Something as simple as differentiating one from two, two from three, involves a profound conceptual leap. Line up stones; count sheep; cut trees in half. Something as compelling as contemplating "one-ness" and "two-ness" constitutes a solid foundation upon which an idealized system—the integers—can be formulated. Of course, we know it doesn't stop there. Fractions, negative numbers, square roots of integers, square roots of negative numbers, various types of infinity, all these constructs have been spun out from a handful of integers.

I do not pretend to have an informed opinion about how we as humans accomplish this feat. Some people believe the mind is a blank slate, absorbing empirical information, conjuring up concepts later. Others take the opposite view: a baby's brain already has much in it that is intrinsic, hardwired so to speak. It is suggested learning to speak a language is an example of hardwiring; again, some scholars argue that the ability to discount present satisfaction in anticipation of greater future rewards is intrinsic.

My invoking the relationship between the material world and the world of ideas stems from a completely different agenda. In these pages, I argue that ideas and material forces interact in shaping economic, political, and religious behavior. In particular, I argue modern capitalism has emerged through a complex interaction with religion. Capitalism consists of a bundle of ideas and material outcomes; religion consists of a bundle of ideas and material outcomes. These bundles are ideologies, two of the most important ideologies shaping the modern world. The clash—or avoidance of clash—between the two bundles in the world of ideas, in the arena of material reality, informs history.

Consider fire. We cook with it. We combine chunks of beef marbled with fat, fresh carrots, cloves, onions, herbs, slowly simmering in an iron pot that draws heat from a fire redolent with the fragrance of burning wood.

We roast a pig, rotating it on a spit, blood-stained oils spilling out over a charcoal infused hearth itself the product of fire. We cast iron ingots in the heat of fire, we clear forests with controlled blazes, we spread the ashes of fires once ravaging our woodlands for future use. We employ blistering fires to manufacture glass. We mold clay into ingeniously contrived shapes over flames. Fire literally illuminates our lives: before electricity candlelight was our dearest friend, allowing us to read, quilt, or play music on dark nights. We savor the warm embrace of a crackling wood fire on a crisp winter day: the fragrance, the subtle heat, cocoons us. We cremate bodies in fire. It was fitting for a Greek hero that his or her corpse was consumed in fire. It was considered far better to revere the dead thus than to consign their remarks to dark, dank, cold dirt.

To be sure, fire can be an implacable enemy. We build watchtowers to look out for its withering spread. We shoot arrows emblazoned with fiery torches, slaying our enemies in battle. We dispatch terror with it; we torture with it. In the medieval era, burning at the stake was designed to send horrific messages to the masses. Commit heresy, you may be next. Be careful of the company you keep. There are those who will walk on fiery coals to demonstrate their fortitude. We oscillate being admiring their holy fortitude and consigning them to the ranks of the mad.

As well fire is in the mind, a potent idea, a springboard for narratives, a metaphor for the sacred and the mundane alike. It is said Hades is bathed in flames. It is said a person has a fiery temperament. It is said a prophet is enraptured in holy fire; that he is illuminated in a blaze of divinity. Distant stars are said to explode in great balls of searing flames. In a pitched battle, you seek colleagues emboldened by fiery passion to protect your back. Prometheus is said to have challenged Olympus by bringing knowledge of how to usefully employ fire to humanity. Fire is symbolic of purification. In the ancient world burnt-offerings of animals slaughtered by priests were said to satisfy transcendental deities. The horse sacrifice was a pinnacle of sacred offering in the Vedic literature; the red heifer in ancient Judaism. People are purified in fire. But they are also baptized in water, which brings fire to its knees, dissipating its fury.

Ideas and material forces are crucial. They interact. Their conjoining drives history. This assumption, this premise, motivates the narrative of this book. Like the Roman god Janus this book draws its inspiration from a face gazing in two seemingly distinct directions.

Note

1 For the importance of symbolism in shaping ideologies see Becker (1973), Bellah (2011), and Deacon (1997). Becker argues that two psychological conditions peculiar to humanity—denial of death, difficulty accepting physical limitations of our bodies (e.g. embarrassment about urinating, defecating, embracing the materialism of sexual intercourse, menstruating)—underpin ideologies like religion. That fear of death cements the hold of religion among a wide range of cultures

is widespread in the literature on religion. After all transcendental pure worlds invoked by religion—Heaven; hell; deities who never age, become infirm, or perish; the existence of a haven of never-ending, absolute goodness—all dispense with human finitude. Denial of dying certainly can help explain why religion remains a potent factor in the twenty-first century within predominantly secular societies. See, for instance, Hitchens (2007). Hitchens, a vocal atheist highly critical of religion, nevertheless accepted denial of death as crucial to the perpetuation of religion in an age when scientific knowledge appears to call into question the validity of religious doctrines of all stripes.

1 Idealism and materialism in economic history

Janus

Over many decades I have labored under a fascination with the god Janus. Janus is an unusual Roman god, a rootless orphan, lacking a pedigree, finding no parallel, in the Greek pantheon. Fanciful to be sure, rampant speculation might say the Romans conjured him up out of haughty patriotism: "see, we were beholden to you Greeks for your past achievements, but past is past. We, not you, represent the future." Janus, head bifurcated, gazing simultaneously to the right and left, taking in both past and future in a single sweep seems to impishly claim to enjoy two very disjointed worlds. Drawing upon the past he foretells the future. He is ancient; he is modern.

Perhaps Janus simply fascinates me because I am a scholar. As a scholar, I struggle to keep up in a field peppered with freshly minted academic publications: present research harkening to the future. Yet I never forget that what seems novel, what is claimed to be strikingly innovative today, often as not is little more than a rehash of an older literature. More to the point, I have come to realize that some century-old scholarly debates linger on, perhaps clothed in fresh finery, undoubtedly invigorated by more recent advances, technical and conceptual, yet not so remarkably different in substance.

Weber and Marx

Take the famous intellectual clash between followers of Karl Marx and Max Weber, between so-called materialists and so-called idealists grappling with the relationship between capitalism and religion. [1]

Let me simplify the two opposing positions.

Both Marx and Weber were trying to explain the same thing: the emergence of powerful merchant groups during the seventeenth and early eighteenth centuries who acquired vast fortunes through global trade and diligent management of domestic resources—time, money, and political connections—paving the way for the first industrial revolution. Particularly successful in the transition from the mercantilism of the seventeenth century to the industrial revolution were the countries steeped in Calvinism, notably

Puritan England that emerged as the technological and international trade dynamo of the period 1750 to 1850.

Writing in the mid-nineteenth century, Marx argued that the transition from mercantilism to industrialization was driven by the primitive accumulation of capital. Under feudalism, avaricious merchants accumulating capital managed to undermine feudal class relations, commercializing associations rooted in hierarchical obligations. On feudal estates, military overlords extracted labor services from the serfs and peasants tied to their land. Successful merchants—acting as commercial intermediaries between urban artisans producing luxuries consumed by the manorial overlords—built financial empires.

As Europe ventured out into global oceanic trade under the aegis of mercantilism, powerful merchant houses acquired monopolies granted by monarchs vigorously competing against one another in politically fragmented Europe. Establishing colonies in the New World, seizing oceanic trade routes, merchant companies chartered by crown governments exploited African slaves in amassing ever greater wealth. Capitalism emerged. To Marx, who believed materialistic forces embodied in technological change and changing class relations, the religious beliefs of the Protestant merchants were part and parcel of their "class consciousness," their collective identity as it were. The political superstructure was erected on the backs of the material substructure. As merchants commercialized rural life, they forced a reorganization of farming, promoting enclosures of land, driving off the impoverished peasantry who subsisted on the margins of the great estates, on the common land. Feeding off their economic exploitation of slaves laboring abroad in colonial possessions and a growing domestic proletariat driven off the fields, the class of merchants aggrandized power. Ultimately, they funded revolutions dismantling decentralized feudalism, replacing it with bourgeois democracy which took the form of nation-states. Capitalism and democracy were inextricably linked. The exploitation of serfs crucial to feudalism was replaced by exploitation of the proletariat under capitalism by capitalists steadfastly devoted to the accumulation of capital, oblivious to the long-term consequences of social stability. Under capitalism, merchants and entrepreneurs extracted surplus value over and above socially defined subsistence wages paid to downtrodden workers, echoing the mechanisms by which their feudal predecessors extracted labor services under feudalism.

Just as feudalism was shattered by accumulation of capital in the hands of merchants, so would capitalism eventually give way to socialism, finally to stateless communism, ultimately handing political power to the mass of wage workers. Capitalism would be destroyed by its inherent instability. Willy-nilly, capitalists continue accumulating capital, particularly fixed capital that displaced workers as mechanization proceeded apace. Workers would be made redundant by the force of accumulation. Thrown out of employment, automated out of jobs, they would ultimately have no other choice but revolution. Key to achieving this great political transformation was the development of working class consciousness, a realization that they were being exploited diffusing its way through the rank and file proletariat.

Noting that established churches in the Protestant countries were justifying nascent capitalism on religious grounds, Marx denounced Christianity itself. Arguing religion is the opiate of the masses, he maintained that its seductive appeal to the downtrodden lay in the dismal reality of lives barren of hope. Religion infused visions—visions of a future paradise in which the poor garner justice, embracing purity while the mighty of the world are brought low, suffering cruel physical punishments in purgatory or consumed by the fires of hell; visions of an afterlife in a more elevated caste; visions of immaterial enlightenment sweeping away the dark, bitter reality that is in essence nothing but illusion; following the golden rule, worshipping your ancestors through elaborate rites and rituals, embracing virtue despite wallowing in poverty—these are smokescreens preventing the proletariat from facing the reality of their economic oppression, throwing up barriers to the forging of revolutionary class consciousness. Religion must be opposed. By impeding the flourishing of working class consciousness, it slows down the inevitable overthrow of heartless capitalism. Under classless communism, ushered when workers seized power, religion become superfluous. It is no longer needed since the blinders have been pulled off the eyes of the workers. Religion should be done away with; it is an enemy of progress. Fighting it goes hand in hand with revolutionary political struggle.

To those convinced by Weber's vision, ideas channeled through social institutions shape economic activity. Religious ideas—recognized as a key cornerstone of culture broadly conceived, every community on the planet making use of them in some way—are crucial to historical change. Whether societies embrace long run economic development or flounder along the path of successfully economic achievement is viewed as cultural. It was in the European West that the right complexion of ideas took hold. The crux of this ideology is remarkably simple: make a virtue out of saving and of working tirelessly and assiduously; accumulate financial resources that can be invested in physical capital; worship efficiency; be as thrifty as possible with the time granted a person on earth; imbibe a doctrine declaring "time is money", eschewing the expenditure of valuable time upon frivolous leisure activities. These ideas emerging under Protestantism, notably Calvinism, play a crucial role in the Weberian paradigm.[2]

In a sense Weber's emphasis on Calvinism is paradoxical. In a profound sense Calvinism is remarkably deterministic. One's future salvation, the hope of a heavenly afterlife, is predetermined. Despite all our best efforts to influence the outcome, we are preordained to go to Heaven or Hell. After all, we mere defiled humans wallow in corrupting sin. How dare we miserable creatures presume to comprehend or question what our pure and omnipotent creator wants for us? By God's grace and that grace alone are we prepared for salvation. God selects who is saved, who is damned. Now the paradox: determinism is destiny; but it is also duty. The community of the elect should display its exalted status through the rectitude of its disciplined behavior. The very thrift-oriented stance Calvinistic communities adopt is actual proof of their blissful selection as the saved. There was a danger that this conviction would lead to antinomianism. Sincere Calvinists knew antinomianism was heresy; it must be countered by due community diligence, by punishments if necessary. Antinomianism was the deceit of the Devil.

Duty, discipline, diligent time management: for Weber Calvinism was eminently rational, relatively bereft of animistic thinking, chary of pointless ritual, suspicious of the very trappings of magic represented by the ceremony of the Eucharist that Catholic priests used to awe and inspire their flocks. By "demystifying" the world, Protestantism opened wide the doors of thought to a decidedly contrary version of dutiful time saving toil, a secular version. Under secularization, obligation, guilt, obsessive concern with the relentless clicking away of valuable time became a routine laden "iron cage" applied to business, factory work, corporate and government bureaucracy. A deep paradox was afoot. One particular religion—not religion in general—ushered in the apparent opposite of religion: secularism. Because the world was demystified, rational, scientific thinking could flourish. The full-scale bloom of modernization could assert itself, pushing its roots deeper and deeper into the social soil. Capitalism as a system went hand in hand with pitiless unrelenting rationalism.

In a nutshell—and for completely different reasons—both Marxism and Weber inspired analyses predicting religion would wither away at least in the West. For both schools of thinking, the possibility that the triumph of capitalism might be limited to the West was real. For Marxian analysis, the presence or absence of feudalism was crucial. Suppose feudalism failed to develop in India or China. Perhaps this implied capitalism would never develop in these arenas. For Weber, the presence of religious traditions—Confucianism, Hinduism, Buddhism, Taoism, and Islam—that oriented devotees away from the type of rationalization of life key to Protestantism might well condemn them to a non-capitalist future.

All of this failed to materialize. Non-Christian countries like Japan, China, Thailand, Indonesia, either became capitalist or embraced communism during the twentieth century. This sent scholars scrambling to refashion the arguments of Marx and Weber. The list of powerful ideals crucial to thrift and hard work was expanded to incorporate Confucianism. Materialistic arguments flourished under new guises. Marxist inspired Frankfurt School thinking emerged. Neo-classical economic arguments cast in terms of relative prices, income per capita, and wages gained ascendency. Geographic or quasi-geographic formulations explaining why some cultures advanced to industrialization and others failed to do so were propounded. Perhaps most intriguing, Neo-Darwinian evolutionary thinking stepped in the intellectual arena with a flourish.[3] Intriguingly evolutionary thinking was honed to explain why religions arise, why they play an important role in shaping economic behavior, and why capitalism has become increasingly dominant, first in the West triumphantly before spreading out into East Asia with a vengeance.

The linchpin of the Neo-Darwinian approach is reproductive success. Why reproductive success is crucial to bolstering religion and economic cooperation deemed crucial to capitalism builds on advances in neuroscience and evolutionary biology. As the root of these fields is an observation Darwin struggled with: why are humans, and some animals, altruistic? If competition for resources is a totally selfish pursuit determining who has the greatest number of offspring surviving to maturity—lowering our mortality risks, lengthening the amount of time we can reproduce, bolstering our fertility—why do we go out of our way to assist others? One possibility is that altruism promotes group fitness—for example, among hunters and gatherers—rendering them more successful in the competition for animal prey and vegetation than competitor groups.

Unfortunately for Neo-Darwinists, genetic transmission from parents to offspring—the Darwinian mechanism of reproductive success playing out at the level of DNA—is not a group phenomenon, it is an individual phenomenon. So why are humans relatively cooperative at the level of groups?

One solution is transcendental monitoring. As Johnson (2016) asserts in his book *God Is Watching You*, fear of divine punishment permeates all religions worldwide. Suppressing selfishness at the individual level enhances an individual's evolutionary success. It reduces the probability that one will be physically punished, ostracized, or accused of wrong-doing by the group. If fear of cosmic retribution and belief in a Just World, in virtue being rewarded and criminality and non-cooperation severely punished—if not in this life but at least in an afterlife—is sufficiently widespread in human populations, most people will suppress their selfishness. But why should that come about?

One line of argument involves recent research on the brain. The idea here is that there are two systems active in the brain. One is the BAS (behavioral approach system). Fueled by what we call positive feedback, it is what we have in mind when we talk about carrots as opposed to sticks. The other system is the BIS (behavioral inhibition system). This system feeds off threats, negative sticks if you will. According to neuroscientists, learning tends to favor the BIS system at the expense of the BAS system. The better educated we are, the more likely we are to favor punishing others. In human populations, enjoying the use of symbolic language—spoken as well as symbolic body language (crossing our arms is a sign of disapproval, as is scowling and rolling our eyes)—informal education takes place within the confines of households; in all groups, no matter what the technological basis for production of goods and services, children imbibe an understanding of deceit, learning how to discern its ugly character in social settings. Children learn to avoid those addicted to deceiving others. As they mature, they learn how to punish liars and connivers. In short, punishing comes natural to us. It is innate. This might explain why we are cooperative. We punish free-riders and malcontents. We make it possible to cobble together public goods beneficial to all of us, albeit the rewards may be captured by some persons in society and not by others. It is not a stretch to imagine how useful to society fear of retribution by an all-knowing, all-powerful, monitor critical of deceit would be. Can this explain the ubiquity of religion?

Behavioral psychologists have weighed in on the issue of transcendental monitoring. Consider the findings reported in Norenzayan (2013). Based on laboratory experiments, participants being primed—or not primed depending on the experiment involved—by religious statements before their behavior is observed, Norenzayan draws a variety of conclusions that he highlights in eight mantra-like assertions. These are: watched people are good people; religion is more in the situation than in the person (we are more altruistic on a day when we attend church, synagogue, or mosque for instance); Hell is stronger than Heaven (fear of divine punishment trumps fuzzy feelings of being loved by a benevolent cosmic force); we trust people who trust in God (atheists are distrusted because they are likely to be free-riders, detracting from group objectives); religious actions speak larger than words (advertise your faith by living it); un-worshipped Gods are impotent Gods; Big Gods for Big Groups; and religious groups cooperate in order to compete.

For materialists, evolutionary claims about religion make for good reading. Groups that do not develop Big Gods remain small. Only those that manage to turn ritual, magic, poetic expression into the service of Big Gods move on successfully from hunting and gathering to settled agriculture with domesticated plants and animals. Ideas are rooted in evolutionary advantage, explicable in terms of the structure of the human brain.

As appealing as this line of research is, I must disagree. Is there not an infinite regress problem here? Do you not have to be fairly cooperative before you can agree on the nature of the Big God? Moreover, what if some people promote a particular god and another group advocates a competitor deity? How do you reconcile that? Materialism overreaches. Ideas matter independently of material forces.

If both material and intellectual forces shape history, followers of Weber and of Marx might both be right; albeit off base in adhering to extreme positions; and also off base regarding predictive power. In fact, there are good reasons for thinking that both Marx and Weber were dead right in some areas. For instance, Marx was correct in analyzing the instability of capitalism; he was right in associating capitalism with the late-eighteenth and nineteenth centuries. He was right in pointing out that automation has a dark side in so far as it sidelines workers and renders useless their hard-won skills. Again, I believe Weber was astute in linking religious thought to capitalism; he was right in arguing that scientific thinking was important. Taking the position that both approaches have bite is tantamount to saying that both material and idealist forces interact in some way. However, going down this road means we must come up with crisp and clear definitions of capitalism and religion. Why? Because fuzziness in defining capitalism and religion opens up a rancid can of worms—scholars arguing with one another without establishing ground rules for fruitful debate. There is nothing worse than a game played without rules.

Definitions

With this in mind, I give two definitions. I define religion as purification buttressed by faith not fact. I define capitalism as the mobility of capital buttressed by credit creation.

In formulating these definitions, I rule out associating capitalism with the operation of relatively unfettered markets. I rule out capitalism being conceived as a system in which an elite group garners income from ownership of capital and land while the non-elite group earns income from labor service, wages for instance. I rule out capitalism being defined in terms of private ownership. For instance, State Capitalism flourishing under Communism: in principle the state being the possessor and manager of capital as a public good supposedly administered in the interests of workers is still capitalism according to this definition. Marx, operating with a teleological theory of progress, assumed that burgeoning trade created social surpluses. In turn, a significant slice of these surpluses was captured by merchants who transformed the surplus they extracted into physical capital in the form of machinery, structures and transport vehicles. If the state secures ownership of capital, wresting it away from the capitalists, it can turn surpluses into physical capital just as well as the private market can. And it can do so without fomenting unemployment provided it sticks to a general full employment plan formulated by state officials, bureaucrats.

What I find compelling in Marx's vision are four ideas: capitalism is decidedly modern, asserting itself at the time of the first industrial revolutions, namely after the mid-eighteenth century; capitalism is unstable, generating booms and busts, downturns spawning unemployment; religion has been, and in some regions of the globe continues to be, a powerful agent of social control that ruling elites wield at the expense of the poor; and dialectic struggle does spawn progress over the long-run. For instance, in my framework dialectics are interpreted in terms of the pendulum swing.

That said, I reject Marxist theory on many grounds. I reject the idea of class altogether. Ironically it is an "ideal type," smacking of the very idealism Marx angrily derided. The problem with "ideal types" is they mask heterogeneity. I believe heterogeneity is crucial to progress in both material and idealist arenas. For instance, invoking "ideal types"—as proposed by Akerlof (1984) and by Akerlof and Kranton (2010) who basically divide populations into insider/outsider groups—is vitiated by its appeal to two homogeneous groups. In Akerlof and Kranton (2010) we have an ethnically defined group—say African-Americans socialized one way—interacting with homogeneous group of non-African-Americans socialized another way. Surely this is smacks of simplistic thinking.

The idea that two homogeneous groups compete for power and economic resources or dispute over ideologies does not preclude heterogeneity. Indeed, it is my argument that competition between two "big tent" alliances—each composed of individuals advancing their own disparate ideas and economic interests—is often the generator of progress over the long-run. The point is that there is heterogeneity within the two opposing groups. It is in the interests of heterogeneous individuals joining a group to combine forces with colleagues who may differ on some points but in the overall picture are natural allies. Without likeminded associates, an individual's hope of achieving any kind of lasting success is doomed, crushed like so many wrinkled up paper coffee cups. Join a group of individuals sufficiently similar in beliefs and material interests, permitting you and your colleagues to illicit the muscle necessary to successfully combat those groups you oppose. According to this logic, heterogeneity is consistent with analysis ultimately based on a kind of binary dialectic.

Moreover, I fail to see how a theory postulating capitalism emergent out of feudalism accounts for what happened in the western world prior to feudalism. A great empire, the Roman Empire, collapsed in the fourth and fifth centuries, ushering in decentralized feudalism and Christian hegemony. However, while in its heyday—from the last two centuries BCE until the end of the second century CE—the Roman Empire was cohesive and large. It spawned specialization and division of labor; it made use of slavery; its impressive road network promoted comparative advantage etched out along far-flung trade routes. In short, in so far as Marx's theory rests on the idea of expansive markets and the exploitation of an underclass giving rise to a social surplus that merchants can extract, making it the basis of primitive capital accumulation, one must ask: why did capitalism only come into its own in the eighteenth century? Why was it not firmly established under Roman rule?

Likewise, I find much in Weber that is admirable. I do agree that science coupled with demystification of the world was crucial to the triumph of capitalism. I do agree that religious ideas coming down from the ancient world were crucial to capitalism as a system of ideas for rationalizing economic production.

As compelling as Weber's thesis is—Weber's approach has spawned a massive literature rivaling that devoted to Marxist analysis – I must dissent on many of the points formulated by Weber and his followers. I sincerely doubt that Christianity had much to do with capitalism. In fact, the originator of the doctrines that Calvinists so devoutly embraced was Saint Augustine. Augustine was writing in the fourth and fifth centuries as the Roman Empire was disintegrating: pummeled by repeated attacks by Visigoths, Ostrogoths, Lombards, Alemanni, Vandals. In the tract that laid down one of the key ideological cornerstones upon which medieval Catholic Church doctrine rested—*The City of God and the City of the World*—Augustine of Hippo advanced a theory of deterministic predestination. God had selected some for salvation. On these he dispensed grace. On the rest of the world He withheld His grace. Some people in the church would be saved; some would not. Who knew whether a diligent churchgoer was one of those selected for salvation? Some people active in the city of the world would be saved. Who knew what their fate was to be? Only God has that knowledge.

In Augustine's dark vision there were two separate worlds: one secular, the other religious. Those destined for salvation—regardless of which world they were active in—would find their souls happily ensconced in the presence of their God when their material bodies perished, leaving nothing more than a soul. Those fated to be damned would not be so lucky. All of this was based on a deterministic theory of predestination, the ultimate basis for the crucial tenets of Calvinist Christianity that flourished in the sixteenth and seventeenth centuries. Were they new? No. In fact, these ideas were alive and well during the waning decades of the Roman Empire.

What did the church, ostensibly committed to Saint Augustine, do with the idea of the soul finding itself once freed of sinful flesh looking to enter Heaven or be consigned to damnation? What the church did with these concepts we know. It fashioned a theory of purgatory. Remarkably, purgatory became a huge money maker for the church itself. It allowed the church to acquire vast tracts of land, to hire mercenaries to fight for it, to contest power with secular authority, to twist the arms of kings lusting for the glories of armed combat.

The argument I make in this book is simple. There was a set of ideas firmly established in the ancient West that ultimately shaped progress leading to full-blown capitalism. These ideas were not Christian. They were Greek. They centered upon what I call the "pendulum swing," an ongoing dialectic in the intellectual world encompassing religion, and in the material world, involving social organization, military affairs, and government. For a while, one school of thought would prevail. Its opponents, having girded their loins, actively opposed the prevailing doctrine, perhaps winning out, perhaps not. Out of the passionate clash of principles, understanding deepens on both sides. Progress takes place. Central to the Greek "pendulum swing" is its taking place simultaneously in the world of ideas and in the world of material forces.

Had the pendulum swing been active only in the world of ideas, it is my assertion that the Western world would not have spawned the same scientific progress and radical experiments in government. Without the scientific progress and acceleration in innovation, the first industrial revolution would not have taken place. Capital would not have become increasingly mobile bouncing around between sectors, seeking its highest rate of return. Key to the pendulum swing in the West is that it never ceased, even after the Roman Empire collapsed. It continued to inform historical change during the medieval period, during the seventeenth century dominated intellectually by natural philosophy, during the eighteenth-century Enlightenment era, and during the first and second Industrial Revolutions.

Three forms of purification: ritual, ethical, and political

What do I mean by purification? To capture the disparate elements swept up into my concept I define three types of purification: ritual, moral, and political. The key point is that each type of purification is justified on tran-scendental grounds. Given heterogeneity—*within* religious communities, *between* religious communities differentiating themselves from one another by dint of ritual, commandments prescribing virtuous behavior, and politi-cal organization—coming up with a comprehensive description for each category is well-nigh impossible. Cursory treatment, a few examples, will have to suffice.

Ritual purification is realized in the physical world. It is materialistic. Not surprisingly rituals around birth and death play a prominent role. Consider death. Disposing of dead, contaminating bodies through burial or incineration in fire, paying costly homage to the memory of the deceased through elaborate mourning rituals, ensuring a peaceful transition to some transcendent realm for immaterial souls, making sure potentially malevo-lent ghosts do not take revenge on the living, are all variants tying a pure transcendental world unsullied by decay to the messy world of human reality. Classical Confucianism, deeply rooted in the natural hierarchy of families—respect for age, birth order, and gender casting its shadow over behavior within and between households—proscribes extremely costly mourning rituals. Consider the idealized model for mourning described by Waley (1939: 94–95)[4]:

> In its full form, the three years of mourning ... involved living in a shed near the tomb of the deceased, abstaining from sexual intercourse, wine, music and visits to friends, and the maintenance, during the whole period, of an air of extreme dejection and decrepitude.

Dying is symptomatic of impurity. Perhaps it is a physical reminder of the sinful nature of humanity. It must be sanctified.

Likewise giving birth: circumcision, abstaining from touching during the period when a woman is menstruating, covering up hair (considered a key physical attribute of sexuality) are good examples from Judaism. In Exodus (4: 24–26), the Lord threatens to slay his chosen leader for the Hebrews enslaved in Egypt, Moses, only to be dissuaded by the fact Zipporah takes radical action:

> Then Zipporah took a flint and cut off the foreskin of her son and cast it at his feet; and she said, 'Surely a bridegroom of blood art thou to me' ... A bridegroom of blood in regard of the circumcision.

Blood is life. Circumcision is sanctification of life, prospective fathers dedicating themselves to the Lord who is eternal, pure, clothing their future act of procreation in purity.

Ritual purification is deeply intertwined with food, the sustenance of life. Justly famous are Jewish Kosher alimentary laws: separating flesh from blood (that is life), avoiding consuming animals "that only chew the cud, or of them that have the hoof cloven ... and the swine ... he is unclean unto you."[5] As well as listing clean and unclean foods, the Hebrew Bible makes it clear that not eating—fasting—is purifying particularly before certain religious holidays like Yom Kippur. Not surprisingly given their debt to Jewish practice, Christianity and Islam recommend fasting as a form of purification; as well banning certain foods pervades Muslim ritual, and the Eucharist or communion, employs the wafer of bread and wine in symbolizing the sacrifice of Jesus, giving up his life, for the benefit of sinful humanity.

Ritual internalized in physical acts—praying with one's head on the ground (expressing submission), contorting one's body in yogi postures, doing repetitive *tai chi* exercises, meditating while seating as stiffly as possible, entering ritual baths, being baptized by the splatter of sanctified water— serve to intertwine physical cleansing with religious devotion. To be sure one can engage in physical ritual without giving a thought to the transcendental. Many persons practicing daily yoga stretching know nothing about the Upanishads, simply wanting to lose weight, limber up their torsos, clear their minds in preparation for a stressful set of business meetings.

Evoking sound—singing hymns, chanting "om," reciting the Lord's Prayer, memorizing a passage in the Torah recited at Bar Mitzvah, channeling the aphorisms of Confucius in pithy refrains—expressed in private or in public ceremonies—to ritualize devotion to the transcendental world goes hand in hand with physical exertion. Meditating; adopting yoga postures; bowing your head in supplication; covering your hair lest it incite lust; being festooned in black robes, walking with eyes cast to the ground in long and winding processions: all these physical acts, all this body language, solidifies and symbolizes pure devotion. So, does establishing a line in the sand between the oceans of secular time and the seas of sacred time. The fact special days—sanctified time—are devoted to doing this in a communal fashion forges within individuals a sense that this is normal, acceptable, socially sanctioned.

In short, achieving ritual purity involves sacrificing resources: time, voice, clothing, buildings, and public space. It comes with a hefty price tag.[6] An individual shouldering the burdens of high political office; a person working three jobs in order to make ends meet (baking bread at the break of day, pumping gas throughout the afternoon, cleaning up horse corrals in the light of a slowly settling sun); a manager heading up a global corporation; all face daily conflicts over allocating their scarce resources. How can I carve out the time to engage in ritual purity? The answer: substitute ethical purity for ritual purity. Apply ethical purity in one's work place. Express purity in a manner that reconciles dutiful work with dutiful religious devotion.

In principle, ethical purity can be conceived of as separate from ritual purity. Indeed, many humanists who subscribe to "religion without gods, religious atheism"—carefully worked out moral codes that they apply on a daily basis—advocate a life devoted to ethical purity jettisoning the completely ritual.[7]

That said, there is no religion that fails to recommend ethical principles, codes of behavior encouraging cooperative behavior. In Exodus (20–21) statements regarding the correct worship of Yahweh (Ywhw)—no graven images, one god alone, remember the holy Sabbath day—are intermixed with lists of banned behaviors. These commandments to not commit certain acts include proscribing the following "crimes": murder; adultery; stealing, bearing false witness against one's neighbor; coveting one neighbor's assets including oxen, servants, or wife; and attacking one's parents, to wit: "And he that smiteth his father, or his mother, shall be surely put to death."

In religions, demarking where ethical prescriptions begin and ritual purity rules cease is a tricky question. Consider vegetarianism. In Hinduism and Buddhism this can be interpreted as ethical behavior arising from *karma*—avoiding eating a creature that once was a human—or an alimentary prescript. The two types of purity overlap, intensifying one another. The Vedic Upanishads clearly link up *karma*-driven caste to ethics:[8]

> Objective morality, according to the Bhagavad Gita is determined by a man's position in caste. Moral conduct is relative to birth and position. It is dharma ... the Brahmin, the king, the merchants, the labourer, and the world-renouncing monk must observe their respective dharmas ... the faithful performance of duties purifies a man's heart and mind by removing selfish impulses.

As noted, diversity rules *within* and *between* religions, vegetarianism being a prime example. Still, several rules appear to be universal to all religions, at least as formulated during the classical period—during the Axial Age between 1500 BCE and 1 CE discussed in the next chapter—the golden rule and the impurity of usury. Both rules have the effect of encouraging cooperation *within* religious groups, while opening up the parallel possibility of reducing cooperation *between* religious groups.

To be sure, the golden rule principle "Do unto others as you would have them do unto you" can be interpreted in many ways. It could justify tit-for-tat behavior as in "an eye for an eye, a tooth for a tooth." You might want to call this the brass version of the rule. It could take the form "Love thy neighbor." This is the silver variant. Or it could take the most radical form "Love thy enemy." Presumably this is the truest gold standard.

In short, adhering to the rule could rationalize violence; at the same time, it could take the form of a bold stance deploring all forms of violence. Indeed, this is what makes it compelling as a principle undergirding cooperation. Murder the murderer, rendering murder an unattractive option (organized predation, warfare, being exemptions from this commandment); proscribe murder, making it abundantly clear that it is inherently evil a veritable despoiler of virtue. Whether we have in mind Buddhist or Hindu non-violence (*ahimsa*), Confucian benevolence, Taoist abhorrence of warfare, Christian advocacy of universal love, Islamic submission to a merciful Allah, the idea of ethical reciprocity—acting in a virtuous manner towards others, thereby inducing them to act virtuously towards you, assuming they are so inclined because they share a common ethical ideology—cuts across cultural divides.

Of course, the various types of golden rules may coexist.[9] Indeed this is probably the typical case, not the atypical outlier.

How does accumulation of economic assets impact ethical purity? Often as not, accumulating wealth goes hand in hand with materialistic greed. It goes against the transcendental grain. From a purist religious point of view, it fails to make a person happy. The Upanishads, notably the Bhagavad Gita and the Katha Upanishad, argue that the Lord uses his lower nature to create material forms, and his higher nature to animate them. Three states exist: the waking state, the dream state, and the dreamless state. The waking state is definitely inferior to the other two. It is tied to the impure material world. Satisfying the desire to accumulate material assets diverts the adept away from experiencing higher reality, from experiencing knowledge of Atman. As a mantra "Wealth can never make a man happy" dictates priorities. A true male Brahmin should give away his or her property, be celibate, be willing to die for his father (eschewing excessive attachment to material existence), and carry out the fire sacrifice.[10]

Above the individual is the community. Every member of the religious community shares a common connection to the transcendental world. Is it right and just that the rich ignore their common brethren in this world? Is a forest not better served if all its trees stand equally tall and erect, each basking in the same sunlight, none so shaded that they subsist as dark, dank underbrush? Does disparity not engender predatory behavior—stealing, or worse, murder—on the part of the impoverished jealous of their wealthy neighbors? Worse does it not encourage wealthy elites to compete in invidious struggles over power and acclamation, the rich flaunting their wealth encouraging their elite competitors to flaunt their riches as well? Wealth should be devoted to the common good, to the promotion of religious virtue, to the propitiation of the deities. So far, so good: but what happens when the religious authorities, the priests, the Confucian elite bureaucrats, abuse the wealth they acquire for the maintenance of the religious cult, divert the funds, loaning them out with interest to the less well off, thereby accumulating personal wealth? What do you do about corruption on the part of those entrusted with the promotion of virtue, or at least ritual supposedly aimed at encouraging virtue?

Examples from the Hebrew Bible make the point. In First Samuel (8: 2–3), the sons of the pious judge Samuel are made judges over Israel at Samuel's behest. However:

> his sons walked not in his ways, but turned aside after lucre, and took bribes, and perverted justice.

In Isaiah (44:9), Yahweh (Ywhw) makes it clear to his prophet Isaiah that persons creating images of deities are doing so for profit:

> Who hath fashioned a god, or molds an image that is profitable for nothing?

The most pious—priests—should disdain profit. That they may be tempted to exploit the fact they are the guardians of assets accumulated in temples and shrines is hardly surprising. It is hardly surprising to find scriptural admonishments to avoid doing so, stating that this is the height of sin, the outrageous flaunting of religious probity.

Typical of the view offered in the ancient Jewish tradition concerning wealth accumulation by the laity is the following diatribe against merchants invoked in the Apocrypha book, Ecclesiasticus (27: 1–3):

> A merchant can hardly keep from wrongdoing, and a tradesman will not be declared innocent of sin, Many have committed sin for a trifle, and whoever seeks to get rich will avert his eyes, As a stake is driven firmly into a fissure between stones, so sin is wedged in between selling and buying, If a man is not steadfast and zealous in the fear of the Lord, his house will be quickly overthrown.

This passage is followed up in Ecclesiasticus 29, with a long denunciation of borrowing and lending funds at interest as opposed to lending for the sake of bolstering the fortunes of the unfortunate. The much-quoted New Testament opinion of Jesus evoked in Luke (19: 24–25) makes this point in a more sweepingly trenchant way, putting it in terms of entering the kingdom of God:

> How hard it is for those who have riches to enter the kingdom of God. For it is easier for a camel to go through the eye of a needle than for a rich man to enter the kingdom of God.

Running through the classical formulations of the world's great religions is a strong bias against accumulation of wealth.

The bias against wealth, hence merchant activity, is particularly strong in the case of usury. Amassing greater and greater piles of wealth because one already controls wealth, thereby enjoying the privilege of loaning out monetized assets (gold and silver coins for instance) at interest, wealth building on itself as it were being anathema. Usury is unusually odious because riches are the fruits of riches, nothing else.

Moreover, wealth accumulation encourages greed. It encourages those expected to be the most virtuous—those closest to the transcendental world—to become avaricious, to devise corrupt ways of securing it, shaking the very foundations of purity upon which religion is based.

Political purity is the third form of purity crucial to religions. What is the relationship between the masses and the religious elite? For instance, the Brahmin caste in India was considered the purest group, the least pure being the untouchables who were not allowed to carry out religious rituals at all. It was considered a violation of Brahmin purity to eat together with an untouchable. The Levites, the sons of Zadok, are a perfect example of hereditary religious elites, instrumental in the formulation of the weighty list of commandments central to the Hebrew Torah.

Who takes precedence: religious or political elites, namely kings and military leaders in the classical period? The struggle between priests and kings pervades all ancient religions. It is the concern of many texts in the Hebrew Bible, particularly the books of Samuel and Kings. Consider the following examples from the Vedic literature, In the Brahmanas, a compendium of ancient Hindu scriptures—there is a tale known as "King and the Priest in the Chariot." It goes as follows:[11]

> Vrisha was the royal chaplain ... of Triyaruna, king of the Ikshvakus ... [he would] hold the reins in the chariot for the king ... to keep him [the king] from doing any harm ... as the two of them were driving along, they cut down with the wheel of the chariot the son of a Brahmin ... they argued with each other about it. The king said "The one who holds the reins is the driver of the chariot. You are the murderer". "No", said the priest "I tried to pull back to avoid him, but you drove the horses on. *You* are the murderer".

A second even more remarkable Hindu scripture, the Bhagavad Gita, describes another great struggle between chariot driver (the god Krishna) and warrior–rider (Arjuna):[12]

> Arjuna ... asks Krishna a lot of difficult, indeed unanswerable age-old questions about violence and nonviolence, this time of the context of the battlefield, questioning the necessity of violence for warriors ... [ultimately] the warrior with ethical misgivings has been persuaded that since war is unreal, it is not evil ... Krishna persuades Arjuna to fight ... [by offering him] devotion ... [renouncing] not the actions but their fruits ... [embracing] actions without desires.

Who drives the chariot? Who takes responsibility for the carnage of battle? These questions haunt all the ancient religious scriptures.

To what extent does commitment to ritual promote ethnic segmentation, inducing ethnic fragmentation? Since much ritual is carried out at the family level—the assumption being that both parents need to be schooled in it from childhood for it to be strictly performed—it is not surprising that taking a spouse from outside the group enjoined to carry on ritual is frowned upon. The Hebrew Bible is ambiguous on this question—the book of Ruth being a primary illustration of the view that a foreign (in the case of Ruth, a Moabite) woman could be accepted in the community of Jews—but elsewhere statements of exclusion appear as illustrated by this passage:[13]

> The people of Israel and the leaders and the priests and the Levites have not put away from themselves the alien peoples of the land and their pollutions, the Canaanites, the Hittites, the Perizzites, the Jebusites, the Moabites, the Egyptians and the Edomites. For they and their sons have married the daughters of these people, and the holy race has been mixed with the alien peoples of the land.

In this case purification takes on the cloak of ethnic discrimination. Examples of this abound, fostering segmentation, even encouraging tit-for-tat predation between neighboring peoples, a theme that runs through all the ancient world religions. It is also a source of segmentation within populations, a prime example being the caste system fostered by Hindu scripture. Caste goes hand-in-hand with requiring marriage to be endogenous to particularly class, occupation, groups. For instance, Brahmins are not supposed to marry outside the Brahmin caste. They forfeit their purity by doing so. One can view this practice through a variety of lenses. One way to interpret it is that raising Brahmin children versed in the Upanishads requires the mother to be actively involved in educating their offspring. A girl not herself raised in a Brahmin household would be hard-pressed to do this.

Notes

1 For followers of the idealist tradition in economic history taking a position on the ultimate causes of the industrial revolution, see *inter alia* Landes (1998), who takes seriously the impact of culture by reiterating arguments of Max Weber; Mokyr (1990, 2002, and 2009), who stresses the importance of Enlightenment thinking; and McCloskey (2010), who favors the norms of bourgeois virtue in explaining why income per capita growth took off during the eighteenth and nineteenth centuries. For materialist arguments emphasizing geographic factors, see Diamond (1997), Jones (2003), Morris (2010), and Pomeranz (2000). Clark (2007) is a materialist of a radically different sort, emphasizing genetically driven reproductive success in explaining why capitalistically oriented elites emerged in England, the first industrialized country.

2 Weber's classical statement of this thesis is in Weber (1958). Also see Weber (1922, 1923, and 1991).

3 For the ins and outs of Neo-Darwinism see the remarkably lucid discussions in the books penned by Dawkins (1982, 1986, 1989, 1996, 1998, and 2009). Dawkins is a prominent opponent of the "accommodationist" position claiming

to successfully manage a reconciliation of modern science with religion. He denies the theory of evolution is consistent with religion, or at least belief in God who has consciously created the universe. See Dawkins (2008). For further discussion of "accommodationism" see Chapter 13, particularly footnote 4 dealing with the views of Coyne (2015).

4 In the *Analects*, a collection of aphorisms attributed to Confucius and one of the nine foundation stones of written Confucianism, it is said "When your parents are alive, comply with the rites in serving them; when they die, comply with the rites in sacrificing to them." This quotation is taken from a list of key Confucian concepts discussed in Van Norden (2002b: 24–28).

5 Alimentary laws are discussed in Deuteronomy 14. In so far as the priests were specialists in ritual it is fairly evident that much of the text in Leviticus, Numbers, and Deuteronomy (the third, fourth and fifth books of the Torah, the Pentateuch) was composed—or subsequently edited and redacted—by priests, or in subsequent editing, rabbis committed to the importance of ritual. Of the twenty-four books of the Hebrew Bible, the first five books (the Torah, the Pentateuch)—Genesis, Exodus, Leviticus, Numbers and Deuteronomy—enjoy a special status, considered the voice of Yahweh (Yhwh) as transmitted to Moses. The Torah text is read in synagogues week after week, the reading completed on an annual basis as a cycle. Contained within it are 613 commandments describing various rituals, some the burden of priestly specialists (e.g. how to carry on animal sacrifices, how to cleanse oneself prior to the sacrifices, and so forth), some to be followed by rank and file members of the Jewish community, all considered to be of sufficient importance to be the subject of learned commentary. The Talmud ("Instruction")—consisting of the Misnah and the Gemara—constitutes a commentary on the Torah; one of its six parts is devoted to Purities (Tohorot). Within the list of purities are rules governing the purity of vessels for eating, the treatment of corpses, preparing ritual baths (mikveh), the proper behavior expected around a menstruating woman. For a discussion of the writings constituting the Hebrew Bible see Chapter 4, especially the first footnote for that chapter.

6 On the importance of the "cost of time" for conditioning the way Judaism is practiced in Orthodox, Conservative, and Reform variants of American Judaism, see Chiswick (2014).

7 Dworkin (2013).

8 Nikhilananda, Volume Two (1956: 7). According to Nikhilananda's interpretation of the Upanishads—as stated in Volume Two of his monumental volume (1956: 10)—"non-injury is the basic moral duty and the mother of all virtues. It implies positive goodwill and kindness to all being ... [non-injury] requires control of greediness ... and control of hate." The principle of non-injury is basically one version of the golden rule. In Volume Two, Nikhilananda (1956: 12) differentiates between Indian ethics and Greek ethics. He notes that Indian ethics stress purification of the mind with the intent of securing liberation from gross materialism—the materialist world being ultimately unreal and therefore unworthy of being a focus of one's life, the expectation being the priestly Brahmin caste constituting the purest members of society will voluntarily accept vows of voluntary poverty in their search for non-materialist truth—while Greek ethics emphasizes the social virtues, especially justice. To be sure this distinction is useful. However, it is overdrawn. Plato's theory of virtue, beauty, and truth has a mystical side paralleling the Vedic interpretation. Chapter 3 deals with Greek purification, taking up Platonic theory among other aspects of Greek religion and philosophy. In Volume Three of Nikhilalananda (1956: 47), there is an interesting discussion of the relationship—positive or negative—between materialistic ritual and idealistic achievement of religious knowledge: "There exists an apparently unbridgeable gap between the ritualistic section of the Vedas, dealing with

the various enjoyments in the phenomenal universe ... and the philosophical section of the Upanishads, describing the Knowledge of Brahmin ... [however] the Upanishads dealing with the upāsanā supplies the bridge. It shows the way to divert the mind from the performance of rituals to the philosophical contemplation of Brahman."

9 In his interpretation of Confucianism, Lin (1943) emphasizes the centrality of the golden rule in Confucian thinking. Lin argues that Confucius thought elites pursuing a universal moral code—freed from vulgar tendencies like greed, pursuit of self-interest at the expense of serving the public order, and disrespect of high officials and princes—would set salutary examples for the remainder of society. Consider the following quotation—given in Lin (1943: 125)—from the *Analects*: "When you repay kindness with kindness, the people are encouraged to be good. When you repay evil with evil, then people are warned from doing bad". Presumably a weak form of the golden rule is marshaled here. Good people set good examples. People not so inclined should be punished, making it clear that bad behavior leads to bad consequences and is deserving of censure. To be sure, Confucius tied his theory of the golden mean to strict observance of ritual. He believed following the proper rituals encourages respectful behavior. For instance, Confucius was a highly accomplished musician. He considered mastering music one of the most useful devices for concentrating the mind, focusing it on pure disinterested achievement. Pursuit of beauty in music ennobles. Despite being ritualistic, it stimulates virtue in elites, thereby setting high minded models for the great mass of humanity.

10 The discussion in this paragraph is taken from various pages in Volume One of Nikhilananda (1956: 64–197).

11 Summarized from the account in Doniger (2009: 140–141).

12 Summarized from the account in Doniger (2009: 282–284).

13 The book of Esdras is included in the Apocrypha. Excluded from the Hebrew Bible, it was included in the Septuagint, the Greek version of the Old Testament (it is included in the Catholic Bible but typically excluded from Protestant Bibles that adhere most closely to the Hebrew Bible). It consists of two books. The quotation appearing in the text is from the First Book of Esdras chronicling the trials and tribulations of the priest Ezra. The background for this book is the struggle between the peoples of the ancient kingdom of Israel wiped out by the Assyrians in the eighth century but still resident in cities like Samaria and those Jews returning to Jerusalem to rebuild the temple erected in Judah later destroyed by the Babylonians (a right granted them by the Persian King Cyrus but subsequently rescinded and not renewed by the Persians until King Darius took over the Persian throne). The Samarians wanted to prevent the rebuilding of the temple, imploring the Persians to support their position. Those returning from the Neo-Babylonian Empire to Judah were staunch advocates of the position that their version of Judaism was superior to that practiced by the rump population of Israelites. Ezra was a priest enjoined to supervise the rebuilding effort, henceforth a lightning rod for animosities directed at the Jews who remained in the former territories of the two kingdoms Israel and Judah. The quotation in the text is said to be Ezra's declaration, indicative of the pressure imposed upon him by the most powerful cliques within the community of Judeans returned from Babylonia. Taken from First Esdras (8: 68) it appears in the version of the Bible edited by May and Metzger (1965).

2 Axial thought traditions
From heroic myth to social control

Religion of hunters and gatherers

Religion exists in all societies. This includes hunters and gathers. Indeed, religion is rooted in the rituals, moral codes and shamanistic practices of foraging groups.

Amongst hunting and gathering populations, religion is the amalgam of magic, ritual, taboo, totemic beliefs, fear of ghosts and reincarnated ancestors, altruistic sacrifice for the greater good of the tribe, the feeling—induced by consumption of drugs or participation in frenzied dances—of being possessed by supernatural spirits, and animism. Largely free of hierarchy—groups are small, specialization of tasks is not entrenched—no formal priestly class, no chief lays down a rigid set of rules governing religion. In a world where there is fear that wild animals—bears, tigers, venomous snakes—might pounce on the unsuspecting person, a world in which other hostile tribes might attack, it is better to assume the worse rather than naively cling to illusions. Acquiring protection from magical figurines, listening to wise tribal elders' instructions on what colorful and elaborate purifying rituals will ward off demonic predators, tribal members weave their way through a myriad of beliefs that serve their interests as individuals. As well, the beliefs contribute to the security of the group as a whole.

Not surprisingly, purity is associated with the luminous sky, with the sparkling stars at night, while earth—where the dead are buried or on which their corpses are burned—is conceived of as defiled. This is animistic thinking, assigning ethical judgment to inanimate objects. To be sure, tribal groups possess an intuitive understanding of physics and chemistry. But in the absence of mechanical devices for probing deeper into the nature of their physical environs, animistic beliefs are the default option.

More generally, purification lies at the root of all aspects of tribal religion. Shielded by magic, warned off incest by taboos, inculcated into adulthood through rituals designed to instruct the young on the mores surrounding hunting, storage of food, and the spawning of offspring, tribal members encounter religion as a relatively disorganized system of practices and beliefs. The physical intertwines with the mental. In frenzied dances, participants experience trances evoking possession by mystical powers. Tattoos convey identity with a cult; taboos shape behavior, investing themselves with the force of divine commandments.

After the Neolithic revolution: predation, trade and gift exchange

All this changes when two things happen to a group: either it settles down or it migrates with its horses and sheep. In the settler case, it increases in size because it adopts settled agriculture with domesticated plants and animals. Population grows as land is converted from marsh, forest, and fen into enriched cultivated land supporting grain fields and yielding sustenance to domesticated cows, sheep, goats, pigs, and chickens. The carrying capacity of the land improves. Reaping a generous surplus far larger than was possible under hunting and gathering, a surplus that elites covet and attempt to monopolize, and thus a clearly etched hierarchy emerges. This is the sedentary outcome. Alternatively, the group remains nomadic, carrying on warfare and trade as two means for generating wealth. In both cases, chiefdoms arise. Hierarchy is established, status exercised around systematized rituals and beliefs. Trade between the two groups enhances wealth creation in both zones.

In sum, predation, gift exchange, and price-driven commercial trade proliferate as agricultural production expands in areas particularly conducive to the domestication of plants and animals.

Trade proliferates because environmental conditions—and attendant human skills acquired in coping with soil and climatic conditions—peculiar to regions give rise to comparative advantage. Olive oil cannot be fruitfully cultivated and processed everywhere; gold, silver, and copper mines are not evenly distributed across the planet; northern climes bristling with firs enjoy a natural advantage in producing wood. Offer up olive oil in exchange for copper; trade logs for copper; trade olive oil for wooden planks fit for shipbuilding. By the same logic, nomadic peoples raising cattle, camels, and horses, acquire through exchange processed foodstuffs like grains, fodder, silks and jewelry from settled large population centers in which specialization and division of labor focused on craft production is well entrenched.

Trade is win–win and attractive for this very reason. But win–lose predation also begins to run rampant when trade opportunities proliferate. Settled agrarian societies enjoy population growth. By converting land into fields bristling with wheat, barley, oats, rye, a plethora of vegetables and fruits, societies so blessed enjoy the potential for human fertility rates to exceed those of mortality. Larger populations can field larger armies; can stimulate expertise in the manufacture of weapons, particularly important after Bronze Age technology gives way to Iron Age technology. As a result, the agrarian world tends to divide into big fish feeding on small fish. Since climate impacts production either negatively or positively, poor harvests in a region encourage those faced with famine to attack their better off neighbors. Vagaries in sunshine and rainfall inevitably encourage predation, particularly when distrust between neighboring peoples squelches opportunities to redistribute food through win–win exchange. Third, predation expands because nomadic peoples enjoying the advantage of horse driven mobility can attack the frontier zones surrounding settled communities. They are attracted by the glittering buildings and fineries accumulated in large settled populations: raiding, perhaps even conquering, appears to be an attractive option. Finally, and most important, predation feeds on predation. Losing a war against an enemy goes hand in glove with rearming to defeat a once victorious rival.

Finally, gift exchange grows because the capacity to carry on transcendental purification ritual grows as populations expand. Consider temples. Magnificent structures dedicated to the worship of gods—typically hewn out of precious metals like gold and silver, fine gems lovingly chiseled into figurines, choice cedar beams secured from elegant forests, jeweled encrustations—come with an expensive price tag. The larger the population, the larger the economy kings and priests draw upon, and thus the more magnificent the structures.

Offering specially designated gifts to the gods—sacrificial animals like the red heifer famous in Jewish worship, the horse central to the Hindu horse sacrifice ritual, the proverbial lamb—requires investment in infrastructure, notably temples. Resources are required; tithes and taxes must be levied; crews of workers—either paid workers or slaves—must be put to work in carefully monitored groups; architects must be brought on board; masters of glass making, jewelry fabricators and painters must be sought out, their talents brought to bear on the task of celebrating the benevolence of a transcendental world lavished upon the community.

Depending on your viewpoint about the effectiveness of gift giving designed to satisfy the desire to propitiate, honor, or advertise a version of transcendentalism—cooperation can be considered an outcome. At the same time warfare between communities differentiated by the nature of their deities or civil unrest brought on within a religious community, sub-groups disputing with one another over theology or proper ritual behavior, can be byproducts of ritualized gift giving. Claiming gift exchange aimed at a transcendental world is "win–win" as opposed to "win–lose" is a matter of opinion.

In short, four kinds of economic activity emerge as the Neolithic revolution proceeds. Subsistence production is basic. On top of a subsistence economy, three other forms of activity develop. One is win–lose predation involving the clash of arms; a second is win–win trade typically organized around markets mediated by price; a third is gift exchange devoted to mediating with the transcendental world. Predation, trade, and gift exchange compete for resources.

In the Appendix, I develop a production function methodology that can be applied to analyzing the transition from hunting to gathering to settled agriculture (enhanced by trade with nomadic chiefdoms), to the Roman economy the most successful economy of the ancient world, and to the industrial revolutions of the modern period. For the reader phobic to mathematical symbolization, let me say: please skip the equations if you must; but at a minimum, please read the text that describes the concepts captured in the algebra.

Chiefdoms

Returning to our discussion of chiefdoms, how do they control their populations? While chiefs have a variety of mechanisms by which they can justify their special status, two stand out: gift exchange and claims to divinity. Elaborately conceived gift exchange, in which the ruler differentiates between the more favored and less favored, effectively ostracizing malcontents, currying favor with priests and warriors who assist him or her in ruling is one option. Another is wrapping oneself with the vestments of heroic status. Claiming to possess transcendental powers that allow one to fend off demons, ghosts, hostile tribes, and give one the capacity to point the group in the direction of purity is an attractive option. In fact, gift exchange and claims of divinity usually go hand-in-hand. Through his devotion, the ruler receives gifts from the transcendental world benefitting the group as a whole. For instance, warm weather, an early spring beneficial to grain planters, an abundant harvest speaking to those raising cattle, goats, sheep, and horses. As ruler, he or she carries out—along with priests appropriately purified, sanctified, robed in regal vestments and jewels—purifying rituals designed to encourage benevolence in transcendental spirits. One way to do this is the blood sacrifice, the offering up of humans and animals to mollify the gods.

Along these lines consider the basic myth of the Central Eurasian Complex characterizing the chief of a nomadic group. It is the story of a hero:[1]

A maiden is impregnated by a heavenly spirit of god.
The rightful king is deposed unjustly.
The maiden gives birth to a marvelous baby boy.
The unjust king orders the baby to be exposed.
The wild beasts nurture the baby so he survives.
The baby is discovered in the wilderness and saved.
The boy grows up to be a skilled horseman and archer.
He is brought to court but put in a subservient position.
He is in danger of being put to death but escapes.
He acquires a following of oath-sworn warriors.
He overthrows the tyrant and re-establishes justice in the kingdom.
He founds a new city or dynasty.

Loyalty unto death was central to the early Central Asian Culture Complex. The oath-sworn friends of the hero were prepared to die for their lord.

Even more striking, in the institution of the *comitatus*, the Praetorian guards, the defenders of the hero were prepared to commit ritual suicide if the hero preceded them in death. The Japanese *samurai* who were heirs to the Complex knew this principle. They channeled it through the concept of *junshi*. Loyalty trumps everything else. A completely loyal retainer proves steadfast devotion by following his lord into the grave festooned with his weapons and riches.

Why embrace this horrid fate? The answer is riches, gift exchange: silk robes laced in gold, jewels, a luxurious life enjoyed in the palaces maintained by the lord. Indeed, this was the key to trade on the Central Asian steppes: the *comitatus* carried on trade in order to secure the beautifully crafted ornaments produced in the civilizations that had embraced settled farming. As well the bond between chief and retainer ran deep. It gave life purpose. In any case an existence spent surrounded by riches was superior to scratching out a penurious fate in dusty villages strung across the vast semi-arid interior of Eurasia.

All of this made Eurasian wide trade both mutually advantageous and potentially dangerous. The nomadic *comitatus* braved the great spaces stretching between the Mediterranean and the Great Wall of China. Either individually or in federations, fighting off raiders, the *comitatus* struggled across frigid steppe lands, over parched deserts, passing through snow covered forbidding mountain passes. All of this to offer up horses, silk, pearls, golden goblets, gems, silver bullion to the elites ruling the great agrarian empires of Eurasia, whether Greek, Parthian, Indus Valley, Chinese, or Roman. At the same time, if challenged, if insulted, the *comitatus* was fully prepared to harass, exhausting their trading partners with feints, bloody incursions, along the string of frontier outposts where goods were bartered.

Human sacrifice

In short, blood sacrifice was integral to the Central Eurasian Culture Complex.

In settled agricultural societies, blood sacrifice was practiced as well. Often it was tied to worship of the great hero who acted as intermediary between deities and the humdrum world of farmers. When Chinese emperors died perhaps twenty or so subordinate officials would give up the ghost along with him or her; when high level officials perished perhaps five or six followers would die. Deposited into the tombs were human bodies, splendid silks, bejeweled swords, gold-laden trinkets.

The Hebrew Bible bristles with accounts of human sacrifice. The scribes and editors tasked with composing the scrolls that were eventually incorporated into the Bible are totally opposed to it, mostly arguing it is symptomatic of Baal worship. For instance, Jeremiah (7:31) claims Yahweh (Yhwh) has spoken to him regarding the practice:

And they built the high places of Topheth ... to burn their sons and their daughters in the fire; which I commanded not, neither came it into my mind.

In Second Chronicles (28:2–4) King Ahaz of Judah is criticized for his sin of sacrificing human flesh:

Ahaz was twenty years old when he began to reign ... but he walked in the ways of the kings of Israel, and made also molten images for the Baalim. Moreover, he offered in the valley of the son Hinnon, and burnt his children according to the abominations of the heathen, whom the Lord cast out before the children of Israel. And he sacrificed and offered in the high places.

In Deuteronomy (28: 53) there is a ferocious account of Yahweh's determination to punish his chosen people by famine, opening the door to cannibalism:

The Lord will bring a nation against thee from far ... as the vulture swoopeth down ... and he shall eat the fruit of thy cattle ... and thou shall eat the fruit of thine own body, the flesh of thy sons and of thy daughters whom the Lord thy God hath given them.

In attacking Baal worship in the Kingdom of Israel, which is said to have involved worshipping before bovine statues, Hosea (13:2–3) states:

And now they sin more and more, and they have made them molten images of their silver. According to their own understanding, even idols, of them they say "They that sacrifice men kiss calves".

Not surprisingly one of the most dramatic heart wrenching scenes in the Hebrew Bible is the account of Abraham's journey up Mount Moriah, the Lord (intent on testing his devotion) ordering him to sacrifice his son Isaac, as conveyed in Genesis (22:1–2):

And He said "Take now they son, thine only son, whom thou lovest, even Isaac, and get thee to the land of Moriah: and offer him there for a burnt-offering upon one of the mountains which I will tell thee of."

These are only examples illustrating a fundamental reality. Before animal sacrifice took hold, human sacrifice was integral to religious ritual.

That blood sacrifice rituals became emblematic of such societies in no way ruled out magic, belief in ghosts, the importance of oracular prediction, the search for miraculous cures from debilitating diseases, spirit possession and the like. Rather these practices and beliefs co-existed with hero cults or were incorporated into hero cults by priests and officials working under the direction of rulers.

Heroic Age

The early heroes of the Axial Age—the period between 1500 BCE and 1 CE—bridge the gap between the divine and the human.[2] Achilles is born of a god and a woman. Jacob wrestles with divine angels. Moses spends time with Yahweh (Yhwh) on the mountain, receiving the divine law. The prophets of the Hebrew Bible repeat the word of their god verbatim. The Yellow Emperor in China slays dragons. The Japanese emperor descends from the sun god. The pharaohs are gods. The god Krishna advises the warrior Arjuna. Bridging two worlds—polluted daily reality punctuated by earthly pain, famines and floods, physical ailment and cruel death—and the purified existence enjoyed by gods who never die and timeless principles that never fail—mythic heroes celebrate the achievements that can be won by inspired warriors, prophets, and priests. In short, the early myths of the Axial Age—often as not initially spoken, recited repeatedly by elites enjoying sufficient leisure to devote themselves to the transcendent—celebrate the military feats of peoples who manage to defeat rival claimants to territory, rationalizing their success by glorifying the special relationship between their military leaders and the transcendental world.

That these primal myths of the Axial Age were elaborated during the period 1500 BCE to 1 CE is not surprising. With the transition from the Bronze Age to the Iron Age, warfare was revolutionized. Conflict between the sedentary civilizations adopting settled agriculture (investing in fixed capital, building irrigation systems, road networks, and walled cities) and the nomadic peoples who carried on long-distance trade that could turn to plunder in the twinkle of any eye, intensified. Threatening the great agrarian civilizations as they came swirling out of the steppes riding on spoke-wheel chariots, the trader–warriors of the Eurasian land mass were prepared to trade horses for elegant textiles, for golden goblets, for jewels. These were the chariot riders celebrated in the *Rig Veda*. Treated with disrespect they could turn dangerous, seizing territory, unseating rulers, and sacking temples. No wonder the Vedic literature makes repeated reference to the horse sacrifice. The horse epitomized steppe wildness.

The age of chariot warfare was frightening enough. But its ferocity pales in comparison to the threats warfare promised once the Iron Age promoted advances in archery. By 1000 BCE, merchant–warriors could flex their muscle when suitably massed in fearsome cavalries. With the onset of the Iron Age, the technology of warfare took a leap forward. A small bow—the "cupid bow"—coupled with cast bronze arrowheads produced en masse according to standardized weight and size—changed all of this.[3] Arrows were simplified and streamlined. Armed with a small bow that could be flexibly operated by archer riding atop speeding horseback, the trader cum warrior was able to dispatch metal tipped arrows in three directions: left, backwards, and forward. Unified into armies through bonds of sworn loyalty to powerful chieftains who made alliances of convenience with potential rivals, the wide-ranging merchant band was capable of carrying goods between the eastern and western reaches of the Eurasian land mass. Good for trade to be sure. But at the same time, the efforts of these steppe warriors created a whole fresh daunting set of political problems for the great agrarian civilizations.

To protect themselves against invasions from the hinterland, the rulers of the agrarian states began to flex their military muscle. They exploited their natural advantage—population size and the size of their social surplus—in an attempt to maximize their security.[4] They pushed out in the borderlands threatened by invasions from hostile trader–warrior groups, defeating these groups whenever they could, incorporating them into their domestic fold if necessary, or paying appeasing tribute to buy peace. They tried to carve out perimeter zones they could fortify, driving out potential threats to their security. Of course, all this required resources. As the length of borders grew, so did protection costs. Along sparsely guarded borders, the nomadic groups enjoyed the advantage of mobility, the capacity to attack at the weakest link along the security chain.

As their empires expanded in size, in the diversity of their economic specialization, and in religious complexity, so did the challenge of securing social control over the peoples they ruled. For rulers using religion—originally shrouded in the myth of the semi-divine ruler–hero but co-existing with a long list of subordinate cults and practices—served as a convenient mechanism for solidifying control. Indeed, had religion not been co-opted by the rulers attempting to fashion large empires it is difficult to see how they could achieve their goals of consolidating control over large and expanding states. What they were inclined to do was "mask" their draconian systems of rules and regulations—putative legal systems—behind a claim that their rule was sanctioned by transcendental forces.

The masking principle

Axial Age China offers an illuminating illustration of this "masking" principle. Three belief systems contended for ruler support during the period when states competed for hegemony over China: Taoism, Confucianism, and Legalism (Realism).[5] Taoism was mystical. It was grounded in the Way of Nature, in a belief that artifice would always fail, that minimal government offers the best rule, that cultivating the pure soul was the best way to live life given the other options:[6]

> The crowd cares for gain/ the honest may for fame/ the good man values success/ but the Wise Man his soul.

The Taoists were monk-like. In their Ideal State, there would be no books, no records save knotted ropes, no machinery, no desire for splendid clothing, and only the simplest of foods. They mocked the Yellow Emperor who "was the first to tamper with men's hearts when he taught goodness and duty." According to the Taoists, the last thing you wanted to do was tamper with the hearts of the people.

This was mysticism. Possession by the natural gods; sheer reliance on the yin and yang principles that undergirded nature itself; rejecting war because it could never achieve its putative ends; in short, Taoism—which at the level of local communities promoted magic, yoga practice, the integration of physical motion with meditation—rejected the myth of the Yellow Emperor. It expressed one end of the heterogeneous religious spectrum.

Confucianism was a contender, rejecting the mysticism of Taoism, rather glorifying the principles of goodness and duty supposedly promulgated by the Yellow Emperor and followed by a few righteous rulers contending for control over China as a region. For Mencius, virtuous rule—benevolence, concern for the fate of subordinates—was the keystone of a good state. Proper observance of rituals—particularly rituals surrounding the death of parents—was essential. If rulers followed the "three years of mourning" upon the death of a parent (especially a male parent), burying the dead with subordinates killed as blood sacrifice, they would be true to, devoted followers of, a Mandate of Heaven. Provided the rulers were benevolent, the common people would prosper, and they too could follow the duties surrounding the deaths of their parents. To purify in the face of death the Confucian school recommended abstaining from sex, living near the tomb of the deceased in a makeshift tent, adopting a dejected face, in short engaging in exaggerated mourning aimed at displaying conscientious respect for the ancestors. In this school, ritual and mollification of the deceased (presumably motivated by fear of ghosts) was paramount. As a practical measure for imbibing the appropriate doctrines, the Confucian school rejected Taoist nihilism, arguing that study of the appropriate written classics was the way to be truly virtuous, truly pure.

The third school—known as *Fa Chia* (Rule of Law) rejected the mysticism of the Taoists as anarchy and the idea of benevolence as naïve. Rulers needed to be tough; people could not be trusted. They must be organized into groups that would monitor each other, mutual espionage being the best way to suppress rebellion, to fasten a tight lid over the boiling pot that was society. Excessive ritual like the "three years of mourning" was wasteful of wealth and human talent. Blood sacrifice was unnecessary and unwise because potentially valuable lives were being lost. Spirits were afoot across the land and should be placated lest they stir up discontent amongst the masses. These spirits were either sent down from heaven, were inhabitants of the hills and waterways, or ghosts of dead humans. The Code of Law must be completely transparent and long, regulating lives in great detail. To the extent possible resources must be preserved—the allocation for military preparation maximized—so that the state is ready to fight off contenders at all times. The plea of the Confucians to follow in the footsteps of ancient kings is naïve because the ancient kings did not have at hand the type of war-making technologies now available to rulers.

Confronted with the choice between these three schools of thought Chinese rulers ultimately elected to pursue Legalism or Realism in practice, while masking it behind Confucian principles. In doing so, they solved one of their chief problems: making sure their subordinate officials carried out the administration of laws in a forthright way. In so far as an official was trained along Confucian lines, the official believed that a fellow official might be truly committed to Confucian rectitude. You do not know for sure. This doubt discourages officials from forming groups that decide to systematically lie, systematically deceiving higher ups. In no way does this policy completely suppress corruption and injustice taking place at the local level. But it does reduce corruption and malfeasance over all. It is a second-best solution to the problem of how to formulate and fairly administer a set of laws that are draconian in fact, not in outward appearance. After all, accusing one of the little people of violating the "Mandate of Heaven" is a powerful threat that can be used to suppress rebellion and discontent.[7]

The idea of religion masking draconian rule applies to most of the great Axial Age traditions but not all of them. How do you employ the ancient myths in which heroes interact with the pure transcendental world in order to secure cooperation and acceptance of poverty for the masses? In the Chinese case, we see one option: masking cruel harsh rule under the guise of benevolent Confucian principles.

In Hinduism, the spread of the caste system offers another option. According to the "Poem of the Primeval Man," a cosmic giant, the Primeval Man, consisted of four parts. Dismembered, it broke into four parts. The mouth became the priests (Brahmins, the experts in sacred knowledge); the arms became the Raja (Kshatriya, the class of warriors, police and kings); the thighs the common people (Vaishya, farmers and merchants); and the feet, the lowest and least pure, the closest to the polluted earth the servants (Shudras, the outsider class). Spreading out into the concept of caste, this system of belief created a social order that could and was rationalized through the idea of *karma* linked to rebirth through transmigration of the soul. If you were situated at the bottom of the hierarchy in one's current manifestation on earth, practicing virtuous behavior rewarded you with good *karma*, opening up the possibility of your righteous soul occupying a higher caste status in a future life. Being virtuous now, being cooperative and accepting your lot in this life, could keep you from being reborn as a worm, a beetle, a wasp. At the local community level, the elite Brahmin castes could exercise harsh control over the lower castes if need be. In any case, the *karma* principle suppressed outbreaks of discontent on the part of the lower orders because the downtrodden occupied the bottom of the social hierarchy where the incentive to abide by your caste destiny was the strongest.

Before turning to the Greek tradition, it is useful to summarize our tentative conclusions about the changing role of religious thinking in societies transitioning from the era of mythic hero–gods to ones regulated by religiously inspired laws and social codes.

Transcendental monitoring remains in force. The deities and heroes of the mythic stage of organized religion are bloodthirsty. Blood sacrifice is rampant at this stage. The gods often as not warrior deities facilitate conquest over forces hostile to society. Fear of these gods—or the divine principles based under belief in the gods—goes hand-in-hand with fear of retribution by an all-seeing force. In short, fear of punishment is a hallmark of these faiths. In so far as the populace remained fearful, believing they will be duly punished by cosmic forces if they fail to be law abiding, encourages cooperative behavior, and the costs of shaping social control incurred by ruling elites are diminished. Monitoring is easier to carry out. Cooperation won through this means does help explain why markets develop during the second phase of the Axial Age, at least in cultures that managed the transition to an Axial Age belief system.

Gift exchange plays a strong role: in Hinduism, the Brahmins are the agents of this exchange, mediating with the divine; in the Chinese case, Confucian officials learn how to practice benevolence in administering government justified by the Mandate of Heaven. However, one form of gift exchange—blood sacrifice—becomes increasingly unimportant over time. It is too costly. It is largely relegated to execution of enemy combatants. In its place emerges the widespread practice of animal sacrifice. But even this is costly. Eventually, it takes on less and less costly forms: abstinence from food consumption at stipulated times of the year being one example.

Religious diversity

Religious diversity is important. Consider the Chinese case. Mysticism and magic mix with possession by the divine: seen as either a good thing (say by Taoists) or a bad thing (say by Legalists or Realists). In the case of Hinduism, the Brahmins who carry out religious rituals—denied completely to the lowly abused Shudras—can pursue mystic union with the godhead or stick to magical incantation. Moreover, for the lower castes the option of becoming a mystic in old age, renouncing materialism altogether, seeking union with the divine, practicing yoga infused meditation: all these became options as Hinduism became a mass-oriented religion in India. For a religion to persist as a successful social control mechanism for large hierarchical societies it has to be "big tent." It should accommodate diversity of expression. Mystics, magicians, governors and rulers, elites and non-elites must co-exist. Those who seek to nourish the soul in mystic union with the divine; those who want a god or religious principle to punish the wicked and reward the pure in heart; those who want to practice magic, dispensing hope and amulets to those aggrieved by tragic deaths of children infected by typhoid, rheumatic fever, or dysentery; all these disparate groups live chock-a-block with one another in the same community.

Where does this diversity come from? Why does it raise its ugly head, churning up treacherous wakes dispelling the myths of "ideal" types? It comes from diversity in temperament, personality, intelligence, and passion. The Axial Age Taoists explained it in terms of yin (negative/dark/feminine) and yang (positive/bright/masculine) mixing in different proportions. Hippocrates imagined it came from combinations of blood, yellow bile, black bile, and phlegm coursing through our physical bodies. Doctors needed to pick up the cues: too much yang might generate fevers just as too much light shining on a glass plate generates heat; too much blood might require blood-letting to restore balance in the humors. Today we speak of anxiety disorders, of hyperactivity, of clinical depression, of anorexia, of insomnia, of paranoia, of sociopathic personalities. We diagnose developmental disorders in our offspring with terms like autism. We have concocted pills and licensed therapies to cope with this diversity of conditions. The point is diversity exists. Whether it is the product of nature—hard-wiring in our brains and nervous systems—or nurture is a matter of on-going debate. That diversity exists is not a contentious issue.

A third feature of religious social control is resource based. Advertising is crucial for successful religions. They need to appeal to their members through structures, symbols, public rituals. To accomplish this, they need capital. They require financial backing whether it comes in the form of hard currency; endowment of land and structures; free labor; or jewelry, stained glass and sumptuous embellishments for the walls of religious structures.

Finally, each of these religious systems must deal with non-believers. Consider gift exchange. A member of a religion gives resources to a priest who intermediates with the transcendental world. How to you know he or she does what you ask? More to the point, gift exchange can easily slip into bribery. For this reason, societies in which religious gift exchange is extensive tend to be corrupt. Bribery goes hand in hand with gift exchange. Not surprisingly, skeptics emerge, disgusted by the corruption. That is one problem. Another problem is religious diversity itself. Schisms are fomented: sects develop, splitting off from the main branch of a faith, spawning new variants. How do you know what is the true practice for the religion? Maybe, you say, nobody knows. Maybe you say atheism is a better option. By atheism here I mean two types. Rejection of a particular set of deities or cosmic transcendental principles: this is atheism particular to a religious setting. A second form is general atheism. You are anti-theistic. You reject the idea of a transcendental world altogether. Thorough going materialists can—but do not have to—fall into this category of atheism.

To be sure authorities—religious, secular, or both working in tandem—can suppress skepticism and atheism in both of its guises. Still they must use resources to accomplish this. Suppression entails costs. Religious police in theocracies play this role: witness Iran and Saudi Arabia. Secular police in contemporary China do this as well. In China, the target is opposition to the Communist Party and its authoritarian ideology. You can do this, but it requires resources: loyal workers; honest intelligence gathering police; how do you trust the information culled by the intelligence gathers? Could they be deliberately lying to you? That is another problem.

Notes

1 On the Eurasian Cultural Complex, see Beckwith (2009).
2 The idea of an Axial Age was introduced when Karl Jaspers set about broadening Hegel's notion of a great axis of historical change ushered in by the doctrines of Jesus Christ (an embrace of cultural relativism that one might impishly describe as proto-politically-correct thinking). Hegel promulgated the idea of an historical turning point in his idealist theory of a historical dialectic. Clash of opposing ideas in the form of thesis contested by antithesis giving rise to a new synthesis. Jasper's argument was that all the major civilizations on the Eurasian land mass experienced Axial change during the period 1500 BCE to 1 CE. In China, Taoism and Confucianism emerged; in Persia Zoroaster preached a dualistic theory of light wrestling with darkness hidden in gross material matter; in India, the Upanishads pioneered an intellectual movement leading to *karma* and *ahimsa*; in Greece, the poems of Homer and Hesiod presented a world in which fate interacted with powerful gods who invested abiding interest in the behavior of warrior heroes; in the Middle East, the Israelites shook off polytheism, eventually declaring themselves key actors in a magnificent cosmic drama wherein they became the chosen few, bearing the burden of history on their own shoulders as it were. Once framed as a key concept in interpreting how ancient civilization came into being, the notion of a distinct Axial Age has recently become a matter of fierce debate as have the validity of interpretations of its very nature. Some scholars thinking along philosophical lines, speak about "thinking about thinking," second-order higher level thought. See the classic presentation in Eisenstadt (1986) and individually penned chapters in two recently published edited volumes, namely Aranson, Eisenstaat, and Wittrock (2005) and Bellah and Joas (2012). See Bellah (2011) for an attempt to explain the emergence and elaboration of religion in evolutionary terms. For the religiously tinted view that the idea of God entered world civilization during the Axial Age, see Armstrong (2006). The interpretation I give in this text is decidedly my own, to the best of my knowledge differing from the views of everyone else mentioned in this footnote.
3 For details concerning horse driven chariot warfare on the Eurasian steppes see Anthony (2007).
4 For the relationship of the impacts of population size, total economic output, and the technological change on the military potential of a society see the discussion of the military power equation in the Appendices.
5 Discussion taken from Waley (1939).
6 Quoted in Waley (1939: pg. 46).
7 For a concrete example of this phenomenon see Kuhn (1990). Kuhn describes horrific punishments and tortures imposed on individuals who are accused of upsetting or undermining the "Mandate of Heaven": the heavy wooden claque placed over the head bearing down on the shoulders; the ankle braces that manipulated by a torturer driving a wedge can eventually reduce the ankle bones to sheer mush; and beating and pummeling in front of colleagues. If this is not enough to turn your stomach consider forms of capital punishment: beheading; strangulation; starvation in a cage; and the most hideous of all—death by slow slicing. So much for Confucian benevolence aimed at propping up the Mandate of Heaven!

3 The pendulum swing in the Greek Axial Age

With these points in mind let us turn to the ancient Greek Axial Age.

Origins

Greek religion—more generally Greek philosophy—is a synthesis, drawing on diverse traditions. Egyptian, Hittite, Persian, Mycenaean, and Phoenician influences abound. A rich metal alloy fused from many minerals. Yet at its core is Proto-Indo-European myth. It shares many features with early Axial Age Hinduism, particularly in its initial stages. Zeus, head of the Greek pantheon is a sky god, sending lightning bolts down onto the earth. Indra, the king of gods—whose heroic presence shows up in the Hittite religion as early as 1400 BCE as well as in Indian Vedas—is a rain god, a warrior god, a slayer of the dragon Vritra.[1] Prometheus, defying Zeus, is the self-sacrificing deity who provides humans with fire; Agni, god of fire in the Vedas, carries oblations from humans to the gods.

In the primordial sagas, chronicling the exploits of Greeks and Hindu heroes and gods are remarkable similarities in the treatment of the mixing of divinity with humanness: some heroes are even begotten by divine creatures; some gods shed their immortality to perish like humans. Achilles, born of a goddess, dares to defy Apollo, arrogantly rages at the Olympians, yet ultimately perishes as a human. The Vedic god Krishna is wounded as a mortal would be, perhaps—depending on the version—dying of old age or leaving the world by withdrawing his divine powers.

The Vedic poem *Ramayana* tells of a great journey by a princely hero Rama who travels in southern India, fighting a world-shaking battle against Ravan in Sri Lanka, losing his beloved wife Sita on the way, continuing tested in bloody confrontations. This mythology parallels the *Odyssey* recounting the adventures of Odysseus returning to his loyal wife. On the way, he fights off the monstrous Cyclops, avoids the seductive singing of the Sirens, passes through the treacherous waters lying between Scylla and Charybdis, before finally dispatching to the underworld the suitors to his wife in a blood-stained finale.

Again, the Vedic poem *Mahabharata* centers around bloodthirsty battles, two groups of warriors fighting for hegemony—at its most dramatic in the famous sequence in which the god Krishna, in the guise of a chariot driver, advises the warrior Arjuna to do his duty despite understanding how meaningless is the bloodshed—paralleling the *Iliad* that seemingly throws up its hands at the brutal tragedies war brings. As well, the *Iliad* illustrates a deeply held aversion to human blood sacrifice in the tragedy of the House of Atreus. In order to launch his great fleet aimed at destroying Troy, Agamemnon sacrifices his daughter Iphigenia. Upon his return, his wife Clytemnestra takes her vengeance, dispatching him in a pool of blood.

Interestingly enough, the evidence suggests both sets of poems, Hindu and Greek, commenced as orally transmitted tales: story after story piled on one another through endless cycles of vocal repetition, perhaps accompanied by music, before taking written form. This is why I refer to these famous sagas as primordial.

Other parallels should not be discounted. Both Hindus and Greeks believed in the transmigration of souls, rebirth in future lifetimes. Both traditions made much of intoxication as a means of being possessed by divine forces in mystical union with the godhead. For the Hindus, soma, the drink offered to the deities along with fire as complementary opposites. For the Greeks, wine: inducer of the frenzied rites of the Bacchus (Dionysus) cult. The Bacchiads—the devotees of wine intoxicated Bacchus—were a cult of mystical ascetics whose extreme rituals could and did turn violent, most notably in the famous accounts of the band of female Maenads tearing apart wild animals in their violent ecstasies. Again, in the early Ionian school of Greek philosophy centered at Miletus on the coast of Asia Minor, the idea of universal wind or breath central to the Upanishads is paralleled by the views of Anaximenes who argued that air surrounds and cements together the universe just as the soul holds together the body.[2]

That said, Greek Axial Age thought and Indian Axial Age thought are profoundly different. To simplify to the point of caricature, Indian Axial Age thought evolved together with the social order into a caste based system relying heavily on the moral ethic of *karma*. Think about this as a horizontal construct, caste pervading all or most Indian kingdoms and princedoms, cutting across jurisdictional lines. By contrast, Greek thought developed most saliently along vertical fault lines, fiercely independent city states differentiating themselves on religious, philosophical, and constitutional grounds.[3] Out of the warring between *polis* factions *within* city states, and out of the warring and jockeying for hegemony *between* city states, emerged a powerful dynamic etched in both ideas and material reality: the pendulum swing.

To illustrate the various ways the concept of pendulum swing became deeply imbedded within the sinews of Greek life I will show how it informed three dimensions crucial to Greek civilization. In politics and military affairs, I will focus on the contrast between Athens and Sparta. In the great run of Athenian drama created during the period of Athenian ascendency and imperial control over a vast Aegean Sea empire (the fifth century BCE from the Battle of Marathon to the late 400s BCE) I will emphasize the oscillation between tragedy and comedy. Finally, in the field of philosophy, I will look at the swings between mystical philosophy and proto-scientific thinking, speculation moving back and forth between the antipodes of Platonic mysticism and Aristotle's proto-scientific approach.

The political pendulum swing

In many dimensions, Sparta and Athens were diametric opposites. Sparta was a rigidly institutionalized military society adept at fighting on the land; innovative in deploying troops (using the peltasts, who were more lightly armed than the hoplites outfitted in expensive armor); a stable oligarchy; and a crafty organizer of war-making coalitions, notably the Peloponnesian War alliance that brought imperial Athens to its knees. By contrast, Athenian constitutions swung between the despotic tyranny of Draco and the democracy of the fifth century. Athens exploited its closeness to the Aegean in consolidating a far-flung empire on the Aegean Sea's perimeter, bringing under its imperial mantle Rhodes, Samos, Miletus, Euboea, Thasos, and the shores of the Proconnesos all the way north to Byzantium. In accomplishing this task Athens promoted its version of democracy, made significant innovations in shipbuilding, and promulgated worship of Athena, its patron deity.

The stability of the Spartan government—a luster that appealed to Plato who imagined a stable utopia in his mid-career masterpiece, *The Republic*—was remarkable, unique among Greek city states (although Crete shared its military orientation). Devoted to war, citizens in the *polis*—exclusive of helots, a quasi-slave underclass whose Laconian ancestors had been defeated by the Spartans—were taken from their families, rigorously drilled in military techniques between the ages of five and thirty, and ordered to eat in common dining establishments with their fellow trainees. Above all, discipline was the keystone of social stability. Sparta had two kings who ruled together as a religious and legal power over an oligarchy consisting of military commanders and an aristocratic council, the *Gerousia*. One of the two kings would take part in military campaigns, leaving the other behind to tend to domestic business, including dealing with the possibility of helot rebellion.

Unlike the stability enjoyed by the Spartan *polis*, Athenian political life was chaotic. During the late-seventh century BCE, attempts to enforce tyranny gave way to the dictatorship of Draco who imposed a harsh law code in the aftermath (hence the word draconian). Feuding among the oligarchs ushered in rule by Solon—statesman and writer of poetry—who encouraged the spread of democracy. Having been drawn into a Greek city state alliance of convenience aimed at repelling a Persian drive for hegemony in the Aegean, Athenian forces proved valiant at the Battle of Marathon in 490 BCE. For the next eight and a half decades, Athens went about consolidating its control over the Aegean, using its mighty navy to exploit its commercially oriented colonies in Asia Minor and northern Greece. Predation and trade marched together as did the spread of democratic constitutions. What were the main features of Athenian democracy? One was the popular assembly, the *ekklesia*. Another was the jury system wherein popular jury members who were chosen and most importantly paid for their services. It is important to keep in mind that Athenian democracy excluded women—who were probably required to be veiled—and slaves, who did much of the grunt work. While it is not proper to refer to the typical Greek *polis* as a caste society, it can be described as enjoying a quasi-caste complexion, enforced by legal code and backed up by military prowess.

Testimony to the extreme jealousy of powerful Greek city states—especially fear of hegemonic rule by any one of their rivals—is their willingness to enter alliances of convenience aimed at defeating powerful rivals. Remarkably, some city states dared to approach their arch enemy, the Persians, in a bid to defeat a Greek rival. Paralleling this is the extreme localness of Greek polytheism. Consider worship of the god Apollo. A priest operating in a temple in one of the city states—say Corinth—would not be qualified to perform rituals in an Apollonian temple in one of the other city states, say Athens or Thebes.[4] The ruler of Corinth ordered its military to drive out the Bacchiads: abject fear of a faith erupting out of the bowels of a competing Greek city state in the Greek world was hard cold geopolitical reality. To return to a point made earlier: one gathers than the institutionalization of Hinduism was extremely different. Caste crossed jurisdictional lines, a Brahmin being a Brahmin enjoying special ritual privileges throughout the land.

To summarize, Greek city state politics exhibits strong pendulum swings both *within* and *between* states. Tyranny gives way to democracy; kings gave way to dictatorships; democracies become absorbed by oligarchies. City states, hyper-jealous of the pretenses of their rival city states, form alliances aimed at whittling hegemonic pretenders down to size. Minnows are rightly terrified of taking up resident in shark filled waters.

The pendulum swing in Greek drama

Athenian drama in the great fifth century characterized by empire building and democracy illustrates the pendulum swing principle in another dimension. In the thirty-two plays that have come down to us, we can see the pendulum swing at work. It swung *within* dramas; and the pendulum *swung* between three different types of drama, namely between tragedies and comic pieces, satyr plays or comedies.

Consider the tragedies of Aeschylus, Sophocles, and Euripides. Aristotle, writing at the dawn of the Hellenistic period, argued that Greek tragedy emerged out of a dithyramb sung by choruses devoted to Bacchus (Dionysus).[5] In short, its origins are religious, not surprisingly drawing heavily from the polytheistic Homeric legends, particularly the tragedy of the House of Atreus. The heroes may have been ancient but the message was contemporary, exceedingly political: at its heart lay the pendulum swing bringing the arrogant hero to his knees, the heroine to her just deserts. There is no better example than the *Oresteia* trilogy of Aeschylus. In the *Agamemnon*, the common folk bristle at the highhanded behavior of Queen Clytemnestra who, in league with her lover Aegisthus, has wrested power from her husband who they have killed. The chorus, representing the people, attacks the queen, the demagogue. For an Athenian audience celebrating its democratic rights, all of this carried a powerful political message: beware of the power we wield, you aristocrats; sheathe your swords; do not dare upset our constitutional applecart! We will check you! Do you think you dare to ignore our religion, our oracles: behold Oedipus, devoid of sight! In Euripides' *Bacchae*, a king excessively absorbed in micro-managing the populace through his despotic laws refuses to carry out his religious obligations thereby sending his city state into a tailspin. At the denouement, he is torn to shreds, blood sacrifice brought on by his failure to respect the checks democracy imposes on a righteous ruler.

The comedies mocked the tragedies. For instance, in Aristophanes' comic *Frogs*, Dionysus is ordered by Pluto—grim god of the underworld, seated around a table with his minions—to judge a contest pitting two of the great Athenian tragedians Aeschylus and Euripides against one another. Who shall occupy the "Best Tragic Poet" seat? Pick from the Greek dramatists currently residing in Pluto's underworld please. Aeschylus triumphs because his verbiage is "heavier"; Euripides is too slick. Again, in *The Clouds*, Aristophanes takes aim at Socrates, gently making fun of the great philosopher.

Greek drama swung between two antipodes. Tragedy always invested with a serious ominous political and religious message could and was counteracted by comedy. The Athenian audience had its cake and ate it too. Skepticism was rife: you always knew the pendulum might swing in the contrary direction.

The pendulum swing in philosophy

Greek philosophy also swung between two poles: religious mysticism and proto-science.[6]

We associate the proto-scientific school with the earliest of the known Greek philosophers: the group of thinkers gathered in Ionian Miletus. Evolutionary and materialist, not deistic, thinking was the hallmark of the views of Thales, Anaximander, and Anaximenes. For Thales, water underlay everything; for Anaximander, the universe consisting of many worlds emerged out of boundlessness and was destined to be reabsorbed into it. For Anaximenes, air was the ultimate substance, binding all matter together in a unity, just as the soul (consisting of air) contains and holds the physical body together. Air is the ultimate cement. While we should not think of this reasoning as overtly atheistic, skepticism about the existence of a transcendental world does pervade it. Or rather, skepticism about any particular theistic vision: the philosopher Xenophanes altogether rejected anthropomorphic representations of deities. He pointed out that Thracians imagined their gods as Thracians while Negros thought the divine bodies were Negroid.[7] Early Greek materialist reasoning was crowned in the fifth century BCE with the speculations of Democritus who conceived of physical reality in terms of atoms, unobservable but still real minute particles.

At the other pole of Greek philosophy was mysticism. Russell (1945: 16–17) traces the mystic tradition back to Bacchus, specifically to the religious cult exalting Orpheus, the Orphics. The ascetic Orphics longed for purification. Outside of eating animal food in sacramental rituals, they abstained from consuming meat. Active in the late sixth century BCE, Pythagoras inherited this tradition. He founded a religion that mixed the purity of mathematical logic to asceticism aimed at guaranteeing the purity of the soul that he reckoned would be reborn in future bodies (transmigration of the soul). Mathematical knowledge came through ecstatic revelation; divinity was embodied in it. It is hard to separate this cult of esoteric knowledge from Gnosticism, the view that privileged elites—and only privileged elites—are granted access to truth, a theory captured in the notion vividly realized in Plato's *Republic*, the typical human consigned to observing shadows cast against the wall of a cave by a fire lit behind their backs, only elite philosophers escaping the dark dungeon to bask in the light of ultimate reality.

The ancient philosophers sought stability. Their agenda rested on a unified firmly rooted foundation, freed from the transient, stripped of speculations reflecting the earthquake-like shaking that humdrum quotidian reality throws up into our faces. In the Greek case, this meant avoiding the pendulum swing. The two most famous philosophers of the Hellenic world, Plato and Aristotle, illustrate this phenomenon. Interestingly enough, their solutions to constructing unshakeable foundations show that this goal can be realized in a totally religious-mystical philosophy (Plato) or along proto-scientific lines (Aristotle). Ironically in proposing radically different interpretations of stability they set in motion a pendulum swing in philosophical thought that echoes through Western thought even to this very day.

Pursuing the vision of Pythagoras, Plato flourished in the late fifth and early fourth centuries BCE. Athenian democracy was under attack by threats of tyranny in his lifetime. At the center of Plato's early writings— *Apology, Crito, Euthyphro, Phaedo, Ion*—is the figure of Socrates, the gadfly of Athens. Socrates had a peculiar attitude toward the democracy Athenians had managed to eke out in the fifth century. To be sure he reveled in the freedom of speech it promoted. The Socratic dialogues are dialectical. They are grounded in the back-and-forth of logical argument. Individual Intellectual freedom was all, leading Socrates to question the validity of the Athenian gods themselves. Indeed, Socrates claimed to have a personal god, his *daimonian*.

At the same time, Socrates had withering contempt for the common person. At heart, he was an elitist, a mystic, a proto-Gnostic. Plato captured the contradictory nature of Socrates in the *Apology*, an account of Socrates's defense against the accusation that he "failed to acknowledge the gods that the city acknowledges" rather "introducing new deities." When pronounced guilty of impiety, Socrates was offered two options: exile or death. Exile was certainly a viable option. Socrates could have removed himself to Thebes where likeminded Pythagoreans thrived, taking in exiles pushed out of a myriad of city-states. Yet Socrates elected death. Why? Because committed mystic as he was, death held out no terror to him. This is the religious vision centered on self-sacrifice of the holy martyr, the religious hero. Not surprisingly, the Socratic choice exerted a peculiar fascination with martyrdom that stained early Christianity. Christian philosophers—notably Saint Augustine and later Boethius, penning *The Consolation of Philosophy* in his prison cell where he awaited execution—were attracted to Platonism, partly due to the edifying example of Socrates, his glorious soul soaring triumphantly over the mundane reality of death.

Mimicking the inconsistency regarding the democracy of Socrates, Plato reacted to the accusation of impiety leveled at Socrates in a seemingly contradictory manner. Ultimately, he appeared to condemn Socratic freethinking. Searching for a way to guarantee political stability, Plato came to idolize Sparta the most stable of the Greek city states, developing his theory of the *Republic* along Spartan constitutional lines. In his account of the ideal utopian city, the polity is divided into three groups. Occupying the apex of the city-state hierarchy is the class of philosopher guardians imbibing mystical truth, able to grasp the forms or concepts constituting ideal reality. Making up the middle stratum is the group of soldiers providing protection for the people. At the bottom are the rank and file commoners, those completely blind to the light. To ensure stability the commoners must be controlled, fed state propaganda fashioned by the elite guardians.

Note the paradox: this is tantamount to banishing any freethinker like Socrates who questioned the mystically pure elite. Reasoning along these lines, Plato argued that the Guardians should practice communism, rejecting private property, sharing wives in common. Shades of Spartan communal military training? Or was it radical invocation of purified monastic rule? Plato's willingness to suppress free thought in the service of stability reached an apex in his late writings, notably in *Laws* where he advocates establishment of orthodox state faith.

At the other end of the Greek philosophical spectrum was Aristotle. Despite having been a student of Plato at the Academy, Aristotle ultimately rejected Platonic idealism, the notion of immaterial forms. Ionian at heart, a keen observer of the natural order, Aristotle was a particularly avid biologist. For Aristotle, matter and form were intertwined. He even speculated about the birth of the soul: was it in the male sperm alone? How important was the female contribution?

Aristotle's aversion to pendulum swing instability encouraged him to develop a theory of government in which the middle class, not the Platonic elite, was the key ingredient to a lasting constitution. To be sure, slaves were inferior. Primarily moved by emotional instincts, slaves were more akin to animals than rational humans and should be guided by their rulers. Key to government is proper balance between acceptable levels for the concentration of wealth and absolute equality. Rejecting communism—only private property induces innovation, thereby improvements in the technological arts—Aristotle argued that the greed and arrogance of aristocrats should and could by tempered by ideology encouraging humility and public mindedness among the economically successful:[8]

> The common people quarrel about the inequality of property, the higher class about the equality of honor ... the beginning of reform is not so much to equalize property as to train the nobler sort of natures not to desire more ... governments which have a regard to the common interest are constituted with strict principles of justice, and are therefore true forms; but those which regard only the interest of rulers are all defective.

Aristotle's pragmatic agenda—considering the realities of human nature, including appreciation that resentment, hostility, and greed cannot be denied or argued away in idealist mysticism—was aimed at preventing the debasement of potentially good forms of governance. Relatively pure societies should not be allowed to degenerate into muck. He viewed tyranny as a perversion of royalty; oligarchy a perversion of aristocracy; and democracy a perversion of constitutional government. In short, he advocated a "middle way" balance between inequality and equality that would stabilize governance in good forms, ones that promoted real world justice.

Aristotle's relentless search for a middle ground was hardly restricted to politics. It pervades his physics as well. In nature, a consensus like that of harmony prevails. Yet everything in the physical world is animated; everything—goats, pigs, birds, rocks sliding off cliffs, water churned up in whirlpools, clouds continually shifting shape as the drift across the horizon—is animated, potentially subject to being moved. How can this animation be reconciled with harmony? After all, motion is not desirable as it corrupts the unity achieved by nature. Along lines similar to those he postulated concerning an ideal political realm, states being prevented from degenerating into impure types, Aristotle postulated an explanation for the capacity of the universe to ward off corruption despite the unending animated movement characterizing the earth. Within the universe is a motionless realm: an outer ring, totally pure, where the fixed stars resided. The four elements—air, water, fire, and earth—seek their proper places in a circular hierarchy of rings located between the world humans inhabit and the outer shell where the stars twinkle in their unmoving glory. On earth, air is somewhat sullied;

only when it reaches its proper location does it exist in a purified form. The same applies to water; the same applies to fire. At the center is the natural realm of earth; above it the realm of water; above that the realm where air seeks to find its motionless state; and above that the natural locus for fire that spews out the comets observed flashing through the heavens. The four elements are mixed together at the center of the cosmos, but they naturally move toward the realms where they enjoy constancy, no longer subjected to rough and ready mixing, no longer forced to move.

What explains the impulse of objects and animated life crossing through the mediums of air and water? The answer: animation within mediums, the air for example. Shoot an arrow through air. The air moves it as it is loosed from the bow; finally—if it does not find a target but keeps on flying—it stops from moving because the animated air puts on the brakes. From this hypothesis, Aristotle deduced an incredibly important corollary: a vacuum cannot exist. The reason is simple. If there is no air, there is nothing to move the arrow, nothing to stop it from moving. This is a contradiction: an arrow cannot occupy two distinct places at the same time. A vacuum is an oxymoron.

Let us summarize. The Greek Axial Age was characterized by pendulum swings: in political life; in drama; and in philosophy. Set in motion by the xenophobic clashing city-states, the principle of the pendulum swing continued to work its way through the Hellenistic era that saw Greek culture spreading from Egypt through Afghanistan to the western fringes of India, and through the dominance by Rome of a sprawling empire stretching from Western Europe—Spain, through Gaul, even across the channel to England—through the Mediterranean into Asia Minor and across the expanse of North Africa.

The strength of the pendulum swing lies in progress, in intensification of thought and action in competing arenas, each working hard to outdo the other. It is impossible to imagine Aristotle without appreciating his tutelage in Plato's Academy. It is impossible to understand Aristophanes without considering the artistic nature and practical real-world politics surrounding Athenian tragedy. Ferreting out the weaknesses in your adversary's position encourages critical thinking and critical analysis that can be turned against your own position, encouraging you to shore up your stance. Like it or not, we strive harder when we are trying to overcome our adversaries. Competition is fine. Cooperation at the cost of retarding progress is not necessarily admirable. As well, its appeal is rooted in heterogeneity. By dint of temperament, native intelligence, nurture, good or bad luck, we are a highly diverse species. Let loose in an environment where we can choose sides, we have options. We form strategic alliances, sequestering our positions under the canopy of a "big tent." Absent a protective umbrella, we have no chance of seeing our pet ideas, our material agendas, become reality. Our colleagues in the "big tent" presumably feel likewise. Consider the alternative: censorship preventing individuals the right to choose. Cast loose in an environment where options are severely constrained, talent and enthusiasm falls by the wayside.

Notes

1 For my discussion of early Hindu mythology, I draw upon Doniger (2009), particularly the first eleven chapters. For the *Ramayana* and the *Mahabharata*, I draw on the condensed versions in Dutt (1910, 1953).
2 For much of the discussion of Ancient Greece and Greek philosophical thought I rely on the various chapters in Boardman, Griffin, and Murray (1986) that deal with Greece, and upon the classic account of the history of Western philosophy penned by Russell (1945).
3 Without a doubt, one can make a geographic argument about why Greek politics, military competition, as well as thought took on an adversarial complexion. The region occupied by the Greeks consisted of a massive peninsula, a mainland crisscrossed by mountain ranges, and a group of islands lying off the Aegean. Ancient Greece naturally found itself divided into regions, each organized around city states dominating their rural hinterlands. Euboea, Laconia, Arcadia, Achaea, Boeotia, Argolis, and Thessaly were all distinctive regions competing against one another, as were the city states of Athens, Sparta, Corinth, and Thebes. The problem with this view is that it is not apparent that Greek civilization began in this crazy-quilt manner. Nor is it obvious that the competition between political entities was driven by geography. It may well have been driven by clashing ideologies. Perhaps changes in the two arenas—ideas and material reality—co-evolved with one another.
4 Whitmarsh (2015: 21).
5 On this point and some of the other insights I offer in my discussion of Greek drama, see Mendelsohn (2016).
6 For the view that philosophy emerged out of religion and science see Russell (1945). I prefer the term "proto-science" to science since most Greek thinking about material substance was purely theoretical, eschewing experimentation and detailed observation, particularly observation employing instruments. Moreover, the reasoning used by the early Greek materialists was deeply steeped with animism. Aristotle, who brought ancient Greek scientific tradition to its apex—his biology was quite sophisticated and insightful—advanced a comprehensive theory of physics shot full of animism.
7 Whitmarsh (2015: 44–47) refers to this approach as theomachy from the Greek term *theomakhia* "battling the gods." His point is that the extreme localness of Greek religion—its highly competitive nature—opened the door to the idea that there might not be gods at all.
8 Aristotle's text as translated and excerpted by Ross (1955: 300–302).

4 God as king in Jewish monotheism

Kings, priests, and prophets

Isaiah (45: 14) says it clearly: "Surely God is in thee, and there is none else, There is no other God." Strict monotheism: nothing can be further from Greek or Hindu polytheism. And so it was always says the Hebrew Bible.[1] "Hear, O Israel, the Lord our God, the Lord is one ..." says Deuteronomy (6: 4). According to Biblical experts Deuteronomy was one of the first books completed by the scribes and priests who wrote the original scrolls making up the Bible. It contains the Ten Commandments. It sets the stage for the Hebrew conquest of the land of Canaan as predicted in Numbers (33: 50–52), an act of determined preplanned predation:

> And the Lord spoke unto unto Moses in the plains of Moab by the Jordan at Jericho, saying 'Speak unto the children of Israel, and say unto them: When ye pass over the Jordan into the land of Canaan, then ye shall drive out all the inhabitants of the land from before you, and destroy all their figured stones, and destroy all their molten images, and demolish all their high places.

So it is clear. The Jews were always monotheistic. They were never polytheists. Never did they worship gods represented by figured stones or molten images placed on high places.

No.

The fact is the Hebrew people started out as polytheists. They made molten images of deities. They worshipped before statues of calves. Their God was originally secondary to a sun god. The god of the Hebrews began its career as a storm warrior god, only later taking on the role of creator god described in the book of Genesis.

Careful parsing of the Biblical texts; recent archeological investigation conducted in the Holy Land; study of Assyrian, Egyptian and Neo-Babylonian texts and inscriptions on monuments; tells us that the original Biblical documents were composed at a time when monotheistic worship of an aniconic god had become well entrenched in Jerusalem, the capital of the kingdom of Judah. This would have been around the sixth or seventh centuries BCE.

To be sure, competitor gods were alive and well in the rituals and minds of some Judeans. However, the political and religious elites—kings, officials, military leaders, priests, and scribes—were committed to the promotion of a temple cult centered on Yahweh (Yhwh). This god retained features of a storm god. Why? Insufficient rainfall spells crop failure. Fear of famine was a horrific reality in the desert lands of the Levant. Yahweh (Yhwh) also bore the trappings of a warrior god. Why? Predation feeds on predation. The geopolitics of the Levant involved constant and continual warfare. Warrior gods protected the people in Tyre; they protected the Moabites; they rallied the Philistines; they were invoked by the Phoenicians.

The reality facing the various nations co-existing in the Levant during the first millennium BCE was this: the peoples were pawns in contests for power initiated by powerful neighbors. Before Alexander the Great conquered much of Asia Minor in the fourth century, the powerful neighbors were Assyria to the north, Egypt to the west, and the Neo-Babylonian Empire to the east. They treated the Levant as a buffer zone. To appreciate the politics of a buffer zone, think Poland, Lithuania, and the Ukraine; think Manchuria; think Albania, Macedonia and the Balkans. Buffer zones have two main characteristics. Win–win trade goes on in these regions, attracting in big powers intent on controlling and taxing it. Contesting control over the region, great regional powers attempt to stake out vassalage relations with the national groups occupying space in the buffer. Not surprisingly, they pursue this agenda by attempting to impose their ideologies upon the peoples they conquer or bully into submission. Their gods mock the gods of the conquered. Nothing is more humiliating to the status of a warrior god than submission to a more powerful deity.

It is unlikely that there was ever a unified state that fragmented into Israel to the north and Judah to the south.[2] The unified kingdom breaking apart upon the death of Solomon is myth dreamed up by editors of the Bible in order to promote a theory, the theory of Yahweh (Yhwh) as a god punishing his chosen people for the sins of their ethically and ritually deficient rulers. Let us call this the "fall due to sin" thesis. It parallels the notion of hubris that brought down the Greek heroes. As far as well can infer from archeology it appears Saul was able to establish some kind of state in the region of Benjamin. It is likely King David led a coup against Saul, perhaps buttressed by Philistine allies to whom he owed vassal service. A dynasty emerged in the north, the Omrid dynasty, making its capital Samaria. According to the "fall due to sin" theory, the Omrid kingdom came afoul of its corrupt rulers. It appears one of their chief sins was worshipping Baal, a Phoenician god that attracted many worshippers throughout the nations of the Levant.

Elaborating on the story line involving the "fall due to sin" is the story of Jehu who—according to the Bible—overturns the Omrids, setting up right-eous rule, banning worship of Baal. The idea here is that after the fall comes redemption. A righteous ruler emerges, conquers restoring purity. In point of historical fact things were very different. It is probable Jehu was a vassal of the Assyrians who began their inroads southward into the Levant during the ninth century BCE.[3] In any event the kingdom of Israel managed to survive and eventually prosper by playing second fiddle to the Assyrians.

Subsequently, King Jeroboam II (787–747 BCE) acting at the behest of his Assyrian overlords, ruled over an economically successful territory enriched by the production of and trade in olive oil. From Bible accounts involving the prophet Hosea it appears some of the people in the kingdom became rich from the proceeds of the olive oil trade, flaunting their wealth, wielding their power over a growing impoverished population. Commencing with this account is a theme running through the prophetic literature in the Bible like a swelling river: the utopian idea that in economic injustice will—should—disappear in a world in which everyone follows the dictates of God. Interestingly enough, Hosea also denounces worship of "calves" in Samaria and Bethel, suggesting that the protecting deity of Israel, the northern kingdom, was represented by molten images, specifically of a bovine form.[4]

In so far as the god of Israel was worshipped in bovine form—in holy places erected at Samaria, Bethel, and Dan—it is likely this practice was an overlay of Baal worship. After all Baal took the form of a bull in Ugarit rituals. That Yahweh (Yhwh) was competing with Baal in Israel is apparent from the Biblical account of Elijah organizing a contest between priests devoted to Baal and himself on Mount Carmel. In the contest Baal is completely humiliated. That said, other gods—El, for example—enjoyed favor in Israel. Jehu, an ardent proponent of Yahweh (Ywhw) according to the Biblical authors could go only so far in promoting the cult in Israel. Moreover, it is likely the cult he did establish as proprietary to Israel was an amalgam of Baal and Yahweh (Ywhw) as attested by the altars set up honoring a bovine statue.

Bristling against Assyrian domination, the last king of Israel—Hosea—attempted to cobble together an anti-Assyrian alliance. He tried to entice the king of Judah, Ahaz, to join his crusade, planning a combined attack against Assyria. Ahaz—perhaps driven on by the encouragement of the prophet Isaiah—resisted, playing an anti-Israeli card. In the aftermath Israel fell to the Assyrians in 722 BCE, about twenty percent of its populace was forcibly relocated to other Assyrian dominated territories, and the former kingdom was carved up into four Assyrian provinces. In pursuing what can only be described as a cynical pro-Assyrian policy, Ahaz enhanced the status of his capital—Jerusalem—at the expense of Samaria. The cults of Jerusalem gained ascendency over the cults of Israel. Jerusalem trumped Samaria.

What prevailed in the Jerusalem cult during the seventh and eighth centuries BCE? According to Römer (2015: 100 ff) in the Jerusalem temple as originally constructed Yahweh (Ywhw) was lodged in a lateral chapel, the main part of the sacred space devoted to Shamash a solar god. Over time the royalty favoring Yahweh (Yhwh) marginalized the solar god, perhaps setting up statues to the god. One reason it is plausible that there were "molten images" of Yahweh (Yhwh) worshipped in Jerusalem is the fact the Biblical authors make the worship of molten images a major reason for the eventual fall of Jerusalem and Judah to the Neo-Babylonian Empire in the early sixth century BCE (specifically between 597 and 587 BCE). Zedekiah was the last king of Judah; the temple was completed destroyed in 587.

According to the "fall due to sin" theory Judah fell because it was impious. It betrayed Yahweh (Yhwh), playing the harlot as prophets like Jeremiah said. Along these lines the history of the kings reigning in Judah between the death of Ahaz and Zedekiah is instructive. Hezekiah is praised because he pursued an anti-Assyrian policy (in doing so he tried to forge an alliance with Egypt, playing off one big power against the others). This enraged the Assyrians who proceeded to destroy most of the cities on Judah, but failing—perhaps by strategic intent, perhaps due to a lack of military muscle—to take Jerusalem.

Buying into the second part of the "fall due to sin" theory—redemption after perdition—the editors of the Bible view the "miraculous" survival of Jerusalem in 701 was a sign Yahweh (Yhwh) had stood steadfast with his chosen people, protecting Mount Zion. Overall—despite the military debacle in Judah—Hezekiah "walked in the ways of the Lord," or at least this is the gloss put on his rule by scripture. On the other hand, his successor Manasseh who ruled for over fifty years was considered corrupt. He reintroduced Assyrian practices. He promoted a cult of Asherah, something that the "wicked" king of Israel had done earlier during the ninth century. He picked the wrong deity.

Fortunately—according to scripture—redemption was in the wings. Josiah became king of Judah, carrying out a sweeping series of reforms.[5] He banned other cults. He drove out the "sacred" prostitutes—both male and female—from the temple. In short, he was a purifier. Along with David and Hezekiah, he was one of the "pious" kings of the Hebrew people. It is likely that the original text of Deuteronomy was composed by priests and officials eager to solidify the cult of Yahweh (Ywhw) along the lines of Josiah. The claim advanced in the Bible—that a priest Hilkiah discovered an early version of the Torah when the temple was being purified under Josiah's rule—is a pious fraud, like the infamous Donation of Constantine of the Medieval Period. Citing ancient sources for newly constructed documents is an old royal game. The Egyptian king Akhenaton played it in the fourteenth century BCE in his attempt to reform Egyptian religion as did the Neo-Babylonian ruler Nabonidus in the sixth century in reconstructing the temple devoted to Shamash.

Unfortunately, Josiah's reforms did not completely take, or rather his successors—Jehoahaz, Jehoiakim, and Jehoiachin—failed to properly follow the example Josiah pioneered. Perhaps Josiah's death at the hand of the Egyptians had something to do with this.

In any case, Judah fell to the Neo-Babylonian Empire at the beginning of the sixth century BCE. More striking, the temple was completely destroyed in 587. How was this catastrophe to be properly explained in theological/ideological terms? Three groups responded to the crisis. It is these three groups that dominated the writing of the scrolls that make up much of the Hebrew Bible. One group—consisting of fiery prophets like Jeremiah—interpreted the disaster in utopian terms. A new era was unfolding. A second group—dominated by priests, Levites, sons of Zadok—sought to place the event in an ongoing cosmic theory of divine action and revelation echoing down from the creation of the universe. Their obsession was ancient origins. A third group—former high officials active in the royal chambers—sought to write a history of the kings, interpreting the history of the Hebrew people in terms of a series of "fall due to sin" cycles.

Diaspora communities under one God

In any event, very little if any of the writing of the precursor documents to the Hebrew Bible was done in Jerusalem. It was done in diaspora communities especially in Babylonia where much of the Hebrew elite was relocated after the destruction of the temple. Some of it may have done in Egypt, Jews having fled there in the eighth century around the period when Samaria fell to the Assyrians, or later when Jerusalem was destroyed and occupied by the Neo-Babylonian. It is not clear exactly when the compilation of documents was achieved. It is likely that this occurred after the Neo-Babylonian Empire fell to the Persians. It was the Persian king Cyrus who invited the Jews back to Jerusalem to rebuild their temple who is celebrated in the final page of the Hebrew Bible, the end of Second Chronicles (35: 22–23):

> Now in the first year of Cyrus king of Persia, that the word of Lord by the mouth of Jeremiah might be accomplished, the Lord stirred up the spirit of Cyrus king of Persia, that he made a proclamation throughout all his kingdom, and put it also in writing, saying: "Thus saith Cyrus king of Persia: All the kingdoms of the earth hath the Lord, the God of heaven, given me; and He hath charged me to build Him a house in Jerusalem, which is in Judah. Whosoever there is among you of all His people—the Lord his God be with him—let him go up".

In short, the Bible closes on a high note. At last redemption has been achieved; out of deep travail, victory has emerged.

Note how this has "fall due to sin" cycle has been achieved. It has come about because Yahweh (Yhwh) has directed other nations—notably Egyptians, Assyrians, Neo-Babylonians, and Persians—to either punish the Hebrew people for their sins or has rescued them. The logical conclusion is that Yahweh takes precedence over the gods of these punishing or benefactor nations. In short, He is the primary god. Or rather he is the only god.

Since all the other gods have been worshipped in the form of molten images, He—the one and only god—cannot be worshipped in this way. Because most of the kings of Israel and Judah ignored this fact they brought famine and defeat upon their peoples. Now that the one and only god has made it clear He cannot be properly worshipped in the form of molten images, that He is transcendent over all other gods, He will lead his people back to Jerusalem to build a properly adorned temple.

This is the period when Judaism takes on the mantle of monotheism. Noteworthy is the fact this occurs when most Jews live in diaspora communities ruled by non-Jewish kings. In short, Judaism becomes a religion that does not require a king to institute and control it. God is the king.[6]

All of this raised huge intellectual problems for the priestly class that thrived on theology. How to reconcile the idea of one and only one God, a creator god, with the idea of a god that takes special interest in a chosen people? The ingenious solution to this problem lies in the way the Torah is composed. In Genesis, the creator God is El. He creates the universe, He creates Adam in his image, He causes the great flood. He is addressed as "elohim". When this God interacts with the various nations—the Arabs descended from Ishmael, the Moabites descended from Esau, the Jews descending from Jacob—he is "El Shadday", the god of the Patriarchs. When he establishes a covenant with Moses He reveals himself as Yahweh (Yhwh) giving the secret of His true identity and name to the Hebrews. Lest the Jews excessively profit from this remarkable covenant, a price is imposed. They are forbidden to pronounce His name. Moreover, they do not need a country or territory. As a diaspora people, they have a king: Yahweh (Yhwh).

Out of the Dead Sea Scrolls

Unfortunately—or fortunately depending on your viewpoint—the Jews were able to reestablish a kingdom during the first millennium BCE: the Hasmonean theocracy cum kingdom that controlled most of the territory originally under Israeli and Judean rulers, even aggrandizing additional territories through military victories. Under the rule of high priests commencing with Judas Maccabeus in 166 BCE it eventually morphed into a kingdom. One king, Alexander Jannaeus ruled the lands for almost three decades (103–76 BCE), earning a reputation for cruelty amongst detractors, a reputation for stalwart leadership as the "Lion of Judah" by supporters. It was a period of civil war, the community of Jews breaking into warring factions, evincing religious heterogeneity of the most extreme decree. The widow of Jannaeus who became queen, Salome Alexandra, swung one hundred and eighty degrees away from the power base her husband had cobbled together, leaving it to her two sons Aristobulus II and John Hyrcanus II to feed off the sectarian strife.

Ultimately, the internecine chaos ushered in direct control by the Romans. The Romans had always been operating behind the scenes—they had signed treaties with the Jewish authorities—allowing the Jewish state to survive as a kind of vassal, acting as counterweight to a Hellenistic Seleucid state in the north. In 63 BCE, the Roman general invaded the territory, took over control of Jerusalem, and entered—to his great surprise—the second temple of the Hebrew people, totally empty, devoid of any statues. Shortly thereafter, the Romans created a province placed under the rule of a Hellenized Idumean Jew, Herod the Great who enlarged—and to a degree "Romanized"—the temple between 27 and 20 BCE.[7] The fact is the original version of the second temple had been a sorry replica of the original Solomon temple. Herod attempted to make it more monumental, more in line with the grand architectural achievements of the Greeks and Romans.

Hellenization was the principal background casting its shadow over the Hasmonean state. It consisted of hard power in the form of military dominance and soft power in the form of Greek ideas.

As hard power Hellenization began with the military victories of Alexander the Great who whirled out of Macedonia, conquered the Greek city states, and pushed his troops through Persia into northwest India. At the time of his death in 323 his empire stretched from Macedonia to the Indus River. In his wake, he left a plethora of newly created cities, notably Alexandria in Egypt. It is quite possible he was poisoned by his own subordinates. Indeed, his troops rebelled, forcing him to abandon his ambitious military plans for conquest of India, a process he initiated in 326 BCE. After his demise, over four decades of fierce fighting ensued amongst his surviving military retainers. It was only after this bloodbath ran its course—predation feeding on predation—that four stable power blocs emerged out of the wheeling and dealing of rival military commanders. These were Ptolemaic Egypt; Seleucid Mesopotamia and central Asia; Attalid Anatolia; and Antigonid Macedon. The principal lands occupied by the Jews were threefold: Ptolemaic Egypt particularly Alexandria; Seleucid Babylonia; and a buffer region contested by the Ptolemaic and Seleucid rulers, including Jerusalem.

Soft power—ideas—probably trumped hard power in shaping the futures of the various regions conquered by Alexander the Great. In particular a significant number of Jewish intellectuals were attracted to Greek philosophy, notably Philo of Alexandria who became a kind of Platonist apologist for Judaism.[8] To a philosopher like Philo, the Hebrew scriptures were allegorical, not to be taken literally. God is imminent in ideas and in all material reality[9]:

> God fills all things; He contains but is not contained. To be everywhere and nowhere is His Property and His alone. He is nowhere, because He Himself created space and place coincidently with material things.

Interestingly enough, despite his strong Platonist leanings and his emphasis on allegory in the sacred scriptures including the Torah, Philo was a staunch believer in following Jewish ritual. His agenda was amalgamating the best of Greek thought with the revelations offered by the Hebrew Bible. He was definitely not an atheist or agnostic.

Whether the Jewish Hellenizers active in Jerusalem were atheists—at least atheists as far as Yahweh (Yhwh) is concerned—is another matter. They were certainly willing to assist Antiochus IV Epiphanes, the Seleucid ruler who viewed himself as a god (hence the name "Epiphanes") in converting the Jerusalem temple into a sanctuary devoted to Zeus. As well they supported his ban on possession of the Torah, ordering copies of the scrolls burned; they supported his injunction against circumcision and ritual sacrifice. These were the individuals the First and Second Books of Maccabees disparagingly identify as "lawless." They were opposed to the theology of the Hebrew Bible; they were opposed to the rituals; they were willing to have the foreskins of their penises reconfigured, removing all traces of circumcision. They rejected Mosaic laws root and branch.

Opposing the Hellenizers was a highly fragmented community of Jewish stalwarts, each pursuing their own political and ritualistic agenda. Attack on the Hellenizers began with a guerrilla war directed at the group. The five sons of a rural priest Mattathias who died in 166 BCE led a military campaign aimed at driving out the Hellenizers, overturning the laws restricting ritual practices of Judaism, and purifying the temple. The most prominent of the brothers—Judas—was known as the "hammer" (Maccabee). His brother Jonathan Maccabee became high priest subsequently assassinated and replaced as high priest by his brother Simon. The Maccabees fought the armies of the Seleucids across the Holy Land. During these battles three of the five brothers perished. However Roman support for the Jewish state kept the Seleucids from recapturing most of the territory they had controlled. In geopolitical terms, the Jewish theocracy established by the Maccabees was a vassal state of Rome.

That said, it was a Jewish state. Which version of Judaism would take precedence? Recall that the Hebrew Bible was a compromise document, satisfying at the minimum the agendas of three groups: utopian prophets; kings and their officials; and priests. One issue that needed thrashing out was the role of the priesthood, the Levites. Were they to retain their traditional monopoly over scripture and its interpretation? Not surprisingly, the party of priests—the Sadducees—supported the Hasmonean regime established by the Maccabees. After all, Jonathan and Simon Maccabee had been high priests. This situation continued when the state became a kingdom. Under Alexander Jannaeus the Sadducees continued to have the upper hand.

One group opposing the Sadducees consisted of "lay priests." They were devoted to the oral Torah. They were the predecessors of the rabbis. They enjoyed considerable popularity in the countryside, perhaps because they were not deeply involved the temple leadership, hence less likely to be corrupted by the gift exchange practices of the Levites.[10] Like the Sadducees, the Pharisees could be cruel. A leader of their faction in the first century BCE, Shimeon ben Shetah, ordered the hanging of eighty women in Ashkelon for witchcraft. Whether this matches the cruelty of Alexander Jannaeus who supported the Sadducees is a delicate matter: he ordered eight hundred Pharisees who had tried to forge an alliance with Demetrius III of Syria in order to overthrow Jannaeus, crucified. Not only were they crucified. They were forced to watch the slaughter of their own wives and children while they were writhing on their crosses.

Hellenizers, Sadducees and Pharisees were joined by other groups. One faction was probably splintered into sub-groups. These were the *Yahad*, religious fraternities. Another group—made especially prominent in the Dead Sea Scroll literature—was the sect of Essenes. Depending on the accounts one relies on the Essenes were: mystical purists, living monk-like existences in desert communities; pacifists avoiding warfare altogether, refusing to manufacture weapons; advocates of extreme asceticism, perhaps rejecting intercourse with women; or primitive communists sharing all their resources in a common pool, dispensing with private property altogether. Perhaps they viewed themselves as recipients of mystical prophetic visions; perhaps they drew succor from visions like those contained in the Book of Daniel. It is interesting that Philo of Alexandria, attracted to Platonic mysticism, was an ardent fan of the Essenes.

Yet other groups consisted of warriors committed to fighting off Gentile rule: the Zealots. These groups became prominent during the war against the Roman invasion of the Holy Land in the first century CE. In some sense, they were the ideological descendants of the Maccabee brothers. Their model of purification was purely political. Drive Gentiles out of the Holy Land. The infamous mass suicide of at the stronghold of Masada that towers over the Dead Sea—undertaken so the Zealots would not be captured by Roman troops—was a Zealot act. Also active were the *sicarii* who specialized in attacking Gentiles with knives. These groups were xenophobic purifiers pure and simple.

We know quite a bit about the factionalism among the Jewish community during the chaotic period 200 BCE to 100 CE because of New Testament and the Dead Sea Scrolls.[11] First discovered by Bedouins in caves near the archeological site of Khirbet Qumran—lying on the Qumran plateau at the northwest corner of the Dead Sea near where the River Jordan enters the Dead Sea—thousands of scrolls have been discovered and analyzed since the early 1950s. They are of unusual interest to religious scholars because they were written at a time when the Jesus Movement, a Jewish faction, commenced in Jerusalem and Galilee.

Once thought to be the product of Essenes occupying the site at Khirbet Qumran it is now believed that these ancient scrolls—the oldest Biblical scrolls in existence—were the product of a variety of groups, some of whom may have buried them in caves when they were fleeing the Roman invasion of Palestine. To be sure they run the gamut. Some predict a final Armageddon-style war in which the "Sons of Light" are pitted against the "Sons of Darkness." Some deal with elaborate baptism-like purification rituals involving emersion in sacred water. Some are versions of Biblical texts that stray far from the texts incorporated into the Hebrew Bible (one, dubbed "the Book of Giants" deals with a period before the Flood when angels procreated with humans). Some deal with the struggle between a pious "Teacher" and the "Wicked Priest": the best guess of scholars being that the "Wicked Priest" is one of the king–priests of the Hasmonean dynasty). One scroll dwells upon exorcism; another is obsessed with the solar calendar, viewed by the sect as preferable to the lunar calendar followed by the priesthood; one deals with a "chosen one" who will be the Revealer of God's Secrets.

Messiah-like figures abound in the Dead Sea Scrolls. Whether this figure is to be a priest-like purifier, a super-prophet; a military leader dedicated to cleansing the Holy Land of unbelievers; or a "son of man" predicted by the ancient prophets is up for grabs.[12] The scrolls are almost certainly the product of a variety of groups, testifying to a theme crucial to the argument of this book: religions are "big tent," encompassing a wide variety of believers attracted to the tent for countless reasons.

The Dead Sea Scrolls also testify to a riddle—a paradox, perhaps a contradiction—that permeates monotheism. How does a believer account for evil? If God is pure goodness, why is there so much strife and wickedness? One solution is to attribute all of this to the deity. To say in effect "the ways of the hand of God is beyond human understanding". Another—the more attractive option, the one more consistently evoked in monotheism—is to attribute the evil to a secondary heavenly figure, for instance a fallen angel like Satan. Historically, the idea of a Satan devil-figure may have evolved from Judaism's war against Baal. In any event it is a solution invoked by the Book of Job; it enters the Torah in Genesis when Adam and Eve are punished for eating from the Tree of Knowledge in Eden; it becomes a key element in the Gospels of the New Testament.

In short many of the beliefs expressed in the Four Gospels of the New Testament are expressed in the literature of the Dead Sea Scrolls, in the Book of Daniel, and in the Apocrypha. The religion of the Hebrew people—its roots in polytheism—gradually evolved into monotheism, begetting two world-shaking religions: Christianity and Islam. Ironically it was Christian belief coupled with Greek philosophy that fueled the ideological transition of the Roman Empire as it lurched from polytheism to monotheism.

Judaism itself was dramatically transformed by the destruction of the Second Temple in 70 CE. The Sadducees lost their lofty positions as priests devoted to animal sacrifice. The Jewish state in Palestine disintegrated. Victim of a religion trap, civil war generated the worst of all political outcomes, state collapse.

At the same time, the Pharisees benefited. They turned Judaism into a religion organized around reading and learning Torah, a mobile form of worship that could be carried on in primary schools and synagogues. Already flourishing in Alexandria and Babylonia, coexisting with Greek and Roman inspired religions, Judaism became a stateless faith. To provide political and social continuity to far flung communities of Jews educating sons so they could read the Torah became a priority of the de facto leaders of faith, the rabbis who had been the backbone of the Pharisee movement. Focus on literacy became a salient feature of those households who remained within the faith, refusing to convert to the other religions proliferating in the Roman Empire.[13] As it turned out the associated emphasis on learning served well the economic interests of Jewish merchants but not necessarily Jewish farmers. In a Roman economy in which the opportunity to carry on mercantile activity was severely limited most Jews continued to toil within an agrarian economy and many converted to faiths that did not require fathers to educate their sons. It was only with the rise of a religion conducive to mercantile activity—Islam in the seventh century CE pioneering merchant capitalism—that Jews came into their own as successful economic actors.

Notes

1 What constitutes the Hebrew Bible is a tricky question. In its current Hebrew form, it consists of twenty-four books, originally edited and redacted by schools of rabbis in the early centuries CE, later on reworked by the Masoretes. The twenty-four books are further broken down into three types of scripture. The Torah consists of the five books of Moses, the first, Genesis, dealing with the creation of the universe and the tales of so-called Patriarchs like Abraham, Jacob, and Joseph; the remaining four books detailing Mosaic history, the exodus of the Hebrew people out of Egypt, their journey through the Levant, and the promulgation of the ten commandments at Mount Sinai.

   The second part (Nevi'im) consists of the subsequent ancient history of the Jewish people, mainly interpreted through the lens of Prophets who attempted to advise and admonish kings. Commencing with the account of Joshua conquering the Canaan region of the Levant, it continues with an account of theocratic priestly rule, notably by Samuel. Once theocratic rule gives way to rule by kings, deterioration sets in because some kings refuse to "walk in the ways of the Lord." A single kingdom ruled first by Saul (anointed by the Hebrew god Yahweh (Yhwh) who comes to regret his decision), expanded on by David who is viewed as exemplary despite committing adultery and dying with much blood on his hands is brought to an apparent pinnacle by King Solomon who organizes the construction of a temple in Jerusalem where Yahweh (Yhwh) can reside. Unfortunately, King Solomon's kingdom is brought low, almost smashed to ruins by his sins. His successors divide it into a northern kingdom Israel and a southern kingdom Judah. All this history appears in the books of Samuel and Kings. The subsequent history of the two kingdoms and their destruction—Israel falling to the Assyrians in 722 BCE, Judah to the Neo-Babylonian Empire between 597 and 587 (when the temple is destroyed)—is covered in the books of Isaiah, Jeremiah, Ezekiel and the short books dealing with the twelve minor prophets.

   Finally, the third part of the Bible consists of the so-called wisdom literature, the Writings (Ketuvim). It includes a number of books of remarkable literary value, notably Job, Song of Songs and Ecclesiastes. Because classical Hebrew was only written with consonants—alef, beth, etc.—there was ambiguity concerning pronunciation of the text. For example, the name of the Jewish God appeared in the original Hebrew test as "Y-H-W-H" (since a tradition had developed around the third century banning the pronunciation of the word for God this was not such a problem for later generations). This led to a practical conundrum: reading the Biblical text required reaching a consensus on correct pronunciation for words not representing God's name. During the sixth to ninth centuries CE a group of scholarly Jews,the Masoretes (in Aramaic the word means "guardians"), arrived at a system of vowels—patah, sere, et cetera—that, once systematically applied to the text of consonants, yielded a practical reading system. In doing so they were forced to make choices concerning interpretation of passages. In effect, they reedited the text. Römer (2015: 25–27) provides a useful treatment of this history.

As well as composing the classical Hebrew text a second version also written by Jews living in Egypt, particularly in Alexandria, emerged. They composed the text in Greek. It is known as the Septuagint. It appeared in the early centuries CE. The Septuagint contains fourteen or fifteen books of Jewish origin known as the Apocrypha. The Apocrypha include several very interesting books, especially first and second Maccabees. The two books of Maccabees deal with the Jewish rebellion against the Greek Seleucids during the second century BCE. First Maccabees begins by describing the efforts of Antiochus IV Epiphanes who undertook the Hellenization of Jerusalem in 167 BCE, countered by the actions of the sons of a rural Jewish priest living in Modiin: Mattahias, the Hasmonean. Carrying on a guerrilla war against Hellenizing Jews, the sons eventually established a new Jewish state, first operating as a theocracy, later as a kingdom. The Hasmonean dynasty of high priests and kings/queens eventually collapses in civil war between the followers of Aristobulus II and Hyrcanus II during the period 67 to 40 BCE.

It is during this period that many of the texts of the Dead Sea Scrolls were put on parchment, giving us remarkable insight into the period when apocalyptic thinking crucial to early Christianity flourished. The Apocrypha does not appear in the Hebrew Bible, but it was accepted in the Catholic version of the Bible in part due to the editing efforts of Jerome. However, it does not appear in Protestant versions, partly because Second Maccabees refers to praying and sacrificing for dead souls (an idea that was instrumental in developing the Catholic theory of purgatory, which is rejected by Protestant churches). In short there is no definitive version of the Bible. Throughout this book I quote from the Hebrew Bible—from the English text of the Masoretic version published by The Jewish Publication Society of America (1955)—except when I draw from the Apocrypha or the New Testament. For these writings, I rely on the version edited by May and Metzger (1965).

2 For most of the material in this section and the next section I draw upon Römer (2015).
3 This paragraph draws upon Römer (2015: 15–17).
4 Perhaps this is the basis for the "fatted calf" story given in Exodus (32: 4): "Aaron fashioned it with a graving tool, and made it a molten calf."
5 For the reforms carried out under Josiah see Chapter 11 in Römer (2015).
6 This theory is advanced by Römer (2015) in Chapter 12.
7 The Idumeans were inhabitants of Edom. Under the expansionary policy of Alexander Jannaeus they had been brought under Jewish state control, forcibly converted to Judaism, subjected to compulsory circumcision.
8 For the views of Philo of Alexandria see Lewy, Altmann, and Heinemann (1960), particularly the section authored by Lewy.
9 See Lewy, Altmann, and Heinemann (1960: 27–28).

10 One of the Dead Sea Scrolls refers to a Wicked Priest—known as "A Commentary of Habakkuk" as translated in Wise, Abegg Jr., and Cook (1996: 114–122)—who commenced his career as king–priest in a righteous manner, only later becoming corrupted by greed and riches. Most scholars believe the Wicked Priest was one of the Hasmonean rulers, perhaps Alexander Jannaeus.

11 On the Dead Sea Scrolls, see Eisenman and Wise (1992), Golb (1995) and Wise, Abegg Jr. and Cook (1996).

12 Chapter 7 in the Book of Daniel, probably composed during the Hasmonean era, has a fascinating description of the god of Israel as an "Ancient One" resplendent as he sits on a throne accompanied by another heavenly figure known as the "Son of Man." The title "Son of Man" was invoked by Jesus of Nazareth.

13 For the details of this argument, see Botticini and Eckstein (2012).

5   Predation, gift exchange, and markets in the Roman Empire

Predation and empire building in the ancient world

Empire building in the ancient world rested upon military predation. This was true of Alexander the Great's remarkable—but transient—Hellenistic empire stretching from Macedon through Asia Minor, Persia, and into the fringes of India. More important it was the cornerstone of the far more stable Roman Empire that arose in the wake of the disintegration of Alexander's territorial acquisitions.

Predation is costly. First and foremost, it requires very high levels of cooperation. In battles soldiers often perish or are severely maimed during their armed engagements. The most successful military campaigns are erected on the backs of recruits systematically drilled into working together in as seamless a fashion as possible. To encourage armed personnel to fight ferociously and fearlessly they must be well fed, adequately housed, provided with avenues for deployment. As well they must be given strong incentives. Predation is win–lose: defeat your enemy you acquire land, indemnities, captured arms, and currencies. Acquiring the spoils of war certainly provides incentives for rank and file warriors. On the other hand, the costs of mounting campaigns are born in advance of conflict; moreover, you incur these costs even when your side is defeated.

In short, the costs and benefits of predation are unpredictable in the long run. One reason why they are unpredictable is predation turning against itself, living by the sword/dying by the sword so to speak. Under one scenario, generals controlling armies may well turn against each other, warring with one another setting off internecine conflicts that may—and often did in fact—lead to the dismemberment of the empire. This was the fate of Alexander the Great's sprawling empire. It is reported "godlike" Alexander gave up the ghost in 323 BCE—perhaps poisoned by erstwhile supporters—and within two years, a period spanning four decades of warfare ensued. Finally, the remnants of empire coalesced into four regional power blocks—Egypt; Mesopotamia and Central Asia; Anatolia; and Macedon—that warred against one another. At times, enmity between rival blocks generated into open conflict. A second scenario envisions successful predation leading to a concentration of wealth and power within a small sub-jurisdiction of an empire, its core as opposed to its periphery. In this case, outside predators may be attracted by the glitter of the gold. A third scenario sees the troops doing away with the general, electing a new leader from their ranks, setting off a chain of internal predatory conflicts within the military itself. It is noteworthy that Alexander's string of conquests in the east came to an end when his own troops rebelled against his plans for further fighting.

Through astute political management, Roman politicians and Roman armies and navies managed to sustain successful predation across four centuries, adding freshly conquered territories onto the frame of the empire between 241 BCE until 199 CE. Use of the political swing—moving from Republican governance to several different forms of rule by one figure—sometimes several sharing power either as equals or as junior and senior—Emperors helped to stave off centripetal tendencies. However, despite the exercise of considerable creativity devoted to crafting solutions hemming in predation struggles, the Romans were ultimately stumped, their political vigor sapped by predation turning against its very self.

A second problem posed by dependence on predation as a strategy for generating income and wealth is the demand it imposes on economic resources. It competes against other uses of the social surplus generated above and beyond the subsistence needs of the population of a political jurisdiction. In the ancient world, most producers were subsistence producers: they raised animals and harvested crops they directly consumed and utilized as energy sources within the confines of their households. The surplus left over was either taxed away or predated away by governments and military organizations to sustain further predation and bureaucratic governance over colonial possessions; or it was turned over voluntarily or involuntarily to religious organizations that engaged in gift exchange with the transcendental world; or it was spent on win–win market commercial transactions.

Competition between the three ways to allocate the social surplus springing forth from the economy of the Roman Empire animated political and ideological pendulum swings. One arena in which the pendulum swung with a vengeance was within the field of gift exchange itself. Had religion and its relationship to the state not been such a contentious issue—first in the Hellenistic world, later within the Roman Empire—disruption arising from the pendulum swing might have been contained within reasonable bounds. A useful comparison is between the Chinese and Roman Empires. The capacity of the Chinese Emperor and his or her bureaucracy to exploit religion—treating it as a mask concealing the brutal exercise of harsh legal and military power—is exemplary. Despite the attempts of Roman Emperors to harness religion in a likewise manner, it was only later—after the empire had fallen into complete decay—that attempts were made to harness Nicene Christianity as an effective masking device.

A third challenge—ultimately weakening compromises hammered out between the three contending parties struggling against each other for slices off the social surplus pie—stemmed from shrinkage in the surplus itself. To some extent this was exogenous, attributable to climate change; to some extent it was endogenous, a byproduct of predation turning against itself.

Despite its eventual collapse in the fifth century CE, the success of Rome in its organizing predation prior to its collapse is truly remarkable. Beginning with conquest over the Latin and Greek communities lying to its south and beating back assaults by Gauls to the north, Roman armies—conscript at first, later professional—destroyed powerful Carthage in the Punic Wars of the third century BCE. In doing so it amassed an effective naval force with which it made a bid—eventually successful after Mark Anthony swept marauders away, ridding the Mediterranean of pirates and potential military foes alike—of dominating all Mediterranean waters. Advancing westward into Iberia, Roman forces took Spain (206–25 BCE), connecting the imperial center to the shores of the Atlantic. Attacked by, and attacking disparate groups of Gauls, Caesar Augustus led troops into the north, triumphantly bringing restive tribes to heel (121–49 BCE). By 90 CE Rome had incorporated the lands subsequently known as France, Belgium, and Germany into its European holdings. Meanwhile separate armies made forays into the east, conquering Hellenistic Greece through eight decades of fierce combat (148–67 BCE), taking Egypt by 30 BCE, and ultimately absorbing all of Turkey. Serbia, Romania, Syria, Jordan, and Western Arabia all fell to Rome shortly thereafter. At its eastern reaches it occupied a bitterly contested frontier, Persian forces prepared to attack if provoked by Roman aggression.

By 200 CE, Rome had consolidated a far-flung empire centered at Rome. Its navy guarded seas: Mediterranean, Adriatic, and Aegean. Its armies were stationed throughout all North Africa, most of Western Europe, slices of British territory, and huge swaths of Asia Minor. Establishing a defensive line stretching from Switzerland to the Black Sea, Roman rulers stationed armies and erected outposts—even constructing a wall in some areas—along this great defense line that guarded a truly grand land area (estimated at around 5,000 square kilometers in 117 CE). Why? To put it simply: predation breeds predation. Like the Chinese empire builders at the other end of the Eurasian land mass, Roman political leaders were not sleepwalkers. They never relaxed their vigilance, consequently fretting over the doings of nomadic Eurasian groups residing along the fringes of their perimeter.

Who were these Eurasian nomads? What was the logic of their mobility? However, imperfect throwing out an analogy to a pool table may assist us in comprehending the land mass stretching from Roman Empire in the west to Chinese empire it the east.

Play pool on this table. As one ball commences rolling it bounces against formations of balls, causing them to spin, fly apart, crashing their way across the table till they reach pockets where they are either absorbed (incorporated into an agrarian civilization) or settle along walls, etching out a niche near the frontier of an agrarian civilization. Something like this is how the cultural map of the Eurasian center evolved during the period leading up to, and continuing through, the initial institutionalization of the Axial Age traditions. Tribes continually clashed, making treaties afterwards, crafting coalitions typically short-lived, the most heroic and bloodthirsty groups eventually pummeling and pushing their weaker adversaries towards the steppe boundaries.

Start at the table's center. This is where the most dramatic break-out occurred. From somewhere in Central Asia—in all likelihood in the region just north of the Black and Caspian Seas—a group speaking a proto-Indo-European language broke out, spreading outward to all points on the compass.[1] Celts, Italics, Illyrians and Greeks moved into the Mediterranean basin; Thracians, Hittites, Luvians, Lycians into the eastward reaches of the Aegean and Anatolia; Slaves and Germanics northward towards what became Scandinavia; and Aryans, Iranians and Indics to the east. Exactly when, and from what homeland dispersion, originated is much disputed. As McEvedy (2002: 100) acridly concludes, speculation regarding timing and original settlement of the Indo-European tribes is "a game without rules."

The gradual dispersion and settlement into ecological niches of the Indo-Europeans pushed them up against various groups: a Western Mediterranean group inhabiting Iberia; a Uralic group in the north; a Elamo-Dravidian group occupying the Indian sub-continent; and a Afro-Asiatic group splitting into Berbers, Egyptians, and Semites in Africa north of the Sahara and the Levant. Through a combination of accommodation and conquest subgroups of the Indo-European peoples settled into the lands passing through the Neolithic revolution. They abandoned nomadic life. The lucky conquerors became priests or warrior–rulers in their new homelands. The less favored being farmers, servants, merchants. Once settled, either they became fierce adversaries of, or trading partners for, their former nomadic brethren.

As populations grew in the great agrarian centers, and as rulers mastered warfare using Iron Age weapons and tactics, empires were carved out on the periphery of Central Asia: China and India on its east; along its heavily contested southern/central zone a sequence of empires (at various times dominated by Hittites, Babylonians, Assyrians, and Egyptians); and in the west, Greek then Roman. As the nomadic tribes of Central Asia jostled about some gradually pushed up against these empires.

For example, consider the west region of Eurasia. Over time several the nomadic groups, further subdivided, established niches on the border of the Roman Empire, basically just northeast of the Rhine. For instance, having been pushed southward by Alans and later Huns, Germanic tribes settled into a zone between Slavic territory and the reaches of Roman control. Circa 300 CE, Saxons, Visigoths, Ostrogoths, Asding Vandals and Siling Vandals staked out territorial claims on the edge of the Empire while Franks and Alemanni managed to gain entry to the Empire itself.

In the east, a similar frontier situation prevailed. At its northwestern borders, Chinese Emperors struggled with the Xiongnu who commanded 300,000 cavalrymen, a formidable threat.[2] By crafting an alliance with another nomadic group, the Yuezhi, Chinese generals dreamed that their combined militaries could quickly bringing the pesky Xiongnu to their knees. Failing in their effort the Chinese generals abandoned the Yuezhi to a horrid fate. The Xiongnu promptly defeated the Yuezhi, killing the Yuezhi chief, crafting his skull into a drinking vessel (a standard way to celebrate victory on the Central Asian steppe). Driven westward and southward the Yuezhi eventually settled in several regions, notably Bactria (today a region shared by Afghanistan and Uzbekistan). Eventually, the once hapless Yuezhi were able to form the Kushan Empire that managed to make inroads into northern India.

In short, the borderlands fringing the great classical age empires emerging out of the Iron Age were potentially unstable. Military pressure from the interior of Central Asia was one problem. Population growth or climatic disruption preventing re-growth of grasslands within its vast interior would certainly set the billiard balls in motion.

As well pressure from the great empires pushing outward into its reaches was a destabilizing element. For example, the greatest economic triumph of the classical age—the establishment of the land-based Silk Road around 14 CE—was largely due to Chinese military victories upon the Tarim Basin rendering relatively safe passage over 2000 miles of the 4,400 miles stretching from Changan, China's western capital from Antioch on the Mediterranean.[3] To be sure, the economic interests of emperors and kings and the interests of the nomadic tribes operating along the Silk Road coincided: rulers secured taxes; the heroic leader of a nomadic tribe received luxury goods he lavished upon his *comitatus*. At the same time as tribes were absorbed into the empires or chased away, even exterminated, in humiliating defeat, they had to adjust to new realities. Many so-called barbarian groups ended up as soldiers employed by the empires that had crushed their former leaders.

That the wealth accumulated in Italy, especially in its metropolitan center Rome, was a shining prize worth considerable risk in capturing, is evident from Table 5.1.[4] Inhabitants of the imperial center, particularly the elites (senators, knights), lived in luxury unknown to the most successful of the nomadic Eurasian tribes.

How did the economy of the Roman Empire function, prospering to the degree it did? Predation was a major factor. Its impact was both direct and indirect. It brought in war indemnities, precious metals, and other spoils of combat. Slaves were captured. Unlike free individuals, slaves had little choice over the amount of leisure they carved out. The estimates in Table 5.1 suggest slaves toiled much harder—or at least worked longer hours—than their free compatriots. Land onto which colonists migrated relieved Malthusian pressures.[5] Low population densities existing in most of the imperial periphery proved a magnet for Roman citizens. Establishing farms in sparsely populated zones was a good deal. It allowed farmers mainly focused on growing grain to set aside fields for the succor of chickens, goats, sheep, pigs, horses,

Table 5.1 Population, population density, per capita income estimates for the Roman Empire; free and slave populations; and elite incomes, circa 14 CE

Panel A: population (P), population density, persons per square kilometer (d), and per capita income (y) in 1990 Geary Khamis Dollars, circa 14 CE: Maddison's Estimates

Subregion	Population P (1,000s)	% of Empire	D	Y
Roman Europe				
Peninsular Italy	7,000	15.9	28.0	857
Iberia	4,150	9.4	7.0	493
Gaul	5,800	13.2	8.0	469
Total	23,100	52.5	10.4	478
Roman Asia				
Greater Syria	4,000	9.1	36.7	n.e.[a]
Total	12,200	27.7	18.3	550
Roman Africa				
Egypt	4,500	10.2	160.7	600
Total	8,700	19.8	19.6	541
Entire Empire				
Empire	44,000	100	13.2	570

Panel B: Free (F), slave (S), and total populations; employment and activity rates (AR), and income per person (y, in HS, *sestercii*), circa 14 CE: Maddison's Estimates

Population Type	Population (1,000s)	Employment		Income per person (HS)
		Activity Rate (AR)	Total	
Peninsular Italy				
Free (F)	4500	.36	1620	790
Slave (S)	2500	.80	2000	300
Total	7000	.52	3620	519

Rest of Empire				
Free (F)	35,000	.36	12,600	790
Slave (S)	2,000	.80	1,600	300
Total	37,000	.38	14,200	735
Total Empire				
Free (F)	39,500	.36	14,220	790
Slave (S)	4,500	.80	3,600	300
Total	44,000	.405	17,820	691

Panel C: Elite incomes (million *sestercii* HS), total number of elites by type, and per person income, circa 14 CE [b]

Type	Total Empire			Peninsular Italy			Rest of Empire		
	Number	Income		Number	Income		Number	Income	
		Total	Per Person		Total	Per Person		Total	Per Person
Emperor	1	15	15	1	15	15	0	0	–
Senators	600	90	.15	600	90	.15	0	0	–
Knights	40,000	1,200	.03	24,000	720	.03	16,000	480	.03
Decurions	240,000	2,000	.008	80,000	667	.008	160,000	1,333	.008
Other	50,000	1,101	.02	17,000	366	.02	33,000	734	.02
Total Elite	333,601	4,406	n.e.	121,601	1,858	n.e.	209,000	2,548	n.e.

Source: Maddison (2007: pg. 35, 40, and 50).
Notes:
• n.e. = not estimated
• Maddison assumes that elite income is the sum of rents on estates and property in the provinces, emoluments, perquisites, and spoils of office
• Knights are *equites*
• *Decuriones* are municipal councilors

and cows. Surely this is one reason soldiers were willing to exert themselves in warfare.

Certainly, favorable weather helped. There is considerable evidence that the early empire enjoyed a "Roman spring."[6] By raising crop yields it increased the surplus that could be extracted out of the economy, enhancing the capacity to carry on predation.

Most important, consolidating a huge empire patrolled by navy and armies and crisscrossed by major roads reduced the costs of carrying on trade: less piracy; a common legal and monetary system backing up the commerce; well defined avenues for delivering goods from one locale to another.[7] Apply the logic of comparative advantage: land, labor and capital can be used more efficiently if they specialize. Grow grapes in Gaul; grow olives in Greece; secure minerals from mines in Spain; extract wheat from Egypt, the great breadbasket of the Roman Empire, major source of the wheat shipped to Rome at the behest of the government committed to dispersing free—or very cheap—foodstuffs to the masses concentrated in the metropolitan core, the so-called *annona*.

Employing an augmented production function elaborated in the Appendices, I provide a comprehensive framework for decomposing non-predation production. Labor input is decomposed into the number of workers, hours worked per worker, and the efficiency with which workers labor; capital is decomposed into a quality component and a quantity component; and land is decomposed into a quality component and a quantity component. Based on my reading of the recent literature on the Roman economy I suggest the following conclusions: (1) labor input viewed in terms of efficiency was not particularly high because education was not widely diffused throughout the economy; (2) slaves worked long hours but free workers did not; (3) land quality was fairly high, enhanced by comparative advantage; (4) capital stock was not of particularly high quality (windmills and waterworks were certainly important but most of the capital stock was concentrated in housing and structures utilized for religious purposes).[8]

What about total factor productivity? As I argue in the Appendices, it reflects three things: the distribution of employment; the level of disembodied technological knowledge; and scale economies in production and distribution. As for the distribution of the labor force the evidence suggests it was primarily employed in farming and predation. As for scale economies, the evidence on manufacturing indicates most of the firms were of very small scale.[9] Finally, consider the state of knowledge exploited by Roman science and its technological applications is simple: I believe it was low. One reason I assert this is the state of knowledge. Aristotle, whose physics bristled with animism, was viewed as completely credible among the ancients. Indeed, even in the writings of medieval scholastics, who relied upon Muslim scholars who in turn were inspired by the learning of the ancients, the acceptance of Aristotelian animism was virtually unquestioned. To be sure, Galen made major contributions to medicine and Ptolemy to astronomy readily incorporated into an Aristotelian framework by Muslim, later medieval Christian, thinkers. But all of this was swept away as if it were mere child's play by the natural philosophy of the sixteenth and seventeenth centuries. The ancients simply lacked the precision instruments that loomed large in the experimental work of natural philosophers. You cannot push technological sophistication very far in such a world.

The view that the performance of the Roman economy somehow added up to capitalism is a view I completely reject.[10] To be sure, the definition of what constitutes capitalism is an issue in reaching this conclusion. If by capitalism you mean markets in which merchants operated, yes, the Roman economy was capitalist. Whenever you have comparative advantage bolstered by specialization and division of labor you have markets. When the scale of the economy reaches a sufficient size you find merchants acting as mediators between buyers and sellers. If what you mean by capitalism is a system in which powerful elites own the means of production and most of the capital and workers provide labor services, you have to wonder. A lot of the land was farmed on a small scale; a lot of the capital was tied up either in miniscule structures—houses crafted from stone, mud and clay—or in religious structures. If what you mean by capitalism is a dynamic economy in which capital is churned around, moving from sector to sector, moving from domestic to foreign uses, then the Roman economy was not capitalist.

Above anything else, the Roman economy was predatory.[11] It was not capitalist. Predation is a risky foundation for an economy. As emphasized already predation breeds predation, bringing the engine of growth of such an economy to a grinding halt. Indeed, this is eventually what happened to the Roman economy.

That the Romans struggled to keep predation from devouring itself alive is clear from the various experiments undertaken by successive Roman governments. Originally a kingdom, Rome became a republic administered by a powerful group of senators. As armies commanded by powerful generals marched westward, southward, eastward, and northward (some staying in the metropolitan center to quell slave revolts, notably the Spartacus revolt), competition between the powerful military leaders selected amongst the ranks of the senators precipitated on-going factional fighting, ultimately dooming the republican form of government. Two triumvirates—power-sharing agreements to divide the empire into regions each under the dictatorial control of a feared general—were cobbled together. Eventually, they collapsed after Caesar was assassinated when he defiantly marched his army back from Gaul into the environs of Rome. His adopted son Octavian was able to establish a centralized system under the nominal control with himself as dictator, renamed Augustus. Still, wary of the senate, he cautiously took the title "*Princeps Civitatis*" (First Citizen of the State) rather than "*Dominus et Deus*", a term that gradually came into common usage later on, formally adopted by Diocletian ruling as emperor from 284 CE to 305 CE.

In an effort to win popular approval for his new form of government, Augustus funded lavish religious celebrations honoring the traditional gods of Rome. His "games of the century" commenced with animal sacrifice— eighteen sheep and eighteen goats had their throats slit, their blood drained away, and their flesh spitting out fragrant aromas grilled at an ancient site supposedly visited by underworld gods—Pluto and his underworld companions—on the opening day.[12] On subsequent days elaborate ritual festivals to various Roman deities—Juno first, then Terra Mater (Earth Mother)—took place in the environs of Rome, capped off when Augustus brought to the Palatine a sculpture of Apollo, voice of the Oracles, his own patron deity.

In the long run, this strategy of masking dictatorial power in traditional Roman gods failed. It succeeded in China. But it proved ineffective in the Roman Empire. Why?

An ideological pendulum swing

The answer lies in the ideological pendulum swing. In the struggle between different attitudes toward the polytheistic divinities of the Greek pantheon that were basically inseparable from the Roman pantheon.[13] Recall that Greek comedy belittled the gods, challenging their virtue. Recall that one whole school of Greek thought rejected the existence of a transcendental world altogether, the atomists, the materialists, the skeptics. Atheism and agnosticism were alive and well in the Hellenic age. None of this disappeared when Hellenism gave way to Hellenistic culture that spread rapidly throughout a far wider region—into Asia Minor, into Egypt, even unto to India—than the Aegean and the mainland of Greece proper. Epicurus picked up the baton from the atomists promoting a materialist theory that gained popularity amongst the Roman nobility. In *On the Nature of Things*, the poet Lucretius pushes this view to its atheist extremes:[14]

> When prostrate upon earth lay human life/Visibly trampled down and foully crushed/ Beneath Religion's cruelty ... /With horrible aspect, first did a man of Greece/ Dare to lift up his mortal eyes against her/a conqueror he returns to us, bringing back/knowledge ... /Therefore now has Religion been cast down/Beneath men's feet, and trampled on in its turn/Ourselves heaven-high his victory exalts.

Not a doctrine popular among learned clerical circles during the medieval era!

Testimony to the appeal of theories of reality devoid of deities for well-educated Romans is the writing of Cicero. In the late 50s BCE, he penned an essay that imagined a debate between a Stoic, an Epicurean, and an Academic. Holding steadfast to the middle ground, the Academic responds: one should act as if the gods existed regardless of whether it is true or not. Practical wisdom some might say; but definitely not an enthusiastic endorsement of the Greek or Roman pantheons.

Adding to skepticism about the Roman gods championed by Augustus was the spread of salvation and mystery cults, particularly amongst the illiterate and downtrodden, amongst soldiers and slaves, both groups facing brutal corporal punishment for disobedience on a daily basis. One of these cults Mithraism appears to have enjoyed Persian Zoroastrian roots. Mithra was Indo-European god, one of the three judges in the Zoroastrian pantheon charged with guiding souls. A variant of his name shows up in the Hindu *Rig Veda* so it is likely he is derivative of proto-Indo-Iranian-European worship. In any event having made its way in the Roman Empire his image as a bull slaying god, Goodness dedicated to defeating Evil, he was worshipped in caves by devotee communities organized along lines similar to early Christianity, bishops, deacons and presbyters taking command of ceremonies.

On top of this religious diversity was the monotheism espoused by Jews living in Palestine. After 63 BCE, the Romans had turned direct rule of their newly created province to the Herodian dynasty. From the outset Herod was not particularly popular with most Jews despite his efforts to render the second temple grander, more imposing, in scale and presentation. He was Idumean, hence a second-class Jew in the sense that he—or his family—had been forcibly converted to Judaism under the expansionary military policy of Alexander Jannaeus. More to the point he owed his kingship to the Romans: to a degree he had to march to their tune. His successors—Archelaus, Philip, and Pontius Pilate—continued his pro-Roman policies. All the internecine squabbles within the Jewish community that had brought the Hasomonean state to ruins continued under Herodian dynastic rule. The only difference was the replacement of Greek puppet state rulers by Roman military figures. The term *kittim* that reverberates in the Dead Sea Scrolls—particularly in the War Scroll—designates the hated enemy, namely the Romans. Before it was used to designate the Romans, it was used to designate the Greeks. New wine in old bottles, so to speak.

It was under the rule of Archelaus that Jesus of Nazareth was born; it was under Pontius Pilate that Jesus was crucified. Jesus—who shared many of the views of the Pharisees—was one of the Jewish radicals fashioning themselves around the image of the great Hebrew prophets. Beginning his movement among the poor and downtrodden in Galilee, he moved on to Jerusalem, where he joined those Jews opposing the temple priesthood on the grounds that the priests were corrupt and mercenary. To his followers he was the Messiah, the righteous one who was destined to usher in a new age.

Jesus was hardly alone in attempting to cleanse the Jewish religion as a Messiah-like figure. His focus was on ethical purification, but others— Zealots, short dagger-wielding *sicarii*—were intent on political purification, driving the Gentiles out, whether Greeks or Romans. They wished to follow a Messiah who was a principally a military leader. After the death of Jesus in 31 CE, the political resistance to Roman rule intensified. In 66 CE, the first Jewish revolt began. Countering it with military force the Roman military systematically began destroying military strongholds held by the Jewish revolutionaries. As far as can be ascertained Khirbet Qumran was one of the military fortifications designed by Hasmonean military commanders to be a key node in an armed shield protecting Jerusalem from attack by foreign troops. It was seized by the Jewish revolutionaries. The Romans destroyed it in 68 CE, moving on to crush into smithereens the second temple in 70 CE. Mopping up the destruction of the first Jewish revolt, the Roman military destroyed the great fortress of Masada in 73–74 CE, the Zealots and *sicarii* committing mass suicide in the face of humiliating defeat. Yet even this did not squelch the fervor of Jewish resistance to Roman hegemony. A second major revolt—led by Bar Kokhba—broke out in the next century. It was only after this revolt was crushed did Jewish military resistance end.

Ironically, it was the man crucified by the Romans at the request of the Great Sanhedrin of judges seated at the second temple—Jesus—whose life and death eventually became the focus of a religious cult dominating the Roman Empire. To most Jews—staying with the faith of their fathers, choosing a Diaspora life edified by rabbis commenting on the Torah—Jesus was simply a failed lay priest, hardly a Messiah savior. A Jerusalem church devoted to the teachings of Jesus was surely a small drop in the reservoir of Jewish sects operating under Roman rule. Perhaps this would have mattered little had it not been for Christian zealots like Peter and Paul who, playing down the importance of Jewish ritual—including circumcision—promoted the new faith among the Gentiles. Of course, it was simply one of the cults—like the Mithra cult—spreading throughout the Roman Empire in the first and second centuries CE. Like the Mithra cult, worship in the early Christian communities was organized along bishop/deacon/presbyter lines. Like the Mithra cult, this faith eventually managed to become popular among soldiers recruited in Roman armies. Indeed, it was a military leader intent on firing up his troops for a major battle who paved the way for Christianity to become the official religion of the Roman Empire.

Notes

1 See McEvedy (2002: pg. 8 ff) and Anthony (2007). Drawing upon an impressive array of information about horses, wagons, chariots, archeological sites, and language, Anthony makes an impressive case for the ancient homeland being situated north of the Sea of Azov, stretching eastward past the Volga and Ural Rivers. See Anthony (2007: 84, 132). Much of the evidence linguistic and archeological brought forth by scholars is used in dating the split-offs of various languages from a Proto-Indo-European ur-language that probably developed circa 4500 BCE. In Kennedy's preferred schema, Anatolian split off around 4000 BCE; Tocharian next; Celtic and Italic next; Armenian and Greek next; followed by the splintering into Indo-Iranian, Balto-Slavic and Germanic. McEvedy (2002: 10) pretty much agrees with the timing of the split-offs—he accepts the notion that it gradually occurred between 3000 BCE and 1500 BCE—but provides a different model. In his framework, there is an initial division into a Hittite group and two Indo-European groups (east and west Indo-European), the latter two groups subdividing into a welter of languages, including Hindi, Farsi, Polish, Russian,

Greek, Albanian, French, Italian, and Spanish. Doniger (2009: 87–95) considers some additional scenarios, including one in which an Indus Valley group responsible for the Vedas was actually the original Indo-European group, subsequently migrating westward and northward.

2 See Liu (2010: 6 ff.).

3 McEvedy (2002: 96).

4 To put these figures in some meaningful context, consider Maddison's estimates of per capita income in Europe. Around 1000 CE, he figures it was $431 (1990 Geary-Khamis $); around 1500, he estimates $753; and around 1820, he estimates $1,202. Scheidel (2012b: 4) warns us against accepting estimates of per capita income for the Roman Empire as completely accurate. I cannot dispute his assertion. The principal reason I report the estimates assembled in Table 5.1 is to illustrate the importance of regional differentials, particularly the largess of the metropolitan center garnered by the elites ensconced in the imperial capital Rome.

5 The typical interpretation of the Malthusian framework emphasizes its dynamic implications: population increase reducing the standard of living provided technology, land, and capital remain unchanged. Perhaps more crucial for human history is its implication for the distribution of income at a particular point in time. Increase the number of workers, wages fall relative to land and capital rents. Increase the amount of land, wages rise relative to land and capital rents. Successful Roman predation in the four centuries between 200 BCE and 200 CE, tended to raise wages—relative to land rents—simply because it added on land, increasing the land base relative to the labor base, to that already under Roman rule. Key to this thesis is the observation that population densities tended to be lower in the newly conquered lands than in the old core regions of the Roman Empire.

6 On the website supplementing Scheidel (2012a)—on the internet at www.stanford,edu/~scheidel/CCRE.htm (accessed on May 2, 2016) by this author—Scheidel provides the following estimates of climatic conditions:

Location	Climatic Condition
Northwest Iberia, 250–450 CE	Warm
Northwest Iberia, 450–900 CE	Cool
Northwestern Italy. 200 BCE–100 CE	Warm
Northeastern Italy, 400 BCE–1 CE	Warm
Northeastern Italy, 450–700 CE	Cool
Central Asia, 100–200 CE	Warm
Central Asia, 200–1000 CE	Cool

7 On the importance of comparative advantage in generating a surplus in the Roman economy, see Adams (2012), Jongman (2014), Temin (2013), von Reden (2012), and Wilson (2012).

8 See Saller (2012) and Scheidel (2012b).

9 See Hawkins (2012).

10 The view that capitalism developed in the ancient world has been vigorously argued by a number of writers providing chapters for the volume edited by Neal and Williamson (2014a). See Jurca (2014) on Babylonia in the first millennium BCE; Bresson (2014) on the Greek city-states during the Hellenic era; and Jongman (2014) emphasizing the importance of rising slave prices in the Roman economy during the first few centuries BCE. It goes without saying that I reject their views.

11 On the overwhelming importance of predation in the Roman economy, see Bang (2012a, 2012b)

12 I draw upon O'Donnell (2015) for this account.
13 The Roman gods are fundamentally identical to the Greek gods: Jupiter is the Latin name for Zeus; Juno the Latin name for Hera; Neptune the Latin name for Poseidon; Saturn the Latin name for Cronos; Venus the Latin name for Aphrodite; Pluto the Latin name for Hades; Ceres the Latin name for Demeter; Minerva the Latin name for Athena; Mercury the Latin name for Hermes; and Cupid the Latin name for Eros.
14 Quoted in Russell (1945: 248–249).

6 One God, one emperor

More political pendulum swings

Between the effort of Augustus to revive the Roman deities as a mask for despotic largely military rule and the invoking of one version of Christianity— Nicene Catholicism—as the official religion of the Roman Empire, an act taken by the Emperor Theodosius at the end of the fourth century, the pendulum swung dramatically. It swung within the field of Roman politics. It swung within the annals of Christianity itself. As it transpired, the two swings, initially separate, were firmly joined together at the hip once the Edict of Milan in 313 CE declared Christianity legal throughout the empire.

The problem confronting early Roman emperors was legitimacy. What Chinese Emperors could achieve by appealing to the lofty ideological notion of a Confucian "Mandate of Heaven"—as justification for their harsh laws, as motivator of their bureaucracy, as spur for their troops supposedly guaranteeing victories—was simply not a viable option in the Roman Empire. Religious diversity precluded it. In its absence, successful predation was the only sure guarantor of political stability.

To be sure, Augustus attempted to appeal to the traditional Roman gods. However, this was the same Augustus who created the elite group Praetorian guards stationed in Rome with the aim of protecting his personage, with the aim of heading off coups instigated by ambitious rivals. As it turned out the Praetorian guards became despoiler, as well as protector, of Augustus's successors.[1] One indicator of the instability arising from the role of the Praetorian guards is the number of Emperors who died by natural causes. From the reign of Caligula to the reign of Trajan, ten individuals were declared Emperor by the Senate. Of these, only three died of natural causes. The typical reign was short. Claudius and Nero both enjoyed reigns of over thirteen years, but Nero, knowing the Senate had condemned him and lacking military backing, ended up committing suicide.

Still, between 96 CE and 192 CE, the Nerva–Antonine dynasty was able to reestablish stability. Trajan was Emperor for almost two decades; both Hadrian and Antoninus Pius managed to stay on the throne over twenty years; and Marcus Aurelius reigned for nineteen years. But this was a period when the empire was still expanding, notably achieving conquests in Asia Minor.

In the wake of Nerva–Antonine rule, the pendulum swung back. In the year 193 CE there were five contenders for Emperor as the Praetorian guards auctioned off the post to the highest bidder. Caracalla managed to hang on for over seventeen years (he was joint emperor for thirteen years) and Severus Alexander was uncontested for thirteen years but most of the emperors between 193 CE and 235 CE enjoyed reigns of less than four years, and almost everyone died of unnatural causes. The empire was no longer growing. Predation was turning on itself. Generals were just as likely to attack each other as to war against the so-called barbarians threatening the empire along the perimeter of the great defensive shield their predecessors had managed to cobble together.

Indeed, over the ensuing fifty years, chaos ruled. Civil wars sapping the ranks of the armies rode roughshod over commerce, as merchants were terrified to travel the great road networks that had fueled comparative advantage during the heyday of the empire. Adding to the woes of the economy was plague (the Plague of Cyprian raged for two decades) and the onset of cool summers, depleting agrarian yields. Testimony to the centripetal forces at work, in 268 CE the empire had split apart into two regions: a Gallic empire consisting of Gaul/Britannia/Hispania (the last sub-region moving in and out of the jurisdiction); and a Palmyrene empire consisting of Syria, Palestine and Egypt. Of the twenty-six claimants to the emperorship, a generous definition of natural cause of death only yields five names (two perishing due to plague), the remainder either killed in battle or overthrown and executed in bloody coups. In fact, two emperors only served twenty-one days in office; two lasted between two and three months; and another ruled under eleven months. The pendulum had swung toward complete disunion as predation became increasingly cannibalistic.

Dominus and Deus

In a successful bid to reunite the empire and conclude the internecine warfare tearing the empire apart, Diocletian took power in 285 CE. He was determined to restructure the bureaucracy and reestablish religious legitimacy for the position of emperor. To achieve the former goal, he created a Tetrarchy consisting of two co-emperors (*augusti*) and two subordinate junior emperors (*caesars*). To quell unrest in the fractured Senate, he banned the practice of appointing powerful senators to high military posts. To cloak military dictatorship with legitimacy to the throne he took the title "*Dominus and Deus*", abolishing Augustus's title of "*Princeps Civitatis*". As well, he worked assiduously to reestablish respect for the traditional Roman gods. In doing so, he earned the ire of the Christians living in the empire as he declared their practices illegal. Without a doubt, part of his animus toward the religious cults popping up throughout the empire was his assertion that they were greedy, jacking up prices just like the merchants and rapacious landlords. At least this is what the language in the prologue to his famous Edict on Maximum Prices (301 CE) suggests. Astute to the end he determined to live out his elderly years in peace, dying a natural death rather than falling victim to ambitious subordinates. With this in mind, he resigned the emperorship in 305 CE, building an estate on the coast of Asia Minor far from Rome.

Now the pendulum swung back with a vengeance. Civil war broke out. In the most famous of the face-offs between the rival claimants to the post of Emperor Constantine, leading an army assembled in the western reaches of the empire took on Maxentius at the Battle of the Milvian Bridge in 312 CE. Without doubt, Constantine was a mythic, charismatic figure—to some Christians he was the thirteenth apostle—but the myth cloaked hardnosed political machinations. Whether he was really committed to Christianity or simply believed that it would be advantageous to select one of the many deities in play throughout the empire as his personal transcendental patron, a deity that many of his soldiers were committed to, is unclear. What we do know is that he decided to make the *chi-rho* insignia (the two letters forming the beginning of the name of Christ (Greek for Messiah) the symbolic guarantor of victory at the Milvian Bridge battle. In anticipation of the engagement he ordered fashioned a tall pole covered with gold crossed with a bar in the image of a cross, festooned on the top with a wreath displaying the *chi-rho* letters, the *rho* intersected by the *chi*. As well, he had the *chi-rho* imagery placed on the shields of his soldiers and on his own helmet. Perhaps all he had in mind was that he required a divine protector for this decisive confrontation, Christ appearing to be the most powerful god he could invoke, hitting upon *chi-rho* symbolism as a solution. That Jesus preached nonviolence did not seem to bother him in the slightest.

In any event, Constantine prevailed at the Milvian Bridge. As a result, he was determined to favor his adopted religion, probably reasoning that it would shower legitimacy over his rule. As co-emperor with Licinius (an arrangement that lasted until 324 CE at which point it end with Constantine's victory over his co-ruler), he legalized Christianity with the Edict of Milan. Moreover, he ordered that a temple to Aphrodite that had been constructed by the Romans near Jerusalem be re-consecrated as the Church of the Holy Sepulcher. Most importantly, he convened a famous council of bishops that met at Nicaea in 325 CE.

The Council of Nicaea

Constantine was politically attuned enough to realize that if Christianity had any chance of becoming an official religion of the Roman Empire someone had to hammer out agreement among the competing variants of Christianity, or at least favor one variant over the other competitors. At Nicaea, the main issue that needed resolution turned on a single Greek word *"homoousia"* (one in being, of the same substance).

What was at stake in a subtle choice of words, specifically in the choice of the *"homoousia."* What was at stake was correctness in ritual. To be precise, correctness in the ritual of baptism that introduced the newly baptized to the Christian world. By dint of priest-controlled ritual, the baptized individual was placed onto a particular path clearly overshadowed by a kind of arithmetic. At the end of the path that for every Christian was life on earth, a mere prelude to a potentially more glorious afterlife, was a moral calculation. The arithmetic involved weighed up a lifetime's accumulated sins up against a list of righteous, virtuous deeds. Think about it as an ethical bank account, with the fate of the soul in a future afterlife hinging upon it.

The fact is the gathering at Nicaea was bent on defining orthodoxy and its opposite heresy. Emerging out of the Hebrew faith at a time when many different views on religion clashed and contested, Christian belief and practice took on decisively different hues depending on the other faiths it interacted with.[2] One version was Gnosticism. According to this view, Jesus Christ was never of flesh and bone. He only appeared in human form, like some apparition. Again, followers of Marcion rejected the notion that Christ had been born of a woman. Not only belief but behavior was at issue. Followers of the gospel according to Montanus—prevalent particularly in Asia Minor where apocalyptic writings like the Gospel of John and the Book of Revelation flourished—practiced strict ascetic rituals, avoiding eating and sex, even following female prophet leaders. In short, Christianity in its initial centuries was highly diverse.

The particular sectarian division that excited the assembled bishops at Nicaea was whether Arius was right or wrong. Arius took the position that the Father was superior to the Son whom he created. The father was eternal but the Son was not: He was the Father's first creation. Hence the word *"homoousia"* should not appear in the creed used at the critical moment of baptism. The Father and the Son were not of the same substance, they were not inseparably bound together in all eternity.

Why did this matter? I can only speculate. In my opinion one reason why Arianism—the theory that Arius's interpretation was correct—was controversial is that it invoked an image of blood sacrifice. The Father creates the Son, proceeding to abandon Him, permitting Him to be killed as a sacrifice.

In any event, whatever connotations Arius's position had for abstruse theology were overshadowed by Church politics. It divided the faithful along geographical fault lines. The eastern branch of the Church, the Greek-speaking contingent as opposed to the Latin-speaking contingent, favored Arianism.

In the upshot, Arius's position was decisively voted down at Nicaea. Arius was exiled to Illyria. His writings were declared heretical. They were to be assembled and burned. Anyone caught holding onto his writings were to be executed. The Nicene Creed incorporating the idea of *"homoousia"* was declared orthodox, the only version that was acceptable at baptism ceremonies.

The Council of Nicaea was not simply concerned with banishing Arianism. It began the process of issuing canon law, declaring among other things that self-castration was unacceptable (some Christian extremists believed castration was required for purification), readmission of lapsed Christians to the faith was acceptable, and priests should be barred from practicing usury. But the most important action it took was the declaring of Arianism as heretical. As it turned out this proved to be much harder to enforce than the bishops and the priests who accompanied them to Nicaea could have possibly dreamed.

After Constantine the Great

Indeed, as soon as Constantine died the Arian controversy was reignited. If Constantine believed that the issue was laid to rest at his deathbed—great sinner that he was, he cleverly resisted being baptized until he was about to draw his last breath—he was naïve. Upon his death, three of his sons—Constantine II, Constantius II, and Constans I—met to carve up the empire between them (an agreement that did not last long as they quarreled, ultimately warring against one another). To guarantee that no other family members could claim a share, they had all other potential rivals executed. Immediately, they split along doctrinal lines. Constantine II and Constantius favored Arianism; Constans I supported the Nicene position. The facts on the ground led to these splits: bishops were becoming increasingly important in advising emperors or co-emperors. Some bishops, particularly those in the eastern region of the empire, were closet if not overt Arians. This reality set the pendulum swinging against Nicene Christianity.

Remarkably, the religious pendulum swung into a new direction when Julian became emperor. In an ultimately vain attempt to reject Christianity he attempted to revive Roman and Greek belief systems. He had a special passion for Neo-Platonism, a dualistic theory that adamantly rejected materialism as corrupt and impure. As well, he was fascinated with Mithraism; espousing belief in the transmigration of the soul, he toyed with the notion that he was Alexander the Great reincarnated. Trying to fashion a politically potent ideological umbrella populated by non-Christian belief systems he issued an edict guaranteeing freedom of religion, encouraging non-Christians to attack Christian communities.

Ironically, at Julian's demise, the pendulum violently swung the other way. The Valentinian dynasty assumed power. Valentinian I supported the Nicene Creed but his co-*augustus* Valens supported Arianism. At least they were Christians unlike "pagan" Julian, albeit Christians of two different stripes. Valentinian II followed: he was raised under the influence of an Arian mother but leaned very heavily on Ambrose the Nicene bishop of Milan. His successor Theodosius I leaned even more heavily on Ambrose. He declared

Nicene Christianity the official religion of the empire; he dissolved the order of Vestal Virgins; he ordered the razing of the Temple of Apollo in Delphi and the Serapeum—devoted to Serapis, a synthetic Hellenistic–Egyptian deity combining Osiris and Apis—in Alexandria.

Were Arianism the only problem tearing apart Christianity, some kind of compromise might have been possible between the two variants of the faith. But this was not the case. A so-called Donatist community of Christians—named after Donatus, a prominent member of the group—was active in North Africa, particularly among Berber tribes. They argued Christians should be pure. The Church is the bride of Christ; it should be unblemished. Sinners should be discouraged from entering its doors. To Saint Augustine of Hippo, this was anathema. He argued that no one could be pure. All of humanity was swimming in vile sinfulness. The best one could do was be humble, hoping God had chosen you to be among the elect whom God in His infinite wisdom had selected for salvation, a decision that was prede-termined and out of your control. Along similar lines, Augustine opposed the views of Pelagus. He maintained Pelagianism was arrogant, assuming people could freely walk righteously by acts of free will. Not surprisingly, monks who aspired to purity found Augustine's position problematic.

Not only did Augustine and Pelagius differ on the issue of free will and determinism. They had profoundly different views about wealth. Pelagius believed that the rich should give away their wealth, following the exam-ple of Jesus and his disciples to embrace voluntary poverty, to live in an Essene-like religious communist community, to dedicate themselves to immaterial gift exchange rather than to grimy, odoriferous animal sacrifice and to the erection of awe-inspiring edifices like the Second Temple. By adopting true Christian values, the fervent believer could walk in the way of the Lord. In contrast, Augustine took a worldly, arguably more practi-cal, attitude toward the wealthy Christian community. He argued that the wealthy should give their riches to the church that would in turn feed and nurture the poor and downtrodden. A church dedicated to reaching out to the masses was a church that was amassing good wealth, mirroring in its mission to the impoverished the treasures awaiting those fortunate persons whose souls were bound for salvation in the afterlife.

"The City of God and the City of the World"

As the Roman Empire disintegrated during the fifth century, as the Vandals poured into North Africa, as Rome was sacked in 410 CE, Christians found themselves on the defensive once again. The "pagan" old guard argued that failure to worship the traditional Roman deities was the reason the empire was drowning. In his reply, Augustine wrote the text that would reverber-ate throughout the medieval period—a book Charlemagne declared was his favorite—*The City of God and the City of the World*. In it he laid out his thesis concerning predestination. God decides who is to be saved and who is to be damned. Those destined for salvation may be active members of the Christian community, or they may not be. They constitute the City of God. Some persons destined for salvation dwell temporarily in the City of the World that is hopelessly violent, hopelessly corrupted by sinfulness. They are the elect and the Church needs to reach out to them despite their apparent unrighteous behavior induced to be sure by the dog-eat-dog reality of the City of the World. Claims that one can voluntarily guarantee admission to the City of God through acts of free will, through extreme ascetic devotion for instance—in short, views advanced by Donatists or Pelagians—are misguided.

Other highly respected individuals holding sway amongst the ranks of Nicene intelligentsia favored a more benign version of Augustine's position. Perhaps simply more pragmatic, they attempted to throw open the doors of the orthodox faith to soldiers and wealthy landlords exploiting slaves. Their variant treated Christ as a benevolent judge that could—and would—pardon the sins of the penitent, in short, a kind of divine emperor issuing pardons on a regular basis.

The bottom line is that the controversies over Arianism, Donatism, and Pelagianism and the sharp demarcation between the City of God (the religious authority) and the City of the World (the secular authority) did not vanish. They became part and parcel of the great ideological pendulum swings of the medieval period.

Notes

1 Many accounts of the lives and (often untimely) deaths of Roman Emperors exist. Still, it is hard to beat the classic account penned by Edward Gibbon, *The History of the Decline and Fall of the Roman Empire* (1776).
2 For a discussion of the various first and second-century Christian beliefs and practices, see *inter alia* Brown (2015) and Madigan (2015).

Part II
Merchant capitalism

7 Islamic merchant capitalism

Consolidating Catholicism and feudalism: The great pendulum swing of early medieval Europe

Between the fifth century and the end of the eleventh century, the western world roiled with ideological and material pendulum swings. Ideas and material forces moved together. In the ideological dimension, fierce competition between Arianism and Nicene Christianity dominated the early medieval centuries, known—somewhat unfairly I might add—as the Dark Ages. Beginning with the seventh century onward Islam emerged as ideological contender with Christianity. As well it loomed large as a military and political threat to the Christian west, ultimately dismembering many of the Christian territories bordering on the Mediterranean Sea. In short order, Islamic armies managed to subdue much of the region that Hellenism followed by Roman armies had conquered. Between southern Iberia running through North Africa, through Egypt, through most Mediterranean waters, across much of Anatolia and the Arabian Desert, through Persia and even into northern India Islamic forces managed to cement together a huge empire rivaling in territorial terms anything Roman forces had been able to hold in sway.

In responding to the challenges of Arianism first—Islam afterwards—the Roman church and its secular military defenders contended with ideological and material swings rampant in the west. On the one hand, the church thrived under decentralized feudalism because it could pit feudal lords against one another, thus cowing secular power. On the other hand, in countering Arianism and in combating Islam, the church depended heavily on convincing secular overlords and kings to do its bidding. Convincing a king who loosely controlled, through bonds of fealty, feudal lords and their knights to convert to Nicene Christianity proved to be an effective weapon in bringing populations under the aegis of the Roman church. Convincing powerful kings to assemble a sufficiently formidable army to hold back Saracen invasions—or hostile Lombard forays—was necessary for Rome and Christian Europe to survive as a potent Christianized zone firmly rooted in the western reaches of the Eurasian land mass.

The pendulum swung back and forth between decentralized feudalism and centralized kingdoms, between Roman Catholicism and Arianism within Europe; and after the early seventh century between Islam and Christianity in sizable zones of the territories once defended by legions of the Roman Empire.

How to civilize the barbarians who rode roughshod over an increasingly Christianized Roman Empire? Compatibility between the Central Asian Culture Complex and Christian dogma had to be managed somehow. One approach was the Church's proliferation of saints and martyrs in the struggle to bring barbarian opponents around to the true civilization. Advertise extreme devotion: hopefully it will trump loyalty to the *comitatus*. Two forms of gift exchange were confronting each other: the trick was how to glue them together.

As it turned out, the concept of purgatory worked wonders for all parties involved. Incorporating views propounded by theologians—by Saint Augustine and by advocates of Christ as a merciful imperial judge—the concept of purgatory as a physical place located between Heaven and Hell evolved in the centuries after the imperial collapse. Ultimately, it rested on fear. The fear was of the Second Coming of Christ, the notion that a Final Judgment was imminent. Souls ultimately destined for Heaven—not Hell—who died without securing sufficient remission from sin during their lifetimes to justify immediate entry into Heaven spent time in purgatory, where their suffering and abasements paid off their debt owed to God. Once arrears were settled, once one's soul was sufficiently purified, it could move on to blessed paradise. Church sanctioned prayers offered for them during their lifetimes and prayers offered by those who directed their contributions to the church in the honor of the deceased could diminish the torturous time spent in purgatory.

What better institutions for organizing prayers for the deceased than monasteries? Monks devoted much of their days to solemn prayer. Surely they could be induced to pray for a powerful feudal overlord who had set aside land for their structures. To boot, monasteries were organized along hierarchical lines, not too dissimilar to a *comitatus*. Under the principle of Benedictine monastic rule the abbot of the monastery became all powerful, meting out physical punishments to underling monks. Loyalty to the abbot's harsh rule was the watchword. This form of organization surely exercised a strong fascination to those following the rigid discipline of the *comitatus*. To the chief of a Germanic tribe the two organizations did not seem so different. Moreover, practical concerns were not insignificant. A *comitatus* chief intent on avoiding wholesale division of his estate among male heirs found convenient the option of dispatching some offspring to monasteries established in the territories under his control. Calculating thusly, local rulers doled out land to monks who were required to toil as part of their training. Monasteries ended up specializing in farming. In principle monks worked in the fields. Or in the monasteries where copying manuscripts and prayer took precedence in the litany of tasks assigned the devout, monks at least managed—while not necessarily toiling on the fields—farmland actually tended by serfs, slaves, and tenant farmers.

Purgatory became big business for the church. According to Brown (2015: 164, 166):

> Except for a few saints, no passage to heaven was easy. The soul required all the prayers that it could get ... the great of the [Merovingian] land ... sought protection for their souls through gifts to the church ... It was this high-pitched view of the Last Judgment that accounted for the mounting fortunes of the church. Contemporary records of donations showed this with clarity.

Purgatory opened the doors of the churches to a massive inflow of earthly treasure. As well, it threw open the doors to the Christianization of real estate, monasteries amassing generous tracts of land set aside by feudal lords for the care of their souls.

In the upshot, decentralized Christianized feudalism spread over Western Europe. With the Christian empire carved up in the West—the Byzantine remnant alone maintaining a dual system of emperor dominance, Eastern Christianity serving as a masking device—Rome had little choice but to compromise with local feudal lords and/or with the kings who tried to weld together loose confederations of recalcitrant rivaling tribes. In accomplishing this they were forced to surrender undisputed control over the churches and monasteries established within their domains. In contrast to the Byzantine situation—secular rule trumping religious rule—Western Christendom ended up with a power sharing arrangement, control over loyalty and resources oscillating between Saint Augustine's City of God and City of the World.

Not only was the Roman Church forced to compromise with decentralized feudalism. It also had to consolidate its ideological hegemony over western Christianity, driving Arianism under the ground, rendering it as a heresy. In this struggle, its main success came from dealing with kings to whom feudal lords owed fealty.

A key breakthrough benefiting the Roman Church came in the wake of the establishment of the Merovingian dynasty who, marching out of lands allocated to them north of the Rhine by the Romans swept aside Visigoths, Saxons, and Alemanni confederations. The Visigoth rulers had committed themselves to the Arian position; the Salian Franks who established Merovingian rule over a huge chunk of central Gaul were not Christian at all. However Clovis—the second Merovingian king who proved remarkably successful in winning battles against other federations—eventually brought under Merovingian rule most of Iberia, all of Gaul, and lands stretching to the Rhine. Prior to one of his major wars, Nicene Christian bishops convinced him he could secure victory if he converted to Christianity. Upon his conversion around 500—reminiscent of Constantine's conversion a century and a half earlier—he and his successors proved loyal to his bishopric advisors, granting lands and structures housing abbeys and monasteries, even members of the royal dynasty choosing to become bishops.

Division of Clovis's territorial conquests among his four sons set in motion a process of subdivision eventually weakening the kingdom. With time royal control over the Frankish lands dissolved, real power falling into the hands of mayors of the palace. Fear of ongoing Islamic aggression in the late seventh and eighth centuries spurred on Pope Zachary to dissolve the Merovingian dynasty in 752, his successor Pope Steven II formally transferring rule to the first Carolingian king, Pepin the Short, in 754. It was an astute move. After all, Pepin's son, the ruthless, despotic Charles Martel, had defeated the Moorish invaders at Tours in 732, turning the tide against the Islamic invasion of Europe.

Even with the creation of the successor to Frankish rule with the formal investing of Carolingian leader Charlemagne as the Holy Roman Emperor by the pope in 800 CE—an act that surely angered the Byzantine Emperor, driving a wedge between the two branches of Nicene Christianity—feudal decentralization and fragmentation remained a grim reality in Western Europe. In the upshot, three parties wrestled for control over the resources allocated to Christian organizations, notably the monasteries and bishoprics: the Holy See in Rome; the Holy Roman Emperor; and the feudal lords.

In effect, gift exchange—either in its feudal guise as fealty or in its religious guise as devotion to the church and its putative commitment to serve the poor and pray for the souls of the departed—came to dominate the division of the social surplus in the west. To some extent, gift exchange fealty served predation. Competing feudal fiefdoms vied with one another; kings overthrew other kings. The Merovingians supplanted the Visigoths; the Merovingians lost their legitimacy, stripped of power by a more powerful legitimating political force, the papacy. Commerce was a much depleted third claimant, particularly as markets collapsed under feudal divisiveness, a fact exemplified by the atrophy—in some regions ultimate destruction—of many of the ancient Roman roads.

The coronation of Charlemagne as Holy Roman Emperor was not simply a response to the ideological dynamics of European Christendom, to the successful spread of Nicene Christianity. Indeed, one of the most important factors lay elsewhere: the rise and spread of Islam. To understand how a religion emerging among merchants and traders spread across much of the Eurasian land mass—eventually capturing much of the territory once controlled by the Romans—the importance of the Silk Road as a conduit between the eastern and western zones of the Eurasian land mass requires our attention.

The Silk Road

In its heyday, the Roman Empire had expanded in all directions: east, west, south, and north. Its legions marched triumphantly into Gaul and Spain; having crushed Carthage in the Punic Wars it took control of northern Africa; it pushed out into the Middle East and the Levant, gaining a strong foothold in Egypt. It expanded to the east, exploiting Silk Road trade opportunities. In accomplishing these Herculean tasks, it drew a militarized barrier, a line in the sand separating its Greek and Anatolian conquests from those possessed by its Persian imperial rivals. Merchants caught in the middle between these two mighty foes—in Syria, Iraq, and the Arabian Peninsula—naturally took advantage of the situation, acting as intermediaries transporting goods from Red Sea ports and merchant dominated cities in old Fertile Crescent to western India and onward to China. Two avenues were available to them. One was the caravan moving through desert lands. The other was seafaring, taking advantage of the winds to traverse the Arabian Sea and arriving at the Bay of Cambay where Barygaza was located.

Great Middle Eastern trade centers flourished under these circumstances. The earliest to emerge as a major commercial powerhouse was Petra, populated by Nabataeans who settled down in a Jordanian ravine, handling the transshipment of goods between the Gulf of Aqaba on the Red Sea and the east. Key to their choice of locale was avoiding the clash of arms between Romans and Parthian/Persians quarrelling over the lands once held by the Seleucid Empire. Eclectic in their choice of gods, the Nabataean faith incorporated Greek, Roman, Mesopotamian, Persian, and Egyptian deities into their shrines, statues and rituals.[1] Along the Silk Road, religions clashed and congealed as merchants came together to truck and barter their wares.

There is nothing like competition—in this case, competition for riches with which jewel-encrusted temples could be erected. Consider the other end of the Silk Road. After the barbarian invasions of the Great Wandering dismembered China, spinning off nomadic dominated dynasties in the north, the Northern Wei Empire established a foothold between the Central Asian steppe and the remnant of the Han Empire now relegated to the south. To differentiate themselves from the Confucian dominated south, the rulers of the Northern Wei chose to base their legitimacy on Buddhism, hoping to make this the dominant religion of a China ultimately unified under their aegis. The carving of monumental Buddhist figures played an instrumental role in their patronage campaign. What better way to advertise your commitment?[2]

Motivated by a similar goal, consolidating legitimacy, the ruler of the once nomadic Yuezhi, also embraced Buddhism, promoting a variant of the faith more compatible with the gift giving practices key to the *comitatus*. The resulting faith, Mahayana Buddhism, promoted the giving of Seven Treasure donations (the luxury goods of the Silk Road) to Buddhist monasteries and stupa, a veritable entry fee to securing a place in the Buddhist inspired paradises populated by Bodhisattvas. Not surprising, over time the carving of Buddha figures spread, skirting along the fringes of the Takla Makan desert, spilling down into what is today's Afghanistan.

In short, the Silk Road trade did increase religious competition for merchant wealth. Is it surprising that eventually a religion justifying merchant activity emerged? To be sure, nothing is inevitable; however, momentum is important. It is difficult to escape the feeling that a religion compatible with the idea of credit creating mobile capital, a religion embracing merchant values, would eventually emerge somewhere along the Silk Road.

The rise of Islam

It did: in Mecca.[3]

Early seventh-century Mecca was somewhat similar to Petra. Christian tribes, Jewish tribes and pagan tribes competed and cooperated. There they watered their camels; haggled over the prices of cloth, wine, leather, grain, spices, and frankincense; and argued over which faith was superior to the others. Like Petra, it was extremely commercial and extremely ecumenical.

To prevent the internecine fighting between tribes that plagued caravan trafficking across the Arabian Peninsula connecting the Red Sea to the Arabian Sea the tribes worked out a clever arrangement. They fashioned sacred space out of what was de facto commercial and diplomatic space. A border of stones was laid around Mecca. Within this space attacks against competitor tribes were anathema. At the heart of Mecca was the Ka'ba a holy temple. Myth and tradition swirled around this structure. Did Abraham's son born to Hagar, Ishmael, sanctify it? That it was mentioned in the Hebrew Scriptures—in Psalm 84 where a pilgrimage to the Valley of Baca is mentioned—suggests it was associated with Abraham the "original monotheist." Was its interior decorated with a painting of Jesus and the Virgin Mary? In any event, during the early seventh century the Ka'ba was under the control of the Quraysh, who worshipped a pagan god, Hubal.

This was the world that welcomed Muhammad at birth. Born into one of Mecca's noble families—his father tragically deceased before he emerged from the womb—Muhammad followed in the footsteps of his tribal elders, becoming a shepherd first, later a highly successful merchant.[4] It was only later that he became the prophet—according to Islam the Last Prophet, continuing a prophetic line staked out initially by Abraham, extended by Joseph son of Jacob, by Moses, inherited by Jesus—establishing an exceptionally pure form of monotheism.

Driven out of Mecca by the Quraysh, Muhammad led his followers to Medina where he consolidated his political base, ultimately returning to Mecca, defeating his Quraysh opponents in a holy war (*jihad*), and ultimately gaining control over the Ka'ba in the name of the one god, Allah. Over the course of his remarkable career, Muhammad progressed—from lowly shepherd to wealthy merchant to suffering prophet attacked by powerful enemies to political leader, even a military leader fierce in leading troops in combat—finally becoming the powerful benefactor to the impoverished, advocate for a type of gift exchange mirroring what Saint Augustine had championed during the collapse of the Roman Empire.

Once more emerges the suffering, Socratic religious hero who—through countless travails and grinding hardship—wrests forth spiritual triumph from an impure world sullied by misconceptions and error. Remarkably, for the first time the suffering hero leaves a legacy extolling the merchant. Granted, acquiring riches for the mere sake of acquiring riches is frowned upon. Granted, the Christians are right in condemning usury. Still, trade itself is admirable. Indeed, submission to Allah means submission to peaceful transaction, to honest commerce.

The Qur'an makes the last point crystal clear:[5]

> Cling one and all to the faith of Allah and let nothing divide you. Remember the favors He has bestowed upon you: How He united your hearts when you were enemies, so that you are now brothers through His grace; and how He delivered you from the abyss of fire when you were on the very brink of it.

Once you were enemies raiding each other's caravans, slaughtering each other out of devotion to false deities whose worship accomplished nothing for you, simply preparing you for an afterlife of everlasting torment and incineration. Now, thanks to Allah's mercy, you are free to trade; better yet, you are freed from fear of everlasting torment in the fires of hell.

There is little doubt that Muhammad—growing up in a world alive with Christianity, Judaism, Manichaeism, Gnosticism, and paganism—viewed the program of belief he fervently espoused as a revelation granted him by transcendental authority, in this case by the Angel Gabriel. Given the earlier religious revelations he drew upon it was natural for him to claim that the one vouchsafed to him was on final stop on the road to purification. The "people of the book" had managed to distort the true message of Abraham. Judaism was tribal, exclusionary; Christians failed at elementary arithmetic, confusing three with one. The Qur'an and the thousands of oral statements (*hadith, sunnah*) made by the prophet were revealed truth, mischievous error having been cleansed. Islam was pure monotheism.[6]

In the aftermath of Muhammad's demise, the problem of how to rule under Islamic principles, how to carry on commerce on Islamic principles, how to carry on warfare under Islamic principles, and how to treat peoples conquered by the Arabs (the first group to embrace Islam), became acute. After all, Muhammad was an unusual religious hero: he was at once prophet, merchant, administrator, and warrior all wrapped up into one. During the first three generations of Islamic life—the so-called era of the righteous *salaf*, of the purest generations, of the righteous ancestors of contemporary Islam—sorting out these issues involved much bloodshed, much disputation, and the planting of seeds of future division and dissension.[7] Still, one thing was clear: Islam was a faith that could be readily exploited as a mask for despotic secular rule. After all, the founder of the faith had functioned as secular ruler and military strategist. In competing against western

Christendom, which was rife with tension between secular and religious authority, Islam had a decided advantage.

From the perspective of this book that explores the relationship between capitalism and religious faith the most important issues involve treatment of non-Islamic peoples; the development of legal theories concerning contracting, credit creation and corporations; and the uniting of secular rule with religious rule. With no claim to a comprehensive treatment a few comments about each issue—admittedly cursory—are essential.

Exploiting weaknesses in the Byzantine Roman and Persian Empires, the territories that fell to the armies of Islamic rulers—the caliph—increased dramatically in the aftermath of Muhammad's demise. Under the first three of the Rashidun, the so-called Rightly Guided Caliphs—Umar, Umar ibn Khattab, and Uthman ibn Affan—Persia, Egypt, and a huge swath of territory was incorporated into the Caliphate governed empire. During the short-lived rule of Ali, son-in-law and cousin of Muhammad, the last of the Rashidun, a fierce civil war broke out between various factions striving to grasp control of the empire. To be sure aggrandizing power was crucial but so was principle. Muhammad had been both prophet, anointed religious leader, as well as administrator and war leader.

Which was more important: a religious devotee listening to the voice of Allah—channeling doctrinal concepts, ideas, onto a secular map—or a materialistically oriented king aggrandizing territory that could exploited through control of Silk Trade routes and promotion of agricultural development, bolstering the foundations upon which religiously oriented gift exchange could thrive? The faction supporting Ali became known Shi'a: they believed in the religious devotee should take precedence. The majority faction, the Sunni, supporting a king dominant model, overthrew Ali's faction after the establishment of the Umayyad Caliphate. However, in pointing to ideological differences between the two schools of thought it is important to keep in mind that the line dividing secular and religious was far thinner—far less clearly demarcated—in Islam than it was in the Roman Christianity consolidated in the fourth and fifth centuries. Far more important, for the first major schism within Islam—at least in the first few centuries of Islamic hegemony over the lands Islamic armies conquered—was interpretation of a particular set of historical events involving Ali. After all, Ali had been the fourth caliph. No deep divide between the City of God and the City of the World.

Under the Umayyad Caliphate territorial expansion continued. Central Asian territory was added on: the Caucasus, Transoxiana, Sindh (the Indus River basin), the Maghreb, and a major chunk of the Iberian Peninsula. Unfortunately, this proved to the Umayyad's undoing. During the mid-700s CE, a faction opposed to Umayyad rule—bankrolled by powerful merchants, relying upon Central Asian Turkish, Persian and Georgian slave troops (the Mamluk)—overthrew the Umayyads, the heir to the Umayyad dynasty fleeing to Iberia where he established the Emirate or Caliphate of Corboda.

In sum, within a very brief period a vast number of communities adhering to diverse religious backgrounds were brought under Islamic rule. The problem was how to treat them. Three options were available: convert to Islam; remain non-Muslim, becoming *dhimmis*, who were required to pay a special tax (*jizya*) for the privilege of receiving military security from the Muslim community; or die by the sword.

There were some advantages to being a *dhimmi*. Under the Pact of Umar *dhimmis* had the option of using non-Muslim courts to settle disputes. Subject to the proviso that they were dealing with other *dhimmis* and not Muslims, the Pact allowed non-Muslims to either access Muslim courts—four major schools of religiously inspired Islamic law existed although in practice it was easy to move between the courts—or to seek judgment elsewhere. Muslims, however, were only allowed to use one of the branches of Muslim jurisprudence. Moreover, because Muslims could not renounce their religion, become apostates, without being subject to capital punishment, Muslims could not escape their own religiously inspired law, largely drawn from the Qur'an and the *hadith*, with reasoning based on rational debate free of scripture playing a relatively minor role in three of the four legal schools.

Another potential advantage of being *dhimmi* was the possibility of practicing primogeniture. Islamic law frowned on it, perhaps because the traditions of the Qur'an and the *hadith* were initially developed amongst trading communities using highly divisible, mobile, capital rather than land. Equal division of inheritance tended to fragment both the holding of mobile capital and land ownership.

The bill of exchange

In any event Islamic law was very favorable to trade. Under the principle that interaction between travelling merchants (*al-Tajir as-Saffar*) and resident merchants (*al-Tajir al-Muqim*) should be encouraged in order to facilitate Silk Road commerce, judgments allowing writing of bills of exchange became the law of the Islamic world by the middle of the eight century. The fact that the Abbasid Caliphate had enjoyed strong merchant backing in its protracted struggle to unseat Umayyad dominance certainly did not hurt the cause of facilitating long-distance, mobile capital, business. As described by Rubin (2010) it became common practice for a bill of exchange (*suftaja*) that required payment of a debt by a certain date to be rigorously enforced by the Islamic courts. Individual A loans individual B a specified sum to be repaid by individual C on such and such a date. In exchange for receiving the funds, B issues a bill of exchange to A. A fee is charged for the loan. Dealing in a common currency—ubiquitous throughout the Islamic world—no currency arbitrage is involved. However, interest is implicitly reckoned in the set of transactions governed by the issue of a *suftaja*. The fee charged is really nothing more than interest cleverly masked.

The bill of exchange was an ingenious device for creating mobile capital linked to credit creation. In principle, the Qur'an denounced usury with greater force than did early Christianity—after all, the Council of Nicaea forbad priests from engaging in usury but not the laity—as is made abundantly clear in a famous Sūrah:[8]

> O you who believe, keep your duty to Allah and relinquish what remains [due] from usury.

The idea is unrighteous profit is bad but exchange is good: interest (*riba*) is unacceptable, presumably because it is exploitative, impure. In practice as opposed to principle Islamic law permitted interest. The bill of exchange is one device for charging interest. The other device is sharing returns on investment. If A wants to secure interest from B because B has an investment opportunity the two parties can agree to share any profits accruing to B's management of the funds. Under this subterfuge A is basically securing interest: the share of profits relative to the amount of funds loaned (to compute the rate one needs to take into account the length of time it takes for the fruits of the investment to be realized).

Moreover, Islamic law allowed for other devices that promoted capital accumulation. One was the *waqf*, the trust. Under Islamic law a *waqf* could be created by a benefactor. Once set up the conditions of the trust were not to be changed. The primary motive for arranging an Islamic trust was charity, a basic principle laid down by Muhammad who ended his life as a benefactor to the poor. Typically trusts were set up for the construction and maintenance of fixed capital, hospitals or schools for instance. Still "cash *waqf*" were allowed, suggesting a degree of flexibility. That said, one of the major themes emphasized by Kuran (2011) is that the *waqf* was not the equivalent of the Western corporation. There are two obvious reasons: most *waqf* were set up to provide the destitute with food and medical services; and the benefactor's stipulations were binding. To be true to the principles of Islam, the state needed a system of welfare. Countenancing the *waqf* was one way to accomplish this goal. Allowing it to morph into a profit-making corporation was not in the interests of the state.

That Islam was highly favorable to credit creating mobile capital is clear from the fact that Karimi merchants became fantastically wealthy under the Mamluk Sultanate of Cairo. Enjoying virtual monopolies in the spice trade, and dabbling in the African slave trade, some of the greatest fortunes assembled (on a global basis) during the period of the late Middle Ages were put together by an elite group of Karimi merchant houses.[9]

Given its trade-driven commercial success during the period of Abbasid Caliphate rule (750–1517 CE), it is not surprising that Islam experienced a Golden Age. Indeed Findlay and O'Rourke (2007) suggest that the blossoming of trade is usually associated with innovation, as it appears to have been under early Abbasid dominance. Irrigation, planting of new crops, bureaucracy all spread back and forth from Persia in the east to northern Africa and Iberia in the west.

During the period 750 to 1300 it was the Islamic world, not the Latin Christian world that translated the Greek writings of Aristotle, Ptolemy, and Galen.[10] It was the Islamic world that built on the works of the great Greek philosophers, astronomers, map makers, and medical theorists, improving their calculations, in some cases disputing the rectitude of their doctrines. It was Baghdad, the Abbasid capital that housed great libraries during Europe's early medieval period. Not Paris, not Rome, not London. It was the Islamic world that developed the astrolabe, an ingenious device used for determining the direction to Mecca—crucial for proper Muslim prayer—also with useful applications for seafaring and land travel.

Given its early lead in developing merchant capitalism why did the Islamic world collapse into an era of stagnation? As Kuran (2011: 68 ff) emphasizes, the share of commerce in the labor force of the Islamic world declined between the period 701–1100 CE and the period 1101–1500 CE. By contrast, after 1200 CE it was Western Europe—not the Islamic world— where commercial innovation blossomed, where major advances in merchant capitalism and science were being made.

One popular theory—that growing religious homogenization due to the decline in the share of the *dhimmi* population in Islamic societies (more and more people having converted to Islam presumably to avoid paying the *jizya* tax or to escape other forms of discrimination or because they viewed Islam as superior to their native faiths)—has been questioned by scholars. To be sure the idea that a purifying form of Islamic fundamentalism gained prominence, strangling innovative thinking is reasonable. The Abbasids were corrupt. Over time the luxury of their court became increasingly abhorrent, outright disgusting, to those steeped in the study of the Qur'an. That a purifying movement aimed at returning Islam to the age of the *salaf* occurred is not only plausible but true seems to bear out the key premise of this thesis. However, the burden of Saliba (2007) is that there is no evidence for a decline in the productivity of Islamic philosophers, astronomers and mathematicians during the thirteenth and fourteenth centuries, precisely the period when the purification movements were in their ascendency.

Other theories point to trade diversion, brought on first by the Mongol invasions of the thirteenth century weakening if not destroying Islamic hold over Silk Road commerce. Later, as a consequence of European trade expansion in the fifteenth and sixteenth centuries, the vitality of Muslim trade was sapped out. Of this there is little doubt.

However, an even more compelling explanation cannot fail to impress: the fact that Islam makes little if no distinction between the sacred and the secular. In his book *Lost in the Sacred,* Diner (2009) makes this claim. The shadow of Muhammad, Islam's great hero, looms over the Islamic community. By contrast, in Catholic Christian Europe a distinction between the secular and the sacred existed from the days of the Roman Empire. Grafting the

Central Asian Culture Complex onto Christianity yielded a feudal Europe in which the divorce between the secular and the sacred actually grew wider, even as Christianity evolved from being a minority religion in the days of Constantine, triumphing to become the only religion of any consequence by the time of the Crusades.[11]

The fact that the ideological pendulum swing did not swing back and forth between the secular and the religious within the Islamic—despite the nuances separating Shi'a and Sunni, despite the treasure trove of Greek thought that fell into Islamic hands—was its ultimate undoing. It is not enough to read the classics of the Axial Age; you must live them, incorporate into them your material and ideological being. This happened in western Christendom. It did not happen in Byzantine Christendom; it did not happen in Islam.

Notes

1 For details see Liu (2010: 24 ff).
2 This paragraph draws heavily for Liu (2010: 76 ff).
3 Mecca emerged as a major trading center after Petra—and Palymyra in Syria, its successor entrepôt conurbation—lost its cache due to fighting between the Byzantine rump of the Roman Empire and the Parthian/Persian Empire to the east. See McAuliffe (2006) for an interesting discussion of the politics prevailing in Mecca at the time of Muhammad's youth.
4 For the life of Muhammad, see Ramadan (2007).
5 Quoted in Kuran (2011: 105).
6 On doctrinal differences between Islam and Judaism see Johns (1990) and Peters (1990).
7 The most important sectarian split within Islam—dividing the Sunni and Shi'a communities—occurred within a century after Muhammad's death. While the split involved the question of who was the rightful caliph (political/spiritual) leader of the Islamic community, it intensified later on. Particularly decisive for subsequent disputes over scriptural authority was the fact that Islamic armies brought Persian and later Indian lands under their control. Before Islam arrived, Persians were mainly followers of Zoroastrianism, a faith steeped in dualism, the forces of pure Light opposing the materialistic forces of Darkness. It was a faith sharing many beliefs with Gnosticism; indeed, perhaps the seeds of Gnosticism sprouted in Persia. As Islam evolved from a core faith largely restricted to Arabian lands to one governing a diverse ethnic community consisting of peoples gradually abandoning earlier beliefs—rooted in Christianity, or Judaism, or Manichaeism, or Zoroastrianism, or Buddhism, or Hinduism—it became a "big tent" religion, housing under its umbrella a variety of potentially conflicting worldviews and a remarkable variety of rituals.
8 Quoted in Labib (1969: 79).
9 See Kuran (2011: 138), Labib (1969:82 ff) and Tsugitaka (2012). Labib goes so far as to argue that the Karimi set up stock exchanges (*funduqs*). It should be noted that in his detailed study Kuran (2011) there is no mention of these exchanges.
10 See Leicester (1965), McClellan III and Dorn (2006), and Saliba (2007).
11 Intensifying the distinction between the sacred and the secular was the Roman Catholic Church's decision to declare itself a corporation, managing its business

according to its own canon law (jus novum). This occurred during the late eleventh and early twelfth centuries, intensifying a split that had been in the making for centuries as the Church struggled over its relationships with the Holy Roman Emperor and the feudal lords. See Brady Jr. (1991), Marcus (1990), Kuran (2011: 102 ff), and Morrison (1969). Rubin (2010) argues that the fact that European merchants could handle their legal affairs through secular courts as opposed to religious courts made it easier for European merchants to build upon the bill of exchange and the fashioning of trusts than was true for Muslim merchants dealing exclusively with religious courts. How important governmental and religious bodies—for instance, courts that adjudicate disputes concerning proper adherence to stipulations laid out in contracts—were in encouraging merchants to cooperate with one another is a controversial question. For the view that merchant groups could and did develop self-governing mechanisms for enforcing contracts and cemented trust, see Greif (2006). Greif pioneered the use of game theory techniques in analyzing trust among merchants. Trendy when he did so, the approach seems tired and frayed at present.

8   The pendulum swings of the
High and Late Medieval West

The pendulum swing of the High Medieval Period:
simony and the Crusades

During the early medieval period, the church bettered its secular opponents, extracting resources from the social surplus at a phenomenal rate. To be sure a powerful ruler like Charlemagne maintained an opulent court, albeit one dedicated to Christian worship. Still under his guidance and the wisdom of his successors, resources were found permitting the court to acquire ancient Greek and Latin texts, scribes being employed in the task of transferring their contents to durable vellum (instead of papyrus).[1] As well, fielding armies was a costly business. Charlemagne induced Pope Leo III to crown him Holy Roman Emperor on Christmas day, 800, because he had led troops over the Alps, defeating Lombard troops threatening the territorial claims of the papacy.[2] The pope was prepared to market titles, to confer legitimacy of secular rulers, provided a material quid-pro-quo was in the offing.

A wealthy church inevitably became a corrupt church. Unmonitored gift exchange, the outright graft that purgatory was becoming, was undermining the values propounded by Jesus. It weakened the legitimacy of the very institution supposedly devoted to espousing the doctrines of its founders. In doing so the corruption called into question the legitimacy the church was conferring on secular rulers.

The church had become big business. Many bishops enjoyed incomes accrued from magnificent estates; often even the rank in file parish priest secured a comfortable living from the wealth accumulated by the church. How pure, how well informed in the doctrines of the church was a typical priest? Not much. Standards were not high. Most priests married or bedded concubines; many practiced magic, sanctifying fields prior to spring planting with non-Christian, arguably pagan rituals, carrying out questionable exorcisms, making money off the sale of forged relics, promoting the cult of the dead, purifying water for the Sunday sacraments for remuneration. The wealth of the church was corrupting its minions. Not surprisingly, the papacy itself was up for sale. Powerful Roman families vied to put their children on the papal throne. A teenager even held the post at one point.

The practice of turning the church's income generating opportunities into saleable commodities is known as simony. Russell describes it[3]:

> It was customary for the king to sell bishoprics; this in fact, provided a substantial part of his income. The bishop, in turn, sold such ecclesiastical preferment as was in his power. There was no secret about this. Gerbert (Sylvester II) represented his bishops as saying "I gave gold and I received the episcopate; but yet I do not fear to receive it back if I behave as I should. I ordain a priest and I receive gold; I make a deacon and I receive a heap of silver. Behold the gold which I have once more … [put back into] my purse."

Under the logic of simony amassing fortunes through the purchase of bishoprics was all too possible, all too tempting to the entrepreneurially inclined. A greed-driven investor could secure ten, twenty, maybe more, placing relatives or hired hands into the positions, using them as a source of lucre. This raised problems. Not surprisingly, the proposals cynical clergy put forward were completely at variance with the proposals sincere reformers advanced. The cynical wanted the church to wrest away the take from the secular rulers; the sincere wanted to clean up the whole mess, purifying the operation of the ecclesiastical hierarchy.

All of this came to a head in the investiture controversy, pitting the youthful Holy Roman Emperor Henry IV against Pope Gregory VII.[4] Setting off the struggle was Henry's appointment of his candidate as archbishop of Milan. Gregory rejected Henry's right to make the appointment, excommunicating Henry. Without a doubt Gregory hoped to turn Henry's feudal underlings against Henry. Henry responded by calling together a synod of German bishops at Worms that issued a declaration accusing Gregory of being a usurper, a polluter of the papal office. In the aftermath a famous arrangement, a cynical arrangement was hammered out between the Holy See and the Holy Roman Emperor, one that echoed down to the nineteenth century when Bismarck used it as a stick to beat upon Catholicism in Germany. Henry travelled to Canossa in 1077 arriving as a barefoot suppliant, a penitent who was requesting forgiveness for his sins, asking for absolution from Gregory. In fact, a quid-pro-quo involving Imperial military support for the pope underlay the exquisite farce. Even more farcical was the ultimate denouement. Gregory gathered up his forces in 1084, sending them across the Alps where they occupied Rome, sending Gregory packing to a fortress in Saint Angelo where the pope put out a bid for support from the Normans. All of this turned dark for Rome. The Normans did beat back Henry IV's forces but they also burned down a third of the city while Gregory ended his life as a virtual prisoner of the Normans who ostensibly were doing his bidding.

Ultimately the investiture controversy was put to rest at the Concordat of Worms in 1122. Under the compromise hammered out bishops were to be elected by the church in accordance with canon law. In return, the Emperor was permitted to witness the actual appointment. In practice, secular authority continued to exercise influence over bishopric politics.

The hard-cold geopolitical reality is that the papacy was caught between a protector—that could and did turn itself against the Holy See when it felt its interests were at stake—and the threat of Islamic invasion. That Catholic Europe was fragmented made it vulnerable to Islamic attack. The fear was not without foundation. Islamic armies had wrestled away Northern Africa, Egypt, and the Levant from the Byzantine Empires in the past; and they were threatening to seize more Christian territory in Anatolia. To the east, Islamic armies had defeated Chinese troops at the Talus River and had turned parts of the Indian subcontinent into Muslim controlled regions.

Not all threats are symmetric. Islam posed a challenge for Christian Europe on grounds largely irrelevant to the peoples of China and India. Caliphs controlled Jerusalem and the Holy Land. How important this bitter fact was to European Christendom is revealed by the fact European maps crafted during the medieval period placed Jerusalem at the world's center. Islamic rulers could and did prevent pilgrims from worshipping at sites holy to both Christians and Jews. Sharing sacred space was a major issue. To cite a particularly striking example: the al Aqsa mosque—erected to celebrate Muhammad's ascent into Heaven—was built on the ruins of the Jews' Second Temple, all but crushed to bits by Roman troops fighting Jewish militants.

Moreover, Christians were second class citizens, *dhimmis,* in the Islamic Empire. From a Christian perspective, they were discriminated against. How valid was the western Christian critique of Muslim oppression of Christians is a contentious issue? Who knows? Few if any Muslims lived in Christian lands. Consider the fact that Christian lands were not particularly hospitable to the Jews, who probably fared better under Caliphate rule than they did in the Holy Roman Empire.[5]

Add to these long festering concerns the fact that the papacy was mired in a complex political struggle with the Holy Roman Emperor, diverse groups of feudal lords, and the Byzantine Patriarch (the great schism dividing the Catholic and Greek Orthodox faiths had just occurred in the mid-eleventh century). With all this pressuring it, the papacy decided to make a dramatic gesture asserting its dominance, issuing a call for Crusades directed against the Islamic world in the closing decade of the eleventh century.

How important economic prowess factored into the reasoning of the papacy is an intriguing question. According to the military power equation elaborated in the Appendices, military potential (M) depends upon the level of overall economic output (Y):

(8.1) $M = (mY)/p_{mf} = (myP)/p_{mf}$

Where m is the military conversion rate (the percentage of total economic output devoted to obtaining human and capital resources used in warfare);

P is population; and p_{mf} is the relative price of exerting a unit of military force (relative to other goods in the economy). Deflating the share of the economy devoted to the military by the relative price of actually implementing action on the battlefield (p_{mf})—the relative prices of swords, lances, horses, armor, the relative costs of building and maintaining castles compared to consumer prices—adjusts the resources devoted to the military sub-economy for their actual effectiveness. It reflects the technology of warfare.

Consider the Crusades dispatched to the Holy Land. They raged for approximately two centuries after Christian forces captured Jerusalem in 1096 CE, pitting feudal knights riding on horseback against Islamic cavalry encased in relatively comparable armor, both sides using swords and lances whose manufacture had been gradually perfected over centuries of warfare. Not surprisingly the combatants employed relatively similar shock tactics in battle since they were basically armed the same way. The monumental account of the Crusades given in Rogers (2010: 446–521) bears this point out. To be sure when the Crusaders first invaded the Levant they faced Muslim armies that employed tactics of fighting the Westerners had not encountered before. Successful use of archery was one such area. Soon enough the Christian forces adapted, introducing techniques employed by their adversaries. Of course, Islamic forces did likewise. Mimicking your enemies is a mainstay of armed conflict.

Think of the military power equation this way: imagine a pie representing total economic activity is cut into two wedges, a military sub-economy and a civilian sub-economy. Resources—human, animal, and inanimate—are employed in both sub-sectors. How this allocation is to be determined and how effective it is depends on politics: upon the individual or individuals ordering the use of armed force; upon who acquires the funds supporting the training and employment of armies and navies.

The easiest case to envision is a non-fragmented system, central rulers raising funds to fight wars. Some of these funds are allocated for purchase of swords, horses, siege machinery, and a navy; some are used to employ soldiers, to pay for their upkeep when they are training as well as when they are in combat. The proportion of the entire economy allocated to military powers—the ratio of the military economy to the entire economy—is **m**. To secure the funds the ruler taxes the population. Under Islamic principles, *dhimmi* were not expected to fight but they paid higher taxes than Muslims, therefore avoiding the call to military service. The relevant population figure the Muslim world was working with was the total population—Muslims plus *dhimmis*—because that constituted its fiscal base. Its base for recruiting soldiers was the Muslim population—and slaves purchased or taken in warfare—under its rule.

In actual fact, political infighting within the confines of the Muslim world had weakened the Caliphate. The days of empire building religious fervor inspired *jihad* were over. The Islamic world had splintered into several competing regions, albeit nothing like the crazy quilt fragmentation of Western Christendom. One of the greatest fissures in the Muslim world ran down doctrinal lines: Shi'a versus Sunni. After the Abbasid Caliphate deposed the Umayyad Caliphate in the mid-eighth century, the Muslim world fragmented. Al-Andalus (at its greatest extent stretching into Iberia and southern France) and the Maghreb were controlled by the Sunni Umayyad, becoming the Caliphate of Cordova. The Berber backed regime of the Idrisid dynasty—Shi'a in orientation—took over Morocco. A swath of territory between Morocco and Egypt—Tunisia, western Libya, and eastern Algeria—was held by the Aghlabids, eventually dethroned by the Shi'ite Fatimids who already controlled Egypt.

That the Shi'a continually fought with the Sunni over territory definitely assisted the Crusaders in their first venture into the Levant. Jerusalem—the crown jewel for the Westerners—had been wrested away from Sunni Seljuq Turkish control by the Shi'ite Fatimids in the late 1090s, just before the Crusaders mounted their successful assault on the holy metropolis, Jerusalem falling to Christian armies in 1099. However, Christian control over the site bristling with structures sacred to Jews, Christians, and Muslims was short-lived, with Sunni-inspired Saladin eventually driving out the Crusader forces.

For Western Europe the question was simple: who was going to bear the costs of fielding troops in the Holy Land? For its part, the papacy imposed special taxes, controversial and resisted by parishioners and secular rulers alike. Ultimately, the church had to secure the commitment of kings who could draw upon feudal retainers for assistance. Kings responded by demanding fiefs and their dependent monasteries supply warriors. Ultimately, the principal supplier of military hardware and personnel was the agglomeration of feudal estates maintaining cadres of knights. The rents earned by feudal lords from their fiefs loomed large in the financing of the military sector of the economy. Cajoling the various actors into participating in a coordinated military action was politically tricky. In short funding and managing the Crusades proved a daunting economic proposition for Christian Europe.

In the event, Rome felt it had little choice: the pope declared Crusades to be a Holy War, the Christian answer to Islam's *jihad*. Offer remission from sins, reduced time in purgatory, guaranteed arrival in Paradise, to the knights. Borrow from the book inspired by the teachings of Muhammad.

Employing the ideology of Holy War as a rallying cry resolved some recruitment problems but did not completely eliminate the problem of economic size. Under a regime in which the technology of killing commanded by military units rests upon an equal technological playing field—the Crusades being a prime example—economic variables—the levels of y, and P (total economic performance Y equaling the product of y and P)—throw a huge shadow over the cold blooded calculus of warfare. Given the Islamic advantage in trade and credit creation—hence a probable advantage in per capita income—European envy of Islamic merchant capitalism is totally understandable.

Learn from your enemies. Imitate those things upon which their economic superiority resides. This is the salutary lesson that the European merchants took from the ultimately futile effort of Christian Crusaders to take control of the Holy Land.

The Europeans enjoying the most sustained and advantageous contact with the rank and file Muslim world were merchants, specifically those residing in the Italian city states of Genoa and Venice. City states cum regional powers dominated by powerful merchant interests, able to keep a lid on pressure of Catholic Church, Genoa, and Venice were actively involved in shipping Crusaders back and forth to the Levant, contesting the eastern end of the Mediterranean with Byzantine and Islamic traders. The saying "a Genoese and therefore a merchant" speaks for itself. Not surprisingly Genoese and Venetian merchants were innovators in adapting the Islamic bill of exchange to the European market.

It is a matter of considerable historical irony that Crusades ostensibly invoked for religious reasons—ultimately ending in military failure for the Europeans—brought the Christian world into direct contact with the Islamic world. That contact laid down the foundations of merchant capitalism in the West; that contact renewed interest in Greek knowledge in the west. In short, coping with the challenge posed by Islam set into motion pendulum swings both material and intellectual: in practical economic relations; in ideas about the nature of the physical world and how best to extract reliable information about that world.

The diffusion of merchant capitalism coming in the wake of Western penetration into the Islamic world played a pivotal role in bringing feudalism to an end. The forces unleashed by the associated legitimization of commercial ideology—expressed in a remarkable explosion of monetary bribes required for success in secular and religious elections—eroded the legitimacy the Catholic church exercised over the operation of gift exchange in European lands. At the same time coming to terms with Islamic learning induced beleaguered church and ambitious secular figures to cope with ancient thought and practice in all its dimensions, ushering in a struggle between Scholasticism and its arch rival alchemy.

The pendulum swing of the Late Medieval Period: merchant capitalism versus feudalism, Catholic Church inquisition versus Neo-Donatist sectarianism, Scholasticism versus alchemy

Once transmitted to Europe, merchant capitalism took off with a vengeance. The back and forth struggle between secular and authority gave it a mighty fillip absent in the Islamic arena.

In fragmented Europe, the bill of exchange was a more potent vehicle for extending credit and charging interest than it was in the Islamic world. Issuing bills of exchange negotiated in a market using a currency differing from that currency where the bill is originally drawn up generates a rate of return. This is above and beyond the return offered by drawing up a *suftaja*. For this reason, the bill of exchange became a more potent instrument in fragmented Europe, where currencies tended to be unique to localities, than in Islamic regions where there was one and only one officially sanctioned currency. One of the consequences was a weakening of the power of rulers. Negotiating bills of exchange ultimately impacted exchange rates between realms. Merchants could undermine and counterbalance the effort of feudal rulers easing a debt burden by debasing the currency of their realms.[6]

The bill of exchange is the progenitor of the bank check. The principal difference is the fact banks deal with many customers who are mostly anonymous, unknown to one other. Pushing the envelope of the bill of exchange, making it the cornerstone for banks charging interest on loans seems like a small step. Indeed, it is provided the religious authorities do not squelch it. In Islam, where state and religion tended to coincide, it was a step merchants and trusts were not easily able to take. They did not push the envelope. In Europe, fragmented and enjoying the use of secular as well as religious courts, the step was easier to take.[7]

Having taken the step in Italy, important improvements and refinements were open for experimenting. The famous hub-and-spoke system creating legally separable partnerships was introduced by the Medici enterprise in the fourteenth and fifteenth centuries.[8] It consisted of a partnership (the hub) managing the affairs of numerous subsidiary partnerships (spokes). The business affairs of each spoke, run by a branch manager, were operated along tracks separate from the other spokes. Theoretically, the entire fiscal umbrella, the hub, bore responsibility for the debts accrued by the spoke managers who bore unlimited liability. In practice—reflecting the fact that each spoke kept its own books and the fact that pursuing legal action against the hub was costly (given the fragmentation characteristic of the hub-spoke system)—creditors assumed the individual branches were independent. This limited the liability of the Medici system as a whole.

This was foray along the path leading to acceptance of limited liability incorporation. In setting up incorporation—an action pursued by the nascent European centers of learning modeled on the trust concept pioneered by Muslims—Europeans pushed the envelope on pooling capital for business purposes. The great trading companies emergent with mercantilism—the Dutch VOC, the English East India and Hudson Bay Companies—drew upon earlier steps taken by universities and banking concerns. The result was the limited liability joint-stock enterprise, gathering in funds from a deep pool of subscribers in order to engage seafarers in global commerce during the age of European exploration and conquest. Mercantilism was a politically infused business; or rather merchant commerce managed in the interest of the state. It is hardly surprising that legal support for the initiatives leading to limited liability joint-stock commerce came largely from secular courts, not Catholic courts.

Not only did the Crusades promote merchant capitalism by putting Christians into direct contact with Islamic merchants. They also led to trade expansion within Europe. As monks, lay people, and knights bristling with chainmail traversed Europe in growing numbers, the wayfarers demanded foodstuffs and services along the way. Market towns sprang up in response to the surging demand. Fairs bringing together merchants from diverse lands prospered. Urbanization was given a strong fillip. So was the mobility of capital.

The gradual transformation of Europe from a system of rural feudal fiefs to a system revolving around market towns and fairs ushered in a reversal in the relationship between secular and spiritual space. Under the feudalism of the early medieval era—the period between, say, 500 and 1200 CE that basically came to an end with the inglorious sacking of Constantinople and the seizing of holy relics (nails from the true cross included) from the Byzantines by the knights of Catholic Christendom—spiritual space mainly consisted of rural monasteries. Many had been set up as the invading Eurasian tribes invading the defunct Roman Empire were incorporated into Christendom. Many of the newly formed monasteries were basically handed over to lay patrons, feudal lords, as part of their fiefs. Into the monasteries went the oblates, the non-inheriting children procreated by feudal elites. The reason was simple: under standard interpretation of Germanic inheritance law estates were to be divided between sons, a fact that undid the Merovingian and Carolingian dynasties. Staving off this eventuality was a major reason why oblates were pushed off into monastic orders. Naturally, powerful lay patrons wanted to draw upon this very same pool of literate elites raised upon their own estates in negotiating with monasteries over who was to be appointed abbots. This was why corruption crept into the ranks of the monasteries, adding to the woes of a church struggling with simony in the appointment of the secular church hierarchy: elites accustomed to consuming luxuries populated the upper echelons of church and monastery alike. This was the reason why the investiture crisis cut such a wide swath across Europe.

Given on-going backsliding, new monastic orders emerged in waves.[9] In each case—Cluny in the tenth century, the Cistercian order in the twelfth century—the professed aim of the founder was purifying monastic life. In each case time eroded the dreamed for commitment to the Benedictine Rule. The Carthusian monks claimed bragging rights because they were less like to deviate from the rule than Benedictines, Cluniacs, and Cistercians.

Not surprisingly as credit creation spread in the secular community the monasteries, increasingly wallowing in materialism, took advantage of their privileges to extract rents. Monasteries carrying the fruits of their vineyards and flour mills evaded paying tolls on bridges maintained by feudal estates. They began to loan out money at interest; they began to borrow to build structures where they could house traveling elites, feudal lords, even powerful merchants. Increasingly they became quasi-secular. Given the decisions hammered out in Nicaea in 324 banning usury, these practices smacked of blatant hypocrisy. Still there was a loophole: the ban on loaning out money at interest applied to priests, not to monks or professional managers employed by monasteries. That the church was deeply mortified about this practice might explain why it extended its ban on usury to the laity at the Third Lateran Council of 1179. Or, alternatively, was the church hierarchy taking this position in an attempt to hang onto a quasi-monopoly over the credit market? In any case, the temptation to take advantage of its vast asset holdings was too appealing. By 1300, lawyers employed by the Holy See came up with a list of thirteen conditions—under the flimsiest of excuses— that permitting loaning out of money at interest.

To some it felt like money was undermining gift exchange in all its dimensions. Fried (2015: 257) writes:

> The beginnings of European high finance are found in the same period … [it got to the point that people replaced] 'Christ' in the old refrain with money 'Money is the victor, money is the king, money reigns supreme over all … [the election of a Holy Roman Emperor following the death of Henry VI] was made possible only by financing it with massive sums in bribery, which Cologne merchants and money brokers … transferred from England to the Holy Roman Empire.

Commerce was taking the upper hand over the gift exchange dominated world of early medieval Europe.

The drift of the church into a commerce and unbridled corruption did not go unnoticed by Christians seeking a pure form of the gospel of Jesus. Reviving the purifying principles of Donatism, breakaway sects spread. While tendencies in this direction had bubbled beneath the waters before the twelfth century, it was with the French Cathar rebellion of the 1100s that the split between so-called heretics and Roman church elite ignited a smoldering tinderbox.[10] Cathar society was divided into two sub-groups, the perfects (*perfecti*) and believers (*credentes*). The perfects committed themselves to chastity. If married, they abandoned conjugal relations. Accepting poverty, they divested themselves of worldly goods, embracing an apostolic life of preaching, missionaries for a true faith.

Along similar lines around 1170 a wealthy merchant named Waldes who became obsessed with the story of the prodigal son, deciding to sell off his property, spreading the monies he received among the poor. Becoming a lightning rod for those seeking a life of Christian purity, Waldes emerged as focus of a growing group of individuals bent on evangelical perfection. Remarkably they concluded that the idea of purgatory—one of the main engines for the accumulation of church wealth—was anathema. It was not mentioned in the New Testament. Equally remarkably Waldensian congregations even allowed meritorious females to preach.

These movements threatened the church's monopoly over Nicene Christian ideology. The Roman church hierarchy sensed it was boxed into a corner. As the neo-Donatist movements spread like wildfire it responded.

First it tried excommunication. When this failed it launched Crusades against the Cathars and the Waldensians, enlisting the assistance of kings and feudal lords. The Cathar stronghold of Carcassonne was summarily attacked in 1209, the Cathars violently expelled. When these methods failed to stamp out once and for all the schismatic flames into dying embers, the Church created the papal inquisition. The avowed purpose of the inquisition was to bring heretics back into the folds of the mother church.

It was the passion of reconverting heretics to Roman orthodoxy that fueled the creation of the Dominicans. From the outset Dominic's strategy was based on impressing the recalcitrant. Advertising their sincerity with the shining example of Dominican purity, members of the order displayed sophisticated argumentation in carrying out their inquisitions, attempting to outthink the heretics placed under their care in inquisitorial prisons. Ferreting out recruits from newly formed guilds cum universities, they specialized in keeping up with the latest knowledge embraced by European intelligentsia. This meant ancient Greek and Latin learning absorbed and modified by generations of Muslim and Jewish scholars active in the Islamic world. Of these the most important writings were those of Avicenna and Averroes, philosophers employed by the caliphs in Cordova, and the Jewish physician and philosopher Moses ben Maimon (Maimonides) whose *Guide for the Perplexed* was devoted to reconciling Hebrew monotheism with Aristotle's collected works. In his deeply thought out treatise Maimonides carefully plucked out those parts of Aristotle consistent with monotheism, discarding ideas like the eternity of the universe that was inconsistent with the notion of a creator god.

Both Islamic and Jewish scholars had managed to bridge the gulf between monotheism bathed in prophecy and miracles and the systematic analysis of natural and political order achieved by Aristotle. Their achievements paved the way for Dominican scholars, notably Thomas Aquinas writing in the thirteenth century. In his *Summa Theologiæ* (*Handbook of Theology*) managed to construct a mighty intellectual edifice reconciling Aristotle's scientific approach with Christian revelation. In so doing, he turned Saint Augustine on his head. Augustine's vision was a Platonic one; Thomas Aquinas's vision was Aristotelian. Although controversial at first—Aquinas's works were burned and condemned—the reconciliation achieved by Dominicans like Thomas Aquinas became the solid foundation on which the ideology of Scholasticism ultimately declared orthodox by Rome was erected.

Dominicans—later joined by the Franciscans who were also utilized by the papacy in implementing the inquisition—became the backbone of the mendicant orders spreading the gospel in the rapidly growing cities and towns springing up in the wake of the commercial transformation of Europe. As the composition of population concentration shifted toward market oriented towns and conurbations, the most dedicated Christians joined mendicant friars, preaching the gospel to city dwellers. And like their monastic counterparts, over time they drifted into aggrandizing rents. One notable example: they began to offer hallowed cemeteries to congregants, cutting into the monopolies once enjoyed by the churches.

During the late medieval period, the symbol of the secularization of space—the eroding of spiritual space at the expense of the secular—was the gothic cathedral standing grand and tall with its flying buttresses and its magnificent stained-glass windows. Above all else these imposing architectural feats testify to the wealth—and not necessarily the fervent devotion—amassed in powerful towns and cities. Funded by tithes, grants from merchants and local feudal lords, the point of the gothic cathedral was to advertise. Come here: you can do business; our people are prosperous; regard our beautiful religious edifices! Perhaps you want to borrow from the very groups that assembled treasure chests for the erection of the massive Church structures rivaling the pyramids in grandeur, surpassing the structures celebrating the power of the Pharaohs due to their Biblical purity? After all, the gothic structures drew directly upon ancient Biblical traditions. Supposedly their dimensions were based on what King Solomon and his priestly advisors worked out in constructing the first Temple devoted to the worship of Yahweh (Yhwh) at Jerusalem. Tellingly, on the outer walls of the gothic cathedrals often appeared figures represented Plato, Aristotle, Galen, and Ptolemy. That they celebrated Greek learning was a material spinoff of the ideas inherent in Scholasticism.

Scholasticism

Scholasticism as a movement designed to counter heresies breaking out in western Christendom had limited success. Part of the problem was inherent in to resolving the tension between natural law and divine law. This is a step onto a highly slippery path. If natural law exists—if it governs motion on the earth, the movement of the planets, the manufacture of iron and steel according to chemical principles, the relationship of the bodily organs to one another; if it explains why people are greedy—what is the purpose of divine law? If natural laws are operating, why do miracles occur? And what are miracles? Why does a deity need to rely on miracles in convincing humanity that it should act in a way that contradicts natural law? Why the confusion?

Not surprisingly Scholasticism was also incapable of holding Catholic Christendom together in a single communion. Reform movements aimed at cleaning up corruption in the Church—at the Vatican in Rome, in the monasteries, in the groups of mendicant Friars—continued to arise, then fail. How could a purified form of Christianity be fashioned? Attempts at radical reform—notably the movement led by Jan Hus in Bohemia—ended in failure. Rome promoted yet another bloody crusade, wiping out the valiant effort of followers of Hus (Hus himself, given a guarantee of safety by Church authorities who proceeded to renege on the deal, was burned at the stake) who barricaded themselves behind wagons aligned in a circle, positioning cannons between the wagons to drive off the Crusaders.

What finally led to victory of so-called heretics like Hus—notably Luther and Calvin—was the printing press. Once relatively cheaply produced bibles appeared the door was thrown open a path promoting a form of Christianity that refused to make use of Church priests and monasteries, a form of worship that appealed to those who had basic literacy. Who needed literacy? And who made use of writing on a daily basis? Merchants of course: they needed to read and write documents; they required written contracts.

Not surprisingly, the rise of Protestantism in the sixteenth century had special appeal to two groups: merchants and local feudal rulers. It appealed to merchants because they could read, because they could advertise their rectitude by joining a congregation committed to fervent promotion of Christian principles in daily life, and because they could openly avoid the ban on usury. Because it gave them an excuse to abolish the monasteries, securing their assets, disbanding their brotherhoods and sisterhoods it appealed to feudal lords who found themselves sinking into fiscal traps, indebted to powerful merchants and their banks. Ironically Protestant sects like Calvinism adopted Saint Augustine's notion of predestination, defiantly throwing up at the face of a corrupt Roman church the ideas espoused by one of their most hallowed founding figures.

A second reason why Scholasticism failed had less to do with faith and more to do to with flaws in the scientific principles laid down by Aristotle. While Aristotle's biological researches were fashioned upon detailed observations, his physics and his cosmology were totally deductive. Classic examples are his claims that nature abhors a vacuum; that the planets revolve around the earth in circular orbits; that complete unblemished perfection exists in the realm of the fixed stars occupying the outer ring of the cosmos. Lacking suitable observations, Aristotle had fashioned his views whole cloth from *a priori* theoretical principles. Eschewing experiments, he had no way of testing out the laws of nature he deduced from his governing principles. How misleading following Aristotelian logic could be is illustrated by an account given in Fara (2009: 82) describing a Scholastic explanation for the outbreak of the Black Death advanced by university physicians in Paris. According to their reasoning, an unusual conjunction of planets had occurred four years earlier. Hot Jupiter had sucked up immoral vapors from the earth. In turn, the vapors exploded into fire by being in the presence of a dried-out evildoing planet Mars. All this celestial chaos corrupted the atmosphere, spreading disease among humans living on the face of the earth.

The Hermetic tradition

The problem is that practical people had been carrying on experiments for millennia. Embracing mundane materialism—smelting metals, cooking, drying out herbs for remedies, cauterizing wounds—groups of inventors flourished throughout Eurasia, busying themselves with experiments. In Western Europe, they were known as alchemists. Convinced that they were privileged beneficiaries granted insight into esoteric knowledge, alchemists operated under principles supposedly granted them by special non-Christian gods. Especially prominent among their host of occult gods was Hermes Trismegistus. Hermes Trismegistus was one of the shadowy gods emerging from a pure amalgamation. On the one hand, the image of Hermes drew from the Greek god of commerce, trickery, deviousness, transformer, associated with the wild frontier. On the other hand, upon Hermes were attached characteristics of the Egyptian god Thoth, conjurer of spirits, adept in Gnostic knowledge, magician *par excellence*. The resulting deity was passed down from Roman times to the European Late Medieval Period through Islamic philosophers. It was known as Hermetic philosophy.

Hermetic philosophy took on the trappings of an underground tradition—underground because it was not specifically tied to Christianity; indeed it was positively frowned on by the Catholic clergy who may have viewed it as a competitor to the magical rituals they performed in the Eucharist—in both European scientific and artisan circles. It was mystical in a Gnostic sense because it purported to unlock esoteric secrets of the universe that only intellectual virtuosi could plumb. In making much of a mystical fifth element, elixir, the pursuit of Hermetic knowledge known as alchemy smacked of magic. Ironically, it inspired icons of natural philosophy like Bacon and Newton.[11]

Alchemy in the variant that reached Europeans in the late medieval period was rooted in Greek philosophy and ancient alchemical practice redacted through an Islamic lens. Aristotle's theories of motion and medicine were the philosophical cornerstones. The basic idea was simple and compelling. There are four natural elements (earth, water, fire, and air) and there are four humors (black bile, yellow bile, phlegm, and blood). Sharing the same number cannot be an accident. They must correspond to one another. Earth corresponds to black bile: it is cold and dry. Fire corresponds to yellow bile: it is dry and hot. Water corresponds to phlegm: it is cold and wet. Air corresponds to blood: it is wet and hot.

Now earth is the realm where everything gets jumbled up. Things are not in their natural places, they are out of sync. They are mixed together in a welter of confusion. The terrestrial world is corrupt, shot through with impurities. It is the place where change can and does take place as witnessed by the motion constantly observed on it, motion involving the transformation of air or water. Purification must be possible because transformation is possible. Evidence one can transform things is abundant: apply fire to water, altering the nature of water, and you turn it into air. Following this logic, impure metals like lead can be transformed into purer metals like silver by rearranging the elements within it. As well, silver can be turned into gold, the purest metal of all.

Islamic philosophers interpreting Aristotle during the golden age of Islam reasoned that a fifth substance—they called it *al-iksir*, the word from which the English term elixir is derived—could produce the transformation.

The existence of this special substance, this elixir, was the core of alchemic mysticism. It has come to be known as the Philosopher's Stone.

As Leicester (1965) emphasizes, alchemy was practiced in many regions within the Eurasian world. The Chinese knew of it. Indeed, Needham (1981: 31) argues that Chinese alchemists discovered gunpowder before 900, dubbing it a "fire chemical" (*huo yao*). Before long the fire chemical was being utilized in warfare, first as flame thrower, later (eleventh century) in the manufacture of land mines, bombs, and grenades. Ancient India knew of it. Certainly, Islamic thinkers thought it important though its conceptual validity was a matter of healthy debate. Having made inroads into Europe via Islam, it became entrenched on European soil. Even if the Church despised it, secular rulers maintained an active interest in it, inviting alchemists to their courts for demonstrations. That rulers had an active interest in it is hardly surprising: turning alloys of metal into pure gold would facilitate issuing of coinage. It would reduce costs. Moreover, proper use of the Philosopher's Stone might well have huge benefits for health and longevity. After all, Aristotle's theory suggested that there were important correspondences between the micro-environment of the human body with its various organs and the macro-environment of the universe.

Given the quasi-religious search for purification central to alchemy, it is hardly surprising that the field could—and actually did—become increasingly wrapped up in mysticism. Indeed, this appears to have been the case in China, where it eventually merged with Taoism and later Neo-Confucianism. It appears to have reached a similar dead end in the Islamic world, fueling philosophical speculation leading onto intellectual cul-de-sacs.

As it turns out, European alchemy did not run into a dead end. Gradually it found itself transformed into chemistry. But before that transformation was effected, it produced illustrious figures who became bitter enemies of Scholasticism. One was Paracelsus. Philosopher, physician, botanist, astrologer, occultist, founder of toxicology, medical surgeon attached to the military, Paracelsus was a remarkable dynamo strutting across the historical stage during the fifteenth and sixteenth centuries.

As a practitioner of alchemy, Paracelsus had great faith in laboratory work, respecting barber–surgeons, apothecaries, the type of people who dirtied their hands in the muck and truck of material reality. Indeed, when he became a professor at the University of Basel he invited these practitioners of the "arts"—think artifice, manipulation of reality, experimentation— a legion of non-academics to illustrate real world phenomena before his students. Paracelsus was an ardent opponent of Scholasticism. For instance, arguing the Aristotle and Galen were totally incorrect in their theory of the four humors, he replaced their key categories with a trinity of essential elements: mercury, sulfur, and salt. A true alchemist, he attached occult meanings to these elements. Mercury embodied spirit and mind; sulfur embodied soul; salt was the essence of the body. Using chemical compounds fashioned from these elements, he professed to cure people of diseases. Imbalance in the four humors—as advocated by Hippocrates and Galen—was not the cause of illness. Rather, disease was due to a dearth of harmony in the body that could be usefully addressed with the chemical and mineral concoctions he created through experimentation.

Alchemists and astrologers akin to Paracelsus flourished in the secular world. In the courts of kings, in the palaces gracing feudal estates, they found ample opportunities to carry on their trades. They were a thorn in the side of the Church, which had adopted Scholasticism. They laid the foundation for practical experimentation that began to loom large during the scientific revolution. Moreover, they spread skepticism about the validity of Scholastic theorizing, a second essential ingredient to the scientific revolution.

The rise of merchant capitalism in Europe was driven by expansion in trade, both within Europe and between Europe and the other great civilizations of the Eurasian land mass. Transfer of technology is the handmaiden of trade. The Silk Road was an avenue along which ideas—the most mobile form of capital—made their way from west to east, from east to west. Indian–Arabic numerals made their way to Spain because Islamic thinkers published books using them, Christian scholars discovering their power. Printing was originally developed in China. Silk reeling started in China, spreading throughout the Islamic region, making its way into Italy. So, it is with the manufacture of gunpowder that was pioneered by Chinese alchemists.

As Islamic advances in credit creation freed up the capital to allow movement across time and space, so it was with gunpowder. Once Europeans discovered innovations made elsewhere on the Eurasian land mass, they ran with them. It was not the Islamic Caliphate; it was not Saladin; although Chinese artisans experimented with gunpowder using bombards, it was not a Chinese general that extended a technique for processing of saltpeter, creating a potent shell that could be readily fired by a gun or cannon, a potent shell that would eventually be mass produced. It was Europeans who did this.

Why, one asks? Because Europe was subject to the political pendulum swing, fragmented into feudal estates that warred with one another, divided into loosely confederated kingdoms that tried to get an upper hand over one another. Warfare was endemic to Europe. Driving down the price of exerting military force (p_{mf}) was at a premium in Europe. Bringing gunpowder into regular use in warfare had massive consequences, comparable to the way the chariot, the stirrup, the saddle, the crossbow transformed combat in the past.

From the late-fourteenth century on, Europeans had to drink from a chalice poisoned by gunpowder. The most important consequence was the gradual demise of feudal knighthood. Use of armed infantry—including employment of semi-skilled mercenaries—gradually displaced use of armed knights riding into combat. As this happened, the door was open for the emergence of powerful states. Particularly in England—blessed by being an island nation difficult to invade—and in France, there gradually emerged powerful kings that exploited statecraft in asserting their power over feudal lords. Once the Netherlands threw off the trammels of Spanish rule, the Dutch republic joined the ranks of states in this case as an entity ruled by an oligarchy. In marked contrast, the Holy Roman Empire remained hopelessly fragmented.

Not surprisingly where merchants had achieved the greatest gains in status, where the promotion of banking and joint-stock financing had made the greatest inroads on the economy, where urbanization had taken off with unusual force, Protestant religions had the strongest appeal. This was the case in both England and the Netherlands. By contrast, France emerged as a strong state primarily on the strength of its rural sector, its farming. To be sure, productivity gains in agriculture occurred in all three countries as open field feudal use of land gave way to enclosed farms experimenting with new crop rotations.

However, the benefits flowing from productivity advance in farming were not the same in all three of the emerging states, England, France, and the Netherlands. In the countries leaning toward Protestantism, productivity gains increased the surplus a typical farmer could produce—a surplus above and beyond what the farmer needed to live on—setting in motion a move of rural dwellers to the cities where the surpluses racked up by agriculture could be consumed. Likewise, many farmers began producing handicrafts and inputs into manufacturing—originally controlled by artisan guilds— employing time of family members freed up from planting and harvesting obligations to engage in non-agriculture activities, increasing the intensity at which they toiled by working longer hours and putting greater thought into how to make each of these hours more productive. In France, farming tended to hang on much longer at the expense of commercial expansion. What was the chicken and what was the egg? Did leaning toward Protestantism encourage the embrace of commerce? Or did the embrace of merchant capitalism plant the seeds of a strong commitment to Protestantism, to inculcating belief in the accusation that the pope was the anti-Christ, and that priests were corrupt, avaricious, perhaps demented?

Notes

1 See Fried (2015: 53).
2 Papal claims over territories and palaces in Italy were based upon an infamous forgery, the Donation of Constantine. That it ultimately was proven a forgery was due to the labor of linguists who pointed out that the Latin appearing in the document was far too crude, shot full of pathetic phrasing that classical writers would have eschewed, to have been composed in fourth-century Rome.
3 Russell (1945: 409).
4 This account is based upon the account given by Madigan (2015: 139–142).
5 According to Stark (2003), Jews were treated equally badly in the Islamic world as they were in the Christian world. He shows that the anti-Semitic violence that besmirched the Christian West during the Crusades was matched by attacks upon *dhimmi* Jewish communities. Speaking personally, I find this unconvincing for two reasons. Prominent Jews, allowed to practice usury banned to Christians,

operated as financiers in the West whereas, as we have seen, under Islam ways around charging interest were well entrenched for Muslims prior to the Crusades. Second, Jews were accused of being the killers of Jesus by Christians; Muslims, denying that Jesus was crucified (and denying that he was a deity), were less likely to despise Jews than the Christians of the Middle Ages, convinced the blood of Jesus was spilled over Jewish hands, were.

6 See Hirschman (1977).
7 For details of this thesis see Rubin (2010).
8 See Kuran (2011: 72–73).
9 On the evolution of the various monastic orders, see Décarreaux (1964), Lawrence (1984), and Wittberg (1994). Coulton (1925, 1989) paints a grim picture of the monasteries, admittedly those surviving into the late medieval period when corruption and cruelty was all too common among the ranks of Abbots and run of the mill monks. As one example of cruelty practiced by Abbots, Coulton mentions the practice of burying alive peasant women and serf women caught stealing. The terrifying conceit was to dig a grave so deep that the stench exuded from their rotting flesh would be snuffed out by the layers of dirt thrown onto their bodies.
10 My discussion of the Cathars and Waldensians draws upon the account in Madigan (2015: 188–195).
11 For the importance of alchemy to the so-called scientific revolution of the seventeenth century see Moran (2005).

9 Mercantilism and the pendulum swing

European merchant capitalism reached its apex with mercantilism.[1] What was it?

Mercantilism

Mercantilism was the upshot of military competition between the emerging states of Europe. Those state rulers best equipped to extract resources for financing the military sub-economy were those that could best survive and prosper in a dog-eat-dog struggle for revenue from international trade and revenue from the domestic economy. Taking three major steps was crucial: transferring rents secured by local units—feudal estates, guilds, monasteries—from the local authorities to the national government, into the coffers of the monarch; increasing the efficiency of all economic actors by eliminating barriers to internal trade and commerce (e.g.: tolls on rivers, bridges, and short roads); and using trade policy to generate a surplus, thereby bringing in precious metals from abroad.[2]

In terms of the military power equation the idea is to increase $\mathbf{m}$ (by increasing the share of rents in the economy taken in by the monarch) and increase $\mathbf{Y}$ by eliminating inefficiencies and expanding commerce abroad, outside of the domestic arena.[3] Embracing credit creating mobile capital was just the ticket. Not only did it give a fillip to foreign trade and international commerce; as well it promoted domestic investment by merchants in rural areas undercutting the power of urban guilds monopolizing local markets.

Undergirding all of this was technological competition. There were two reasons why this was true, both involving the zero-sum logic of predation. By reducing the costs of fielding troops and naval forces—taking advantage of improvements in ship construction, ballistics, and the lethality of weaponry—military capacity was enhanced. By attracting trade and economic activity away from potential rivals, states bolstered the size of the pie from which they extracted taxes and rents.

Fighting wars successfully cannot be done on the cheap. The bigger the economy one commands the easier it is to secure the wherewithal to carry campaigns of conflict on over years, even decades. How do you encourage exports, discouraging imports, bolstering your bottom line? Promoting novelties and niche products that competitors do not know how to make is one approach. Improving quality, avoiding a reputation for shoddy output is another. The deeper the cornucopia of techniques you can draw upon, the more likely it is that you can come up with winners. To be sure what is in the interest of the state focusing on the average quality engendered in the aggregate economy is not necessarily in the interests of local producers—weaving guilds in Liverpool or Lyons for instance—who may prefer exploiting regionally protected monopoly rents. This is why mercantilist policy makers worked assiduously to destroy local monopolies, to encourage competition within their entire jurisdiction, to ramp up the scale of monopoly to the state level. Granting a state level monopoly was an excellent way to transfer rents from localities to monarchs. Encouraging the success of state level monopolies by underwriting research and development in technology naturally went hand in hand with this strategy.

Not surprisingly, opposing the drive toward mercantilism were institutions extracting rents from local markets. The guilds are a prominent example.

Guilds

The guild—merchant guild or craft guild—came to fruition in an environment where the imperative of finding a way to purify commercial and manufacture activities, to stave off Church hostility, was paramount. Remarkably the survival of institutions in a world colored by the Christian concept of purgatory furnished a solution. Guild membership helped address these concerns. Guilds were both religious and commercial organizations. They adopted as guild names referenced to patron saints or specific Christian events. For instance, in the English census of 1388 craft guilds dedicated to the Blessed Virgin Mary, Corpus Christi, Saint Nicholas, Saint Katherine, Saint John the Baptist, Saint William, Saint Lawrence, and All Saints appear.[4]

As religious institutions, they attended funerals and dirges for deceased members, placed burning candles in churches, paid priests to perform functions, and gave alms. They paid for masses dedicated to the souls of deceased members with the aim of limiting the suffering of the deceased member in purgatory. At the same time, they advertised their membership as good Christians, following the commandments, eschewing the seven deadly sins, being truthful, avoiding theft. Lest they be thought of as corrupt and deceitful, they committed themselves to producing high quality goods and selling them at fair prices. Having the right to inspect the operations of all guild members, they claimed to prevent the manufacture and dispensing of shoddy goods. In short, bundling together piety and profit had two important consequences. It discouraged members from violating manufacturing standards by raising the cost of being dismissed from the rolls of the guild or voluntarily abandoning the guild, taking guild secrets upon exiting for greener pastures.[5] As long as one remained a guild member, one could reasonably expect to have alms given, masses held, and prayers organized by one's colleagues upon one's death, when one presumably moved onto purgatory. Moreover, as quasi-religious organizations, guilds advertised the commitment of their members to purity in commercial dealings.[6]

Guilds functioned as cartels. In so far as they combined piety with profit, they exercised tight—oppressive, it could be argued—control over their members. The cost of being driven out of the ranks of the guild being high, most members toed the line. The fact that guild members tended to cluster in a district made it easy to monitor one's colleagues. No wonder guilds were sometimes attacked as monopolies: a cartel in which cheating is absent functions as monopoly. As a result, the more perfect the cartel, the closer it could act as a monopolist—and a single buyer of labor in its region—and the better it could extract rents.

Thus, guilds played a crucial role in conditioning European labor and product markets. Under the rules of the guilds, masters who owned their own shops could take on a limited number of apprentices who were contracted out to the master. In principle, the master taught the apprentice skills, thereby augmenting the human capital of the apprentice. Masters charged fees to compensate them for their efforts. As well, masters benefited from the labor services of the apprentices. Upon completing their apprenticeships, the apprentice became a journeyman, often tramping around through a network of towns and rural communities in search of work. The lucky journeymen became masters, enjoying the full rights of membership. Following this logic, Epstein (1988) argues that guilds played a key role in improving the quality of human capital throughout Europe between the twelfth and the eighteenth centuries. As well, he argues that the circulating of journeymen gave a fillip to the diffusion of best practice technique within fields like hide tanning, iron working, silk reeling, wool weaving, tailoring, tiling, even clerking or tax farming.

It is important to separate out labor training from technical innovation and diffusion of best practice technique. To be sure, some skills were passed on by masters to their apprentices. But—and this is a big "but"—was the master equipped to teach? Moreover, was the master willing to give up all his secrets and clever time-saving practices to an apprentice who was likely to become a competitor? More to the point, viewing the transmission of innovations from a selfish angle, did a guild of wool spinners in London that innovated within a field want to see its technological advances mimicked by a wool spinning guild in Antwerp? If the whole point of the guild exercise was to offer beneficial goods and services to the community it served—goods and services superior and better priced than those that could be imported by merchants from elsewhere—did it not have an overriding incentive to monopolize guild secrets?

In actual practice—as opposed to Christian posturing—guilds practiced rent seeking, hardly surprising in a regime in which the secular clergy and the monasteries were also capturing rents. Apprentices were exploited, cheated by masters who refused to reveal trade secrets. Mercers and wool sellers raised prices for their wares when were shortages appeared in the marketplace. Guilds held onto trade secrets as long as they could.[7] Jaundiced journeymen organized their own associations, attacking guild elites, attempting to exploit any special techniques they had gleaned from observing their masters.

Initially established during the late medieval period, three institutions attempted to counter the stranglehold guilds had over markets: state sponsorship of science and technology; private patronage; and patents. The fact that they took the form they did reflects the political fragmentation of European and the desire of strong monarchs to counter that fragmentation, pushing the pendulum away from localness toward strong state consolidation.

Appreciating the problems imposed on communities by craft guild rules in late medieval Europe, astute individuals and opportunistic organizations interested in promoting technological innovation lobbied for alternatives to guilds. In launching attacks on the craft system merchant guilds were important players. Securing influence over—or direct political control upon—European political institutions through bribery or threats to take their business elsewhere was one weapon in the merchant arsenal. After all, merchants benefitted if the prices they paid craft guild suppliers for the goods they exported to other communities were lowered through technological improvements bolstering labor productivity. Not surprisingly, governments—whether city, ecclesiastical township, princedom, duchy, or monarchical state—offered prizes and subsidies to innovators in response to merchant lobbying campaigns.

Patronage

To be sure, government investment in technical research predates has a long history predating its flourishing in the late medieval era. Driven by astrological concerns, monarchs and emperors maintained observatories to chart the stars. Royal mints experimented with metals alloys. What late medieval and early modern Europe brought to the table was a remarkable profusion of quasi-governmental institutions subsidizing research: Royal Societies armed with grants; university grants; royal promises of lifetime pensions for successful inventors; cross-fertilization yoking together guilds, learned societies and city administrations.

Government and university subsidy was especially important for innovation in precision instrument production.[8] While some of the advances made were mainly applied to empirical philosophy in the first instance—scientific observation—some were generated by commercial endeavor, mainly on the high seas, and all of them eventually had practical application. Navigation, surveying, medical practice, the construction of steam engines, the manufacture field weapons all benefited from the telescopes, microscopes, air pumps, pendulum clocks, and refined balances.

European oceanic exploration illustrates the general phenomenon. It was one important driver for the explosion of investment particularly by governments. Reflecting the intense competition between the emerging states of Europe the push to improve navigation aids went hand in hand with burgeoning demand for devices that sailors could use to accurately observe activity on potentially hostile ships. Henry the Navigator assembled a group of mathematicians and navigation experts with the aim of improving the astrolabe thereby enhancing the capacity of the Portuguese fleet to explore the coast of Africa and the islands off its western shoreline. As a result, the mariner astrolabe came into being. Galileo originally developed the telescope with the aim of marketing it to Venetian merchant houses who wanted to improve their ability to observe the goods and personnel aboard rival ships. Colbert, French Minister of Finance commissioned Christaan Huygens to invent a marine chronometer for accurately measuring longitude at sea during the 1670s. Ultimately, a prize offered by the British government in the early 1700s yielded a successful device. John Harrison, a Yorkshire carpenter turned clockmaker earned a £20,000 reward for his successful submission.

Patents

Finally, there was the patent.

Sometime in the late medieval period—in the fourteenth and fifteenth centuries—European monarchs, smaller governments and cities alike began issuing patents. Monopolies of a sort insofar as their recipient enjoyed exclusive rights over a production technique or the manufacture of a specific product for a limited duration, say ten years. It is said that English kings promulgated royal grants of patent to foreigners with the express aim of encourage them to immigrate to England. It is said the Italian republics granted patents for the making of glass and the construction of barges with sophisticated gearing. Trivellato (2008: 222) notes that the Venetian Senate issued at least 1,900 patents of invention between 1474 and 1788. Once Italians became familiar with the patenting institution they exploited its potential for blackmail: grant a patent to me and my colleagues or we will go elsewhere, securing an exclusive manufacturing opportunity in another realm. Late medieval Europe, still highly fragmented, was the perfect soil upon which the patent system could set down roots.[9]

Securing a reputation for refining materials—smoothing the surface of glass, perfecting the balances used by assayers—was good advertising. As well, securing patents was good advertising. For the artisan and his or her shop, the award of a patent typically sent out a market signal: the recipient took precision seriously. Market opportunities were proliferating. Rich patrons sought beautifully made devices. As commerce began to flourish in the aftermath of the Crusades, enjoying the taste to differentiate the tasteful from the crass became a sign of refinement amongst elites. Monarchs, dukes, princes, wealthy burghers were certainly interested in possessing beautifully made trinkets that they could shower on guests as gifts; that they could employ in attracting politically influential spouses, essential for monarchical diplomacy. Ironically, monarchical diplomacy managed through marriage alliances had been widely practiced by the *comitatus* following the logic of treaty making on the steppes of Central Asia by trading brides along with material riches.

One wonders: what made European manufacturing so special that patents would become spread across jurisdictions in a pre-industrial world? The answer is simple: some European artisans were keen to perfect what purchasers could obtain from their private establishments. They wished to operate outside of guilds. They were unable to secure patronage. Their university posts generated earnings insufficient to fund their research activities. They wanted to build up their own laboratories. In all this, the demand for precision was present.

A central mission of mercantilist planners was to scale up the size of the economic base on which rents could be extracted. Encouraging the creation of a global East India Company, a Royal African Company, a Hudson Bay Company, or a Dutch VOC allowed national authorities to extract rents. Monasteries, feudal lords, and guilds had done this in past. Now states in the business of selling charters to globally oriented merchant enterprises were aggrandizing the rents. As well they enjoyed the side benefit that the arming of the mercantilist merchant companies brought to the table.

Predation

All of this was in the service of state military potential **M**, that is was in the service of national power and national status. 400 years after Europe struggled with military fragmentation in its futile attempt to wrest the Holy Land away from Islamic rule, the centralized mercantilist system—ideologically committed to wiping out the vestiges of feudalism—profoundly transformed the political nature of the military power equation.

Mercantilism was the highest form of merchant capitalism, far overshadowing the small-scale merchant businesses that flourished under Islamic rule.

How important was Europe's merchant capitalism to the emergence of modern capitalism as it evolved later with the first industrial revolution of the eighteenth century and the second industrial revolution of the nineteenth century?

According to Marx's classic work *Capital*, a lot:[10]

> The circulation of commodities is the starting point of capital. The production of commodities, their circulation, and that more developed form of their circulation called commerce, these form the historical groundwork from which it rises. The modern history of capital dates from the creation in the 16th century of a world-embracing commerce and a world embracing market.

and:

> The discovery of gold and silver in America, the extirpation, enslave-
> ment, and entombment in mines of the aboriginal population, the
> beginning of the conquest and looting of the East Indies, the turning of
> Africa into a warren for the commercial hunting of black-skins, signal-
> ised the rosy dawn of capitalist production. These idyllic proceedings
> are the chief momenta of primitive accumulation. On their heels treads
> the commercial war of the European nations, with the globe for a thea-
> tre. It begins with the revolt of the Netherlands from Spain, assumes
> giant dimensions in England's anti-jacobin war, and is still going on in
> the opium wars against China.

For Marx capitalism went hand in hand with predation.

Notes

1 For an extensive treatment of mercantilism, see the classic account of Heckscher (1955) and Chapter 5 of Findlay and O'Rourke (2007).
2 On the inefficiency of the guild form of organization see Ogilvie (2000, 2004, 2007).
3 For the details of this argument, see the second item in the Appendices.
4 See Richardson (2005) and Richardson and McBride (2009).
5 This is the thrust of the argument made by Richardson (2005).
6 In late medieval Venice, the institutional relationship between guild and religious brotherhood was a bit different. A religious brotherhood was known as a *scuola*, while the craft guild corresponding to it was called an *arte*. In practice, the over-lap between *scuola* and *arte* was very high. See Mackenny (1987).
7 On guild rent-seeking, see Ogilvie (2000, 2004, and 2007).
8 On the development of scientific instruments see Anderson, Bennett and Ryan (1993); Daumas (1972), Hawkes (1981), Morrison-Low (2007), and Turner (1990).
9 The career of Leonardo da Vinci illustrates how competitive fragmented Europe had become by the time of the late medieval period. Commencing his career in Florence as an apprentice in a Florentine painter's guild, the Company of St. Luke, Leonardo went on to work under the sculptor Verrocchio, who took in commissions of all sorts: art, armor, jewelry, and church bells were all part of the business. Showing no loyalty to Florence, Leonardo moved on to Milan, where he advertised himself as a military-engineer (in a letter to Duke Lodovico), apprised of secret techniques for manufacturing catapults, chariots, and can-nons. In Italy, divided into a myriad of squabbling city states, an artist had to go where the patronage was good, the opportunity to bring in commissions strong. Accepting the patronage of Cesare Borgia, Leonardo traveled throughout Italy, eventually ending up at the Vatican in Rome. Returning to a Milan in 1515 that was recaptured by Francis I of France, Leonardo ended up living in France, where he died.
    In terms of the theme of European pursuit of precision, it is worth mentioning that one of the most remarkable features of Leonardo's painting is its remarkable attention to detail. Characteristic of the late medieval period, Leonardo acquired a detailed knowledge of anatomy based on years of studying cadavers and skulls. Beyond this, it was in the late medieval period that painters pioneered the concept

of perspective, allowing them to give the illusion of depth on a flat surface. In this endeavor, mathematical logic was put to work solving a problem in pure aesthetics. As well consideration of Leonardo's story illustrates the how the fragmentation of Europe gave patronage leverage in competing with guild attempts to control technology and training during the late medieval ages.

10 Marx (1936: 163 and 823). The astute reader will note that I have used two different versions of Marx's *Capital* in preparing this book.

10 Japanese merchant capitalism

Remarkably, at the far eastern end of the Eurasian Silk Road there emerged a fresh variant of merchant capitalism. It occurred in the early seventeenth century in Japan. How much it owed to the global trade initiated and perfected by the European mercantilist powers and how much it owed to purely domestic forces is an interesting question. Suffice it to say that trade and technology transfer between the European powers and Japan blossomed in the sixteenth century. In principle imitation of a powerful new form of commerce was a possibility. In principle, the Japanese might have been attracted to Western institutions because Japanese ideology was relatively close to Western European ideology.

The Japanese pendulum swing

Indeed, in unraveling the nuances of the Japanese case, one should not slight outstanding similarities between Japan and the West. Two important similarities stand out: separation of the secular from sacred; and the perpetuation of the Central Asian Culture Complex as instituted in Japan's version of feudalism. This was true with a vengeance in the refined version of feudal rule institutionalized during rule by the Tokugawa shoguns (1600–1868 CE).[1]

Secular power was concentrated in the hands of warlords. First among the warlords was the shogun; fiefs—approximately 300 were created under Tokugawa rule—were placed under rule by lesser warlords, *daimyo*. Under shogun and *daimyo* alike were warrior–bureaucrats, notably the *samurai*. Under the hegemonic rule of Toyotomi Hideyoshi, that preceded establishment of Tokugawa control, *samurai* were forced to withdraw from the countryside, forced to reside in the castle town of the *daimyo*, who they served in *comitatus*-like fashion. Loyalty to the warlord chief was crucial; it was embodied in the cult of *bushido* (the "way of the warrior").

Compelling the *samurai* to live in castle towns had profound economic consequences. It stripped them of land. Required to give up their claims to farms, they were compensated by allocations of rice that was taxed away from the villages in their fiefs. The upshot: internecine feuding between armed villages came to an end. Finally, irrigation ditches could be carved out deep in valleys, into areas remote from rivers. Villages near the mouth of an irrigation line were no longer able to monopolize the flow further along the line by dint of arms, effectively charging a toll for water usage, extracting rents from villages less favorably located. Rice cultivation increased in leaps and bounds. So did population, the carrying capacity of the land having been richly improved.

To quell dissent among the restive *samurai*, the policy of granting them the exclusive right to carry weapons, namely two swords, was imposed on both fiefs and shogun-controlled lands alike. In concert with this rule, guns—the greatest threat to feudal retainers, as the transformation of warfare from one dominated by cavalry to one dependent on massing infantry in Western Europe proved—were banned. Japanese artisans who had jumped into manufacturing guns during the sixteenth century, meeting the demands of rival warlords fighting over hegemony, had no choice but abandon a field that was proving highly lucrative. Indeed, they were even selling muskets to western visitors to Japan before the ban. That the shogun introduced these policies kept feudalism alive in Japan at the very time it was experiencing its death rattle in Europe.

The sacred was far more complex in Japan than it was in the Christian West. It was supported on two stools: Neo-Confucianism and Shinto, the imperial cult.

Drawing upon Chinese—ultimately Chinese and Indian—religious traditions, Neo-Confucianism soared to ascendency as one of two officially sanctioned faiths. Neo-Confucianism, first developed in China during the Tang and Sung dynasties, was an amalgam of Confucianism, Taoism, and Buddhism.[2] Incorporating the magic and mysticism of Taoism and Buddhism with the wisdom/ritual orientation of Confucianism, Neo-Confucianism evolved as a "big tent" doctrine appealing to illiterate masses and sophisticated elites alike. At a practical level, Tokugawa-era Neo-Confucianism served commoners and *samurai* elites on separate platforms. Buddhism was the popular religion, and Buddhist temples were supported by fief resources and donations from the faithful. Confucian concepts were promoted for the *samurai* elite. Indeed, by the close of the Tokugawa period, the *samurai* mimicked Chinese Confucian officials in the sense they were uniformly graduates of fief academies, reading the Confucian classics in classical Chinese.

Shinto, a nature cult tied to the emperor who was its head, was also supported by a host of priests performing rituals in temples, paralleling the network of Buddhist temples serviced by monks. Since the Emperor was the only domestic personage wielding authority in the religious field, he—or she—was the closest analogue to the Catholic pope. In theory, the emperor was a descendent of the gods; in practice, he lent his aura of divinity to the Shinto cult. In any case, the shogun and the emperor were de facto rivals during the Tokugawa period. The Emperor's official residence (the imperial place) was in Kyoto; keeping a careful watch on the Emperor's comings and goings were officials serving the shogun, residing a few blocks away from the imperial place.

Complicating the separation of the secular and the sacred was the Buddhist monastery. Many were heavily armed, threatening both the warlords struggling to be shogun and the imperial cult alike. Indeed, Oda Nobunaga, a powerful warlord who attempted to establish hegemonic authority over Japan in the mid-sixteenth century, a predecessor to Hideyoshi and the Tokugawa, actually burned many of the monasteries populating the mountains north of Kyoto.

In short, Japan, recipient of several versions of Axial thought as well as the Central Asian Culture Complex, enjoyed strong similarities with Western Europe. That said, one should not underplay profound differences. Islam and Christianity played no significant role in the evolution of Japanese merchant capitalism. True, some Japanese warlords converted to Christianity during the warring sixteenth century. In the southern island of Kyushu where Spaniards and Portuguese carried on business with Japanese and Chinese merchants, the doctrines of Catholicism made inroads. It was precisely for this reason that the shogun banned Christianity. It was a threat to Tokugawa hegemony. Would being Christian send a message? Would it resonate with *daimyo*, who may have viewed the Catholic ideology as a potential vehicle for recruiting *samurai* retainers?

Fearing that the sword might follow the cross, the Tokugawa regime banned the faith, requiring Japanese living in areas contaminated by Catholicism to tromp upon a picture of the Virgin Mary. Concern that the pope might be a contender to the Emperor could well have figured in the minds of the shogun. To ensure the masses avoided Christianity, compulsory registration with a Buddhist temple was imposed. To make the point clear to the Spanish and Portuguese, Japanese crucified a few priests upside down on crosses, placing them on an island ships passed by on their way to Japanese ports. Negative advertising—with a vengeance—a person might be tempted to say.

Trusting Protestants to skirt the delicate issue of religious conversion, sticking to the truck and barter of commerce alone, the shogun's regime graciously permitted the Dutch to maintain a small island known as Dejima off the coast of Nagasaki (a town under the direct control of the shogun). This was Japan's sole window to the West during the two and half centuries of Tokugawa rule. Indeed, by keeping at bay meddling Western powers, the shogun introduced a close country policy. In effect, the shogun wanted to maintain a monopoly over all international commerce Japan participated in. How much was due to having a controlling hand over diplomacy and how much was due to extracting rents from trade is difficult to say.

Closing the country was a dramatic example of the Japanese pendulum swing. The sixteenth century had been wide open. Trade and cultural interchange with the West flourished. But so did internecine warfare. Restless *samurai* ravaged the countryside, pitting villages against one another.

Attempting to control their minions, *daimyo* struggled to reign in their retainers. Alliances of convenience between *daimyo* were formed, only to fragment. Clamping down on the *samurai* was inextricably linked to creating a balance of power system within the country. As it turned out, the Tokugawa system of dividing the country into fiefs, requiring *samurai* to be resident in the castle towns serving as fief capitals, stripping them of guns, doomed most of the *samurai* to penury. They bore the vestiges of political and social power. At the same time, they struggled to make ends meet on their rice stipends. A military caste that set much of the agenda for the sixteenth century was brought to heel under the aegis of a military government.

Merchant houses

As well, the closed country policy conditioned the evolution of Japanese merchant capitalism. It flourished in a closed country environment. In stark contrast to Europe, international trade played little if any role in its growth and success. True Japanese merchant houses may have enjoyed a slight glimmer of the business practices of the Dutch VOC that visited Dejima from time to time. However, it is difficult to believe this contact loomed large in their notable innovations in corporate structure and marketing.

Japan's merchant capitalism was nursed into being by the organization imposed first by Toyotomi Hideyoshi, subsequently refined Tokugawa Ieyasu founder of the Tokugawa confederation style of government. The basic problem in managing a confederation of squabbling fiefs, cajoling *samurai* resentful of being uprooted from their rural farming villages, and peasantry turning over approximately 40% of their rice production in fief taxes, was balancing supply and demand for rice at the local level. Creating a market where fiefs could warehouse a portion of their output was the logical conclusion. A centralized spot where fiefs enjoying a surplus could sell it to fiefs experiencing a shortfall due to the poor harvests was the obvious solution. With this in mind, Hideyoshi assembled merchants from the area surrounding Osaka (the site of his imposing castle), carving out an island in the Yodo River for the building of warehouses. The merchants were instructed to service the rice market, dealing with emissaries from the various *daimyo* represented at the island. But once the Tokugawa shoguns took control of the country, they chose to maintain their capital elsewhere. They established their castle town on the Kanto plain, their original territorial base. At first this new capital was nothing more than a tiny sleepy fishing village known as Edo, later to become known worldwide as Tokyo.

Osaka was the first merchant capital of Japan. By the nineteenth century it was one of the largest cities in the world, with a population of over 300,000. It was in Osaka that the powerful merchant houses of the Tokugawa era put down their roots. Inspired by the principles of fief rule, they innovated, creating internalized labor markets linked to an ingenious franchising system. The idea was to recruit apprentices (*detchi*), winnow out the lazy by promoting the hardworking apprentice to clerk status (*tedai*), and reserve promotion to the coveted position of chief clerk (*banto*) to the most ambitious and committed recruits. It was the chief clerk who opened new franchise units, basically branches off the main trunk. Reminiscent of the Medici enterprise employing a hub-spoke framework, the franchising of major merchant houses was a vehicle for diversifying into new types of businesses. For instance, Mitsui started out in the dry goods field, eventually becoming a major financier of fief and shogun-managed enterprises. Indeed, in the latter half of the Tokugawa period, fiefs—finding themselves strapped for funds due to the denuding of forests used to construct wooden cites and the onset of diminishing returns to creating new rice fields—began to assign *samurai* the task of actively engaging the market for foodstuffs, fertilizers, and natural resources.

Edo, the shogun's capital, grew at an even more voracious pace than Osaka.[3] The reason: the shogun's fundamental distrust of the *daimyo*, particularly those whose ancestors had opposed the Tokugawa takeover of the shogun's position from Hideyoshi's son and heir. *Daimyo* were required to perform compulsory attendance at the shogun's Edo castle on a rotating base. They were required to maintain lavish estates in Edo where their wives and children resided year round, effectively hostages. They were required to travel to Edo on shogun-controlled roads bristling with checkpoints where *daimyo* and travelling retainers could be searched for weapons. To use a succinct phrase, it was a "guns out, wives in" policy. The shogun kept on-staff spies who watched out for any subversive activities on the part of so-called loyal feudal underlings. To service a host of servants, artisans, and merchants gathered in the shogun's capital.

By the last decades of Tokugawa rule, Japan still a non-industrial country, had reached levels of urbanization few if any other pre-industrial countries had attained. To provide foodstuffs, textiles, lumber for constructing housing, and swords for the warrior elite, a vast network of merchants and artisans had grown from a small base in 1600 to a huge array in the 1850s.

Merchant capitalism, commencing in Islamic lands, further refined in Western Europe, had come into its own in the Far East.

Notes

1 For details on all the points made here, see Chapter 2 in Mosk (2008). Also, see Hayami (2009, 2015).
2 For Neo-Confucianism in China, see Berling (1980) and Ch'ien (1986). As an illustration of the eclectic nature on Neo-Confucianism, the school of Lin Chao-en described by Berling stressed the importance of undergoing nine steps of mind cultivation, basically a derivative of Buddhist meditation practice, itself a distant relative of yogi meditation developed in Hinduism.
3 It appears Edo's population reached the half million mark, partly because servants and casual labor flocked to the capital to service the estates of the *daimyo*. For estimates of population size for, and a discussion of population growth in, the great metropolitan centers Osaka and Edo, see Mosk (2001: 46–50).

Part III
Technological capitalism

11 The pendulum swing in natural philosophy

Technological capitalism

By the term "technological capitalism" I mean investment in technological progress funded by credit creation. Inherent in technological progress is the spawning of new ideas, fresh skills, and the employment of fixed capital in building and outfitting machines, structures, and transportation vehicles. In effect concepts are embodied in physical capital. Idea and concrete matter are conjoined.

Grasping concepts—learning how to use blueprints for the organization and implementation of production—is the most important component of technological capitalism. Concepts, the memes of intellectual capital, are inherently mobile. Provided they are in the public domain they can be taught through many channels: masters convey ideas to apprentices in guilds; managers instruct shop floor workers in factories; books describe shop-floor blueprints in exhausting detail; schools offer instruction in the concepts in a classroom setting. Moreover, workers jump from one job to another; industrial espionage occurs. As a result, even when ideas are not in the public domain the potential for their intended or unintended diffusion—for leakage flowing from one organization or individual to another—is considerable despite the best attempts of organizations and inventors to monopolize the ideas. No form of capital is more mobile than technological capital.

Reflecting this reality—much of the capital inherent in technological capitalism taking the form of highly mobile capital almost impossible to keep bottled up—there exist incentives to not undertake the costly investment in new technologies. Widespread concern about being unable to capture rents accruing from one's innovative activity can and does stymie technological capitalism.

One way around this problem is creating a positive feedback cycle, progress feeding on progress, invention fostering invention. Say a first step is taken by agent A. Suppose A knows that agents B, C, and D will utilize the first step without incurring the costs of innovation that were incurred by A—a disincentive from bearing the costs, to be sure—but also expects that B, C, and D will make improvements on the step taken by A (by carrying out their own costly product development), ultimately benefiting A in the long run. In short, suppose expectation of unending progress saturates the community. In this environment, technological progress can flourish.

The paradigm for positive feedback—the one that emerged in Europe after the Crusades—is one in which technological improvements fostering gains in scientific knowledge in turn lay the groundwork for improvements in technology. Instrumental to the spawning of this positive feedback cycle is the fact that the rewards attractive to shop floor inventors are different from the rewards appealing to scientists. Scientists pursue prestige, status within the community of their peers. Often prestige translates into riches: a boast in salary, funding for travel to give lectures, control over laboratories. At a minimum, power and influence act as a motivator. To be sure, some are less mercenary, enjoying the thrill of discovery for discovery's sake. In any event, the typical priority a scientist works with is to make knowledge public. Believing that constant criticism and debate stimulates further gains in scientific knowledge, most agents working within the scientific community possess a compelling incentive to spread new discoveries far and wide.

Typically, an inventor/innovator wants something else: material rewards, amassing resources for financing further invention. Finding a way to reap a long stream of financial benefits from their work naturally leads them to want secrecy, or in the absence of secrecy, a mechanism of profiting from what they have accomplished.

Creating an institutional environment in which both communities—innovators and scientists—can benefit one another means creating a community in which expectations of progress flourishes. This is the essence of technological capitalism.

Technological capitalism emerged in Europe during the sixteenth, seventeenth, and eighteenth centuries. It thrived in Europe based on a political and material pendulum swing pitting mercantilist states against fragmented local monopolies extracting rents in cities and market towns. It continued to thrive within Europe because mercantilist states actively opposed each other in military and economic affairs, thereby inducing technological progress. It thrived in Europe because competition between radically different scientific ideas set in motion a pendulum swing in the intellectual field. Finally, it thrived in Europe because a key element in technological progress involved precision, namely, the exact measurement of time, distance, acceleration, mass, temperature, the nature of the microscopic world and the nature of the cosmos.

Natural philosophy

The so-called European scientific revolution of the sixteenth and seventeenth centuries drew upon progress in precision measurement—a material phenomenon—that was wedded to progress arising out of ideological disputes.[1]

Both types of progress moved in tandem. Pendulum swings between opposing positions were active in both arenas.

Consider the importance of precision. Begin with a tantalizing question: why did alchemy run into dead ends in China, India, and the Islamic world, yet blossomed into chemistry in Western Europe? The answer lies in the technology of precision instrument making. As Leicester (1965: 82 ff) points out the reason alchemy morphed into the experimental field of chemistry was the command over precision reached by European artisans. In the mundane field of material craftsmanship Europeans had gone far down the road of experience. They were adept at making glass freed of mineral impurities that could contaminate chemical mixtures. They were well versed in creating accurate balances and scales used by assayers and alchemists alike. Accurately weighing outputs from alchemical experiments created a body of quantitative knowledge that experimenters of all backgrounds, including wealthy amateurs, could tap into, could use to display their erudition, to bolster their social status.

Holders of professorships in mathematics, mechanics, astronomy—natural and experimental philosophers specializing in science—devised most of the precision instruments whose applications in the fields of surveying, optics, fluid, and gas mechanics established a foundation upon which the English industrial revolution rested.

For instance, Edmund Gunter professor of astronomy at Gresham College invented a one hundred link chain for surveying. With this device, the costs of accurately laying out the dimensions of private plots and private toll ways fell. It made it easier to specify the cheapest paths for road beds and the optimal placing of bridges spanning rivers and tunnels cutting through mountains. In short, it was just one of the many specialized technical instruments—joining telescopes, back staffs, sextants, and the like—making for improvements in transport infrastructure (surveying) that reduced the costs of moving goods and people.

In the fields of measuring pressure professorial research was in the forefront. Daniel Bernoulli, Professor at the University of Basil, invented a device to measure blood pressure. Robert Boyle, wealthy Anglo-Irishman and patron of the "invisible college" in London that eventually morphed into the Royal Society of London for Improving Natural Knowledge, extensively experimented with air pumps, eventually showing that the volume of gas varies inversely with its pressure. His protégé, Robert Hooke, worked as an assistant to Boyle, eventually becoming the curator of experiments for the Royal Society, earning an annual gratuity that allowed him to carry on his research. Interestingly, he corresponded with Thomas Newcomen regarding the construction of a steam pump that could be used in pumping out mine shafts. Hooke suggesting creating a vacuum through condensation of steam might be effective.

Research in optics carried out in the late-seventeenth century—the work of Isaac Newton, Lucasian Professor of Mathematics at the University of

Cambridge stands out—had important spinoffs in practical fields. To be sure, in the short run applications for the manufacture of telescopes and microscopes were mainly limited to the practice of science itself. However, spectacle makers also benefited from the demands that science placed on lens grinders. Mass production of spectacles had huge pay-offs: it extended the economically productive lives of artisans, clerks, merchants, and seamen.

States, universities, and monarchs supporting institutions like the Royal Society were not the only public or semi-public institutions dispensing grants and prizes for innovation. Pérez (2008) shows that the eighteenth-century government of Lyon was actively involved in encouraging invention in silk manufacturing: 170 of the nearly 900 inventors who applied to the French national administration for a privilege of invention or a reward came from artisans in the city. In the case of Lyon, the major guild in silk production, the Grande Fabrique, worked hand in glove with city administrators, the national government, and merchants in coming up with grants and prizes rewarding innovators.

Outside the world of institutions was the private patron, the wealthy merchant, the duke, the prince, the gentleman scientist. Turner (1990) provides many examples of the purchase of precision instruments devised by wealthy individuals executed by master craftsmen. Some of these individuals became private patrons for scientists; some gave grants to learned societies like the Royal Society in London. Hooke was the beneficiary of an annuity funded by a patron. Early in his career, Francis Bacon, advocate of public funding for practical advances in science and engineering, benefited from the patronage of Lord Essex. The *Gentlemen's Magazine* of the late-seventeenth and eighteenth centuries carried advertisements for philosophical instruments. People of means purchased their own cabinets containing microscopes, measuring devices, and telescopes. The fourth Earl of Cork and Orrery became the patron of John Rowley. Rowley was a gifted instrument maker. At the Duke's request, he copied the work of George Graham, a highly respected member of the Royal Society who worked on devising the Greenwich Observatory, creating a model of the Copernican system that mechanically demonstrated the movement of the known planets. Marketed as an "orrery", the model created a veritable splash in elite circles: Queen Anne commissioned one that she gave to Prince Eugene of Savoy; brass and steel versions resting in expensive mahogany cases were snapped up by the wealthy; cheaper knock-offs flooded the market.

It is difficult to pinpoint when and why the European fascination with precise measurement started. One likely contender is the measurement of time.

Measuring time

How much Christianity had to do with a European fascination with precise measurement of time is an interesting question. Landes (1983: 58 ff) argues that it does. Landes points out that pious Jews pray three times a day, but not at set times. Similarly, in Islam five prayer times are deemed crucial, but they are set by a natural clock (dawn, right before noon, before sunset, after sunset and after dark). Without any natural guidelines on prayer, monks were inclined to pray all the time. Presumably, praying continually was a sign of devotion; those not showing such devotion were viewed as laggards by their colleagues. To free up time for work in the fields and for the copying of manuscripts, something had to be done. Tertullian recommended prayer at set times: at the third, sixth, ninth hours. The Benedictine rule adopted this model, paving the way for its acceptance by other monastic orders. Hence, a strong interest in developing mechanical timepieces that could be readily reproduced for use in far flung rural locales—unlike massive water clocks favored by Chinese emperors—that could be employed by bell ringers laboring in Church towers or belfries.

In short, the monastery played an important role in pushing forward Western technology. Outside of creating a demand for timepieces, other potential links between monasticism and technology have been suggested. One lies in the field of glass manufacturing. Churches and monasteries alike required elegant glass, especially so in the late medieval period when the great Gothic cathedrals with their beautiful stained glass illustrating scenes from the Holy Scriptures were under construction. Another possible link: managing gravity water systems. Magnusson (2001) makes a strong case for the view that the monastic orders demanded fresh, clean water flowing out of taps at fountain heads. The result was a demand for pipes both bronze and wooden, holding tanks, elaborate pressure-releasing cisterns and the like. Since the monastic orders were centralized, innovations obtained at one monastic site tended to spread rapidly to other locales through the agency of the order.

In any event, the upshot of the monastic management of time was immense: by the late medieval period a stream of innovations in time measurement were available on the European market. Chamber clocks, timepieces, all types of mechanical clocks competed for funds of discriminating elites. By the fifteenth century, spring-driven clocks; and by the early-sixteenth century, miniature watches were being manufactured by skilled artisans.[2] It is instructive that seventh-century scientists like Galileo and Huygens invented pendulum clocks with the aim of making time measurement increasingly precise. Indeed, natural philosophers like Galileo worked together with craftsmen in perfecting scientific instruments: geometric compasses, hydrostatic balances, and most famously telescopes.[3]

Remarkably, in fifteenth-century manuscripts the Cardinal Virtue Temperance is depicted as wearing a clock on her head and eyeglasses in her right hand. She stands on a windmill.[4] Precise instruments abound in this concept: miniature gears finely manufactured to measure time, lenses ground the better to see, massive gears converting wind power into a vehicle for grinding grain. Seeing clearly; being punctual; employing machines to extract power out of nature, manipulate nature—representing these as virtue incarnate, cloaked in the sacred, is in keeping with the secular fascination with mechanical precision.

In sum, during the late medieval and early modern periods the European supply of precision instruments vigorously expanded. Whether guilds hindered this growth or harnessed it is a matter of considerable debate.[5] In any event, outside the guild institution were other sources of supply: work funding by governments, learned societies, universities and their laboratories, private patrons, and patents. Over time the guilds became less influential. The Reformation eroded belief in purgatory, weakening the power of piety—an essential glue of the guild; the Inquisition promoted by the Counter Reformation stifled creativity in the guilds located in Catholic lands.[6] The spread of great cities like London spawned suburbs where artisans could escape the control exercised by the powerful guilds assembled under the umbrella of the London Livery Companies. Incipient industrialization created new metropolises free of guild control; all of this meant that the patent, universities, and government loomed larger and larger in the supplying of precision manufactures. Finally, governments of freshly minted nation-states, intent on weakening local sources of influence and power that could challenge their authority, legally abolished the guilds. Patents, universities, and government became the hallmarks of incipient technological capitalism.

Patents, universities, government are institutions. Ideas are generated through and by them because they compete for resources, supporting the individuals and groups who generate the ideas. In turn, competition in the world of ideas determines how the institutions reach decisions about what individuals should receive funding. The pendulum swings in the field of natural philosophy during the seventeenth century illustrate these principles with a vengeance. The story begins with the struggle between Scholasticism and natural philosophy.[7]

Attacking Scholasticism

Natural philosophy as a method of thought went hand in hand with humanism. Humanists thought Greek and Roman philosophy had reached the pinnacle of human thought, but that did not necessitate slavish adherence to Aristotle. In 1417 the poem of Lucretius *On the Nature of Things* was rediscovered by humanists.[8] The lure of atomism had returned. Combine atomism with the idea of a time-calibrating clock, a mechanical device regulating the flow of hours, minutes, ultimately seconds. The essence of natural philosophy is in your hands: you are led to imagine a mechanical universe—one following mathematic laws of physics—that can ultimately be explained in terms of minute atoms. In succeeding with this agenda, the shadowy clouds of Aristotle and Scholasticism were finally lifted away. This could not help but drive a wedge between the Catholic Church and natural philosophy. However—quite surprisingly, I might add—it did not drive a wedge between religion and science. This wedge was not decisively driven in until much later, until the nineteenth century.

The attack upon Aristotle was not the first major step in demolishing Scholasticism. Remarkably, the first step was taken by a Catholic cleric living in Cracow: Copernicus. An accomplished student of mathematics (astronomy and mathematics were conjoined in medieval thought), Copernicus took on a project assigned by Rome: reform the calendar so a definite date for Easter can be determined. Principally relying on observations made by ancient astrologers (Timocharis, Hipparchus, Ptolemy) and their Islamic successors (Arzachel, al-Battani)—he himself made only a few independent observations on his account—Copernicus followed rigorous mathematical logic in working out a heliocentric theory of planetary motion. In doing so, he incorporated epicycles to explain contrary motions carved out along circular orbits just as Ptolemy had done centuries before. However, his theory required fewer epicycles, a clear victory for aesthetically pleasing simplicity. In doing so, he rejected the thesis of a geocentric universe held by both by Aristotle and Ptolemy.[9] As it turned out, the idea of a heliocentric theory of the universe was even known to Greek philosophy. It just was not the mainstream view. The original contribution made by Copernicus was pointing out that while both heliocentric and geocentric theories were consistent with the observations made by stargazers, the mathematics was cleaner under the heliocentric model. As well, Copernicus felt his theory was superior for the purposes of creating an accurate calendar. It was on this basis that he consulted with Pope Clement VII in 1533 regarding his theory.

It is important to keep in mind that Copernicus did not dispute Aristotelian principles of physics. He was astrologer cum mathematician, not a protophysicist. It was Galileo who went after Aristotelian physics with a tooth and nail vengeance. His initial attack involved the problem of acceleration and de-acceleration. It was well known to Scholastic philosophers—notably Oresme—that Aristotle's theory of an active medium (air or water) causing motion of bodies was inconsistent with change in motion. Indeed, these philosophers modified Aristotle's theory, arguing the speed of motion explained by Aristotle only applied to the average speed over the space traversed, faster at the outset, slower at the end. As well the philosophers had come to reject the notion that the speed of a falling body is proportional to its weight, a view maintained by Aristotle.[10] To be sure, observation must have had something to do with their conclusions, but it is likely the main thrust of their reasoning was logic itself.

Galileo, however, did experiments from which he arrived at conclusions concerning the speed and acceleration of falling bodies. Having done these experiments, he came up with a simple mathematical expression for speed, namely speed is equal to one half of the product of acceleration multiplied by the square of time. In short, he attacked Aristotelian principles on both mathematical and experimental grounds. He crossed a huge intellectual chasm by proposing a simple mechanical law of inertia, throwing away as secondary concerns about friction and resistance inherent to media like air and water. Of course, the next step is to remove the resistance of air by creating a vacuum devoid of resistance. Aristotle had claimed nature abhorred a vacuum. But Aristotle was wrong about motion. Why believe in his theory of a vacuum?

Galileo was not only a natural philosopher of genius, mixing mathematical logic with observation. He was also an ideologist, a harsh critic of Scholasticism and of Aristotle in particular. Not surprisingly he was impressed with the theory Copernicus. That he turned his telescope to the heavens—years after he used it to show Italian merchants that they could employ it for commercial purposes, gathering information regarding the makeup of approaching ships at a distance—discovering new satellites orbiting around Saturn (which he named the Medician stars, after the Medici family who had supported his ventures), discovering spots on the sun, discovering that the moon had a rocky surface, only added fuel to his ideological fire. The telescope seemed to prove was that Aristotle's notion of a pure celestial realm was nonsense. But Galileo was already convinced Aristotle's theory was full of errors. Galileo was no alchemist, but in company with the alchemists he was bent on demolishing Scholasticism, lock, stock, and barrel. It is for this reason that he ran afoul of the papal inquisition. After all, Thomas Aquinas had been canonized a saint, and his synthesis of Aristotelian thought with Catholic faith was widely respected by the Vatican. In his polemical *Dialogue Concerning the Two World Systems* published in 1632, a feisty Galileo, ignoring the politics of the church, lampooned a naïve medieval Aristotelian he named Simplicio, who was revealed a fool in his debate against a rival natural philosopher. Tried by an inquisitional court, Galileo was placed under house arrest, still ending his life in comparative luxury. His treatment at the hands of the clerics sent a message to cultivated thinkers throughout Europe.

How far can one go in confronting the Roman church? It might be argued that the spread of Protestantism rendered free thinking more acceptable. Not so. Luther railed against Copernicus. In fact, because the early Protestant sects were absorbed imbibing the gospel of Jesus, they were inclined to dismiss the philosophical god of Scholasticism as well as anything that threatened their belief in miracles.

In this pugnacious attitude toward Scholasticism, Galileo reminds us of Paracelsus. Indeed, in venerating the common knowledge of engineers and artisans, Galileo does fit into the Hermetic tradition. Nor was he unique among the great thinkers of natural philosophy. Francis Bacon, the so-called architect of empiricism, was an avid supporter of Hermetic knowledge and a dedicated occultist. His agenda was wedding the practical knowledge of artisans and alchemists to the interests of the state. He was mercantilist to the core. Ironically, Hermetic methods and beliefs proved anathema to the younger generation of natural philosophers touting the importance of careful experiment. Boyle is a case in point. An atomist and a devout Anglican, he carried out countless chemical experiments, working with an air pump to create vacuums and test theories about the relationship of gas pressure and volume. In laying down an experimental agenda that did not dabble in mysterious forces, he and his colleagues at the Royal Society of London for Improving Natural Knowledge laid the foundation of an experiment-oriented philosophy devoid of the superstitions of alchemy.

Newton versus Descartes

Raised by Jesuits and mindful of Galileo's fate, Descartes took a different path from Galileo in his approach to demolishing the veneration of Aristotle. Rather than simply attack the ancient philosopher as Galileo did, Descartes did him one better. Descartes attempted to replace Aristotle. Taking on the mantle of a new Aristotle, reasoning from first principles, deriving conclusions consistent with the state of art in experiment and observation, he aspired to a grand synthesis in which soul, mind, and matter coexist in a grand mechanical harmony. Consistent with the principles of Descartes's own analytical geometry, matter consists of atoms extended into space. There is nothing between the atoms consisting of three types. No vacuum separates one from another. The atoms push one another; they form vortices in space, accounting for the movements of comets in the celestial realm. The universe is completely mechanical, devised by a rational God who designed it in accordance with physical laws. Non-human animal bodies are machines lacking souls. Human bodies are machines as well, differing from lower animals by having an immortal soul, the pineal gland located in the brain.

Descartes never claimed to know exactly what the actual mechanical laws governing the mechanical operation of the universe are. He imagined a kind of wall of human knowledge. Many laws might be consistent with what humans observe, ferreting out these observations through precise experiments. God—God alone—knows the true precise laws; mere mortal humans speculate on the nature of the laws based on their experimental observations. True, we are mere humans; still, we do know quite a bit. We know the universe is a machine operating very much like a clock. We know one God designed it. We know that once He designed it he did not have to intervene in its future operation. Like a clock it was wound up, running in accordance with the springs, gears, and wheels that God created. That the universe is atomistic does not mean one should subscribe to atheism. Indeed, the reverse is the case. The mechanical operation of an atomistic universe reveals the grandeur of God's plan.

While Descartes was spinning out his mechanistic accounts of the solar system based on his theory of atoms pushing violently against each other, generating huge whirlpools—vortices—in space, empirical and theoretical advances in astronomy and astrology were undermining his approach altogether. Not surprisingly, he ignored these advances. Not surprisingly, his arch-opponent Newton did not ignore these advances. As it turned out, the new findings—captured in Kepler's three laws of planetary motion—conformed very nicely to Newton's anti-Cartesian agenda. Unlike Descartes, he imagined space as a void in which masses resided, pulling toward or away from each other by spiritual forces, occult principles in action. Newton's atoms did not clash into each other. Rather, they were bound together by force expressed at a distance. Gravity was such a force. Whether Newton actually observed an apple falling toward the center of the earth or whether he simply imagined the idea of the center of an apple attracted toward the center of the earth really does not matter. What is clear is that he had a picture in his mind of how natural law operated, one that he could explain in terms of elegant mathematics.

What were the advances in astronomy that Newton felt lay sprawled across the entrance to a royal road revolutionizing the field of natural philosophy? These advances were both materialistic—telescopes, observatories—and idealistic, specifically mathematical, arguably Platonic. Most important were the great giants on whose shoulders he stood: Galileo, Brahe, and Kepler.[11] The analysis proposed by Copernicus was based on crude observations: his precision did not exceed ten minutes of arc. With support from the Danish crown, Brahe launched a massive data-collecting project in a beautifully designed and fashionably equipped observatory on a Danish island lying off the coast. His naked eye observations were remarkable for the time. He reduced error in measurement to the point where theory could catch up with data. Brahe himself advanced a theory based on his wide-ranging, minutely observed records that combined Copernican theory with Ptolemaic theory. In his model, the sun and moon orbited around the earth, the planets orbiting around the sun. A much-derided speculation today, Brahe's figures were precise enough to command respect for his system during the seventeenth century. In the longer run, Brahe's speculations were ridiculed. However, this was only after his erstwhile assistant Kepler, brandishing Brahe's hard-won data, constructed a more compelling model of the solar system.

Kepler was one—if not the first—of the group of serious astronomers accepting Copernicus's heliocentric model of the universe. He came to it through Platonic mysticism. In his *The Cosmographic Mystery*, published in 1595, he argued the solar system was organized in Russian doll fashion. Five distinct Platonic solids were organized in a hierarchy—the innermost seated closest to the sun at the center, the remainder placed one on top of another, each solid representing a path of motion for one of the known planets. The sun was the symbol of God the Father. Kepler was a committed Protestant, totally sincere in his Christian faith, trying as did Boyle to explain how a divinely inspired universe operated. In short, Kepler approached astronomy as a Platonic mathematician would.

That said, Kepler wanted to use the most precise data to further his speculations. It was with this in mind that he negotiated with Brahe, the leading empirically oriented astronomer in Europe. He became Brahe's assistant, appointed to the post with the aim of explaining the orbit of Mars, the planet exhibiting the most convoluted path in the Copernican scheme. Through subterfuge, Kepler ultimately obtained Brahe's full body of observations—Brahe was not interesting in sharing his treasure trove of observations with anyone else—after Brahe died. Kepler was now free to continue his mathematical investigations.

Equally committed to mathematical simplicity and to precise measurement—after all, God designed the universe, leaving only traces of His divine plan to mere humans in observable phenomena, the more precisely measured the better—Kepler kept tinkering with his analytical models until he finally arrived at his three famous laws of solar system mechanics. These are: (1) Elliptical orbits: the orbit of a planet is an ellipse—not a circle—with the sun as one of its two foci; (2) Equal intervals of area corresponding to equal intervals of time: a line stretching from the sun to any one planet sweeps out equal areas during equal intervals of time; and (3) Square/cube law: the square of the period of the orbit is proportional to the cube of its orbit axis. With the first of these three laws, Kepler dispatched the belief in circular orbits, a holdover from the ancient Greeks and Romans, who believed in the purity of circles. With the second law, Kepler came close to developing integral calculus. With the third law, he provided a mathematical equation that—in the hands of an inspired mathematician like Newton—can be deduced from first principles, namely the idea of gravity.

Newton arose to the occasion, deducing all of Kepler's laws from his theory of force, inertial mass, and acceleration (force equals mass multiplied by acceleration). That Newton could formulate a simple equation that not only explained Galileo's experimental observations but also accounted for Kepler's three laws is remarkable. It is certainly the crowning achievement of natural philosophy before it morphed into science during the eighteenth and nineteenth centuries. Surely this is one reason Newton's reputation is clothed in heroic mystique: a god-like, disinterested individual, dispassionately observing the mechanic operation of the cosmos, completely above the messiness of the intellectual pendulum swing.

Nonsense.[12] From the outset it was Newton's goal to discredit Cartesian thinking. He thought it was "vulgar," pointing people down the path to atheism. In the classic experiment, he himself carried out at a relatively early point in his career—in later years he employed an assistant, John Cesaguliers, to carry on experimental investigations—he set out to show sunlight was composed of a variety of colors, basing his reasoning on ancient harmonics, exactly seven in number. Countering Descartes' rival hypothesis that light appears colored because it passes through objects—for instance, through a prism—Newton shined sunlight through a prism, breaking it up into separate colored beams that fell onto a screen. Drilling holes in the screen, Newton then experimented with the colored rays, allowing each to pass onto a separate prism that passed the ray onto a second screen. Demonstrating that the colored rays sent through a second set of prisms did not change color established proof that the colored rays are the actual basis—conjoined together—from which sunlight is assembled. Newton's reasoning was that the colored rays are made up of atoms held together by "active principles." In short, according to Newton, Descartes' entire theory of atomism was misguided. Atoms do not push against each other in the absence of an ether-like void. Rather, atoms of a particular type are attracted to form rays because of the forces binding them to each other through the void. To a Cartesian, Newton's idea amounted to occultism. To Newton, who was an aficionado of Hermetic alchemy, there was nothing wrong with occult forces. Indeed, they were proof divine forces were active in the universe.

After Newton's death, his scientific followers—stimulated by Desaguliers who spread the Newtonian gospel through private schools and Newtonian centers, using the orrery to demonstrate how Kepler's laws worked according to the gravitational logic of Newton—carried on investigations in an ever widening field of investigation.[13] Using Newton's equations, anatomists explained how signals travel back and forth from the nerves to the brain through an ether-like fluid situated in the nerves. Using Newtonian logic, Hume sought to build a psychology on experimental and mathematical foundations. Likewise did Adam Smith. In fact, Smith's theory of moral sentiments is pretty much a carryover from Newton's atomism. Individuals are social atoms bound together by altruistic forces. That Smith elaborated a theory of how an economy could best function if individuals pursuing their own selfish interests (but connected to one another through altruism), buying and selling in price-driven markets, that he felt was Newtonian speaks volumes. It demonstrates why Newton himself was a symbol of the British moderate enlightenment. Newtonian mechanical logic was fully consistent with individualism, an idea gaining increasing force in seventeenth-century Britain (think John Locke). Moreover, it did not threaten the Anglican faith. After all, Newton believed God actively intervened to keep his system operating. Without the deity's guiding hand, the solar system would collapse into itself due to the powerful gravitational forces at work.

Newton's invoking the actions of a deity clashed with the Cartesian idea of a divine architect winding up the clock of the universe, leaving it to operate according to the mechanical laws devised by the all-seeing, perfect creator of the universe. According to Cartesians like Leibnitz, Newton's God was not perfect. Why would He invent a universe that He needed to fix on an ongoing basis? Both Newtonian and Cartesian theory led to deism, a belief in a universe guided by mathematical laws devised by an omniscient deity. Miracles did not really make sense in this world, a point Hume emphasized in his writing. In this sense, both Cartesian and Newtonian schools completed a process set into motion by Scholastics like Thomas Aquinas who made a clear distinction between faith—ultimate wisdom—and analytical philosophy designed to ferret out and explain phenomena discovered in physics and biology. Of course, both Cartesian and Newtonian schools dispensed with Aristotle altogether.

In the pendulum swing unleashed by Newton, Newtonian and Cartesian philosophies became locked in a fierce competition that served as the capstone to natural philosophy at the beginning of the eighteenth century. Ultimately, Newtonian principles defeated Cartesian logic. Why? One reason is its ability to explain Kepler's laws. Another reason is the first industrial revolution in England. Just as the mechanical clock was the symbol of natural philosophy, so the steam engine was the symbol of the first industrial revolution. Was it not designed along Newtonian principles? Well, not really. In fact, it was not Newton that was important for the steam engine. It was Boyle—and the chemist Joseph Black, working with vacuum pumps, gas pressures, and temperature gradients—who pioneered the way to the steam engine. Still, Newton was a convenient symbol. And symbolized he was.

By way of summary, it is useful to display a table capturing the pendulum swings back and forth between different competing schools of natural philosophy. Of course, the main pendulum swing involved the swing away from Scholasticism. By the end of the seventeenth century, no serious natural philosophy subscribed to Aristotle. At a more general level, no serious student of natural philosophy was comfortable basing their theories on what the Greek and Roman philosophers had actually written. To be sure, Newton believed that there was lost, ancient knowledge anticipating the discoveries of natural philosophy. In fact, this was certainly a pipe dream. Still, even Newton, alchemist and theologian, could not produce evidence that the ancients had revealed Kepler's laws of planetary motion or developed the calculus.

In Table 11.1 I separate key figures of sixteenth and seventeenth century natural philosophy in two competing schools: persons specializing in observation and experiment, drawing upon the practical arts mastered by artisans, a school that owed much to alchemy and the Hermetic tradition; and persons mainly inspired by deductive mathematical reasoning. To oversimplify, in making an analogy to ancient thought I call the first school materialist (think Aristotle emphasizing material factors, relying on observation albeit imperfect given the paucity of measurement instruments), and the second school idealist (think Pythagoras, Euclid, and Plato). I want to emphasize that I concede that several individuals listed in this table crossed boundaries, working in both materialist and idealist modes. Still, I believe I am correctly emphasizing the main thrust of their contributions.

The burden of the table is to hammer home a theme running through the entire body of this paper. Over the long history of Western Europe, pendulum swings were in continual motion. Beginning with the Greeks, the process had continued in both material and intellectual realms. The pendulum swings of the heyday of natural philosophy are a perfect example. Commencing with the pendulum swing in which Scholasticism was drubbed into submission by figures like Copernicus and particularly Galileo (heir to the Hermetic tradition which mocked Aristotle), further pendulum swings were set into motion. Atomists like Boyle attacked Hermetic philosophers like Bacon. Careful experimenters like Boyle were skeptical of overarching

Table 11.1 Key figures in two competing schools of natural philosophy

Materialist		Idealist	
Individual, key works	Comments	Individual, key works	Comments
		Copernicus (1473–1727) *De revolutionibus orbium coelestiam*	Mathematician and astronomer, advocate of heliocentric theory of the universe
Galileo Galilei (1564–1642) *The Assayer (1623)* *Dialogue Concerning the Two Chief World Systems (1632)*	Telescope, pendulum, thermoscope, experiments on falling bodies, laws of acceleration and mechanical motion; condemned by Inquisition, house arrest after 1634		
Tycho Brahe (1546–1609) *Introduction to the New Astronomy*	Last of major naked eye astronomers; great accuracy of observations In Tychonic system planets revolve around sun; sun and moon revolve around earth	Johannes Kepler (1571–1630) *The Cosmographic Mystery* *Epitome of Copernican Astronomy (1617–1621)*	Inspired by Platonic theory of solids in early work; belief in sun as a symbol of God the Father; magnetic soul to the solar system Assistant to Brahe Three laws of planetary motion
Francis Bacon (1561–1626) *Novum Organum (New Method) 1620* *New Atlantis (1627)*	Hermetic philosophy, interest in occult "Father of empiricism" Advocate of state support for developing practical knowledge as key to enhancing state power	René Descartes (1586–1650) *Discourse on Method (1637)* *Geometry (1637)* *Description of the Human Body (1648)*	Atomist; mind–body dualism problem; developer of analytic geometry and theory of cubic equations Human body as a machine with a soul located in pineal gland Deist

Table 11.1 Continued

Materialist		Idealist	
Individual, key works	Comments	Individual, key works	Comments
Robert Boyle (1627–1691) *The Sceptical Chymist (1661)*	Alchemist and atomist; Anglican theologian and one of the founders of the Royal Society; director of East India Company Air pump; Boyle's law of gases Advocate of careful experiments	Isaac Newton (1643–1727) *Method of Fluxions (1671)* *Philosophiae Naturalis Principia Mathematica (1687)* *Opticks (1704)*	Mathematician and natural philosopher developed calculus and model of mechanics combining Galileo's acceleration principles with theory explaining Kepler's results Believer in spiritual forces causing atoms to be pulled gravitationally to each other
		Gottfried Leibnitz (1636–1716) *"New method for maximums and minimums" (1684)* *Monadologie (1714)*	Developer of calculus Sufficient reason; law of continuity; theory of nomads; best of all possible worlds Cartesian as opposed to Newtonian

theories like that of Descartes. Newton emerged as a pugnacious opponent of Cartesian thinking. After his death, natural philosophy divided into two schools deeply divided over the nature of deism. Ironically, God was soon knocked out of the picture altogether.

That God was knocked out of the picture was ultimately due to the political pendulum swing.[14] The French Revolution took place in the late-eighteenth century. One of its strongest tenets was anti-Catholicism. In its most violent phase—the Terror of the mid-1790s—Rousseau-style philosophy was all inspiring to the radicals. Reason was the new god. Following the Protestants, the state claimed assets and income streams once aggrandized by the church. The British Protestants had accomplished this task during the reigns of the Tudors and the Stuarts. Now it was France's turn to disinvest the religious authorities. Secular authority was trumping religious authority. While the trend away from religious gift exchange was similar in both countries, a crucial difference between the way secularization was ushered in Great Britain and in France is noteworthy. In Great Britain, the Glorious Revolution that drove out Catholic-leaning James II in 1688 set the stage for alternating two party—progressive Whigs versus conservative Tory—contested parliaments dominating over a monarchy much weakened by the political swings of the seventeenth century. This back and forth Whig versus Tory political competition moderated the British political swing.[15] In France, absolute monarchy wedded to a strongly entrenched Catholic Church was overthrown by an increasingly radicalized revolutionary movement. The pendulum swung much more violently in France. Indeed, France quickly passed through virtually every political form of degeneration mentioned by Aristotle, ultimately leading to dictatorial rule by Napoleon.

Emerging from the chaos of the French revolution, the French Newton, Laplace, proposed a completely secularized version of Newtonian physics. As he confided to Napoleon, he did not need the hypothesis of God in designing his celestial mechanics. That said, Laplace took over, lock, stock, and barrel, the mathematical formulations advanced by Newton. The equations did not markedly change; the idea of attractive forces held together by gravity and other inter-atomic forces was not discarded; but the deity was banished. Laplace envisioned a totally materialistic universe. With Laplace, the nature of deism became irrelevant for science. The way forward to a totally materialistic theory of nature was firmly established. Darwinism, organic chemistry, and the first industrial revolution pushed materialism even further into the forefront of philosophical and scientific thought.

The pendulum swing in the first Industrial Revolution: scientific ideas and material forces conjoined

With the first industrial revolution, the weight of the pendulum swung away from theoretically oriented natural philosophies, Cartesian or Newtonian. The reason is industrialization, the growing use of machines of all types in producing material goods, the mass production of textiles, the substitution of coal for charcoal in metal working, the factory system. Why? Because operating, servicing, and improving on machines installed in factories provided—not by intention, but as a kind of by-product—thousands of experiments.

The best example is the steam engine.[16] The evolution of the steam engine went through many phases, but three are of utmost importance: the Newcomen engine, the Watt steam engine with separate condenser, and the high-pressure steam engine with multiple boilers. My focus here is on the first two engines.

At the beginning of the eighteenth century, the practical engineer Newcomen, engaged in building pumps to draw water out of mineshafts, contacted Boyle. Boyle suggested using a vacuum pump. So advised, Newcomen proceeded to design a massive pump with an oscillating beam that pulled up, lifting containers filled with water out of mines, then swung in the opposite direction, dropping the containers back down into the shaft. Steam was injected into the cylinder from which the pumping device moving the beam back and forth emerged. In this phase, the cylinder was hot. Then cold water was poured over the cylinder. The steam condensed, and the semblance of a vacuum was created. With the cylinder then evacuated the pump did its job, swinging the pendulum beam. Once this phase of the back and forth motion was complete, the cylinder was heated, water being injected first, steam filling the cylinder. The pumping device was set into motion once more. Imagine doing this in an Aristotelian-inspired world, in which no one believes in creating vacuums. Not likely. The point is, ideas concerning the construction of vacuum pumps must exist before you go about the practical business of building the devices. So much for a Greek or Roman world convinced that Aristotle knew what he was talking about.

Heating a cylinder with water in it requires fire. Creating fire requires wood, coal or charcoal. The less you have to heat the cylinder, the less fuel is required. Enter the practical engineer James Watt, assistant to the chemist Joseph Black. Black is working on measuring temperature. Heat water and you get steam. There is a precise temperature at which water turns to steam without the temperature changing. Black dubbed this "latent heat". If you overheat the water you not only get steam. You also get higher temperatures. If you want to efficiently heat a Newcomen engine, you need to know the latent heat required to exactly turn water into steam without overshooting. Watt learned this from his labors under Black's guidance. He applied it in devising prototype stream engines for experimental work. Once set along this road—a practical one, because it deals with reducing the amount of heating required to secure the requisite amount of steam—Watt continued to follow the trail further. At some point, he realized that constructing a separate condenser would reduce the costs of generating pumping motion even further. Separate hot cylinder from cold condenser. Operate on the temperature differential between the two media. You reduce heating costs. Of course, fashioning steam engines with the requisite valves is not trivial. Practical engineer that he was, Watt was up to the task.

In pursuing the logic of driving down costs and—diligent as a tightwad, perhaps to a fault—Watt went even further in his experiments on steam engines. It dawned on him that an expansion principle was at work. The steam rushes into the cylinder. The rushing motion has the potential to do work. Harness this potential by cutting off the injection of steam at a relatively early point. In doing this, you cut the amount of steam you need to operate the device. You save more money.

In order to get tabs on all the variables involved in his steam engines, Watt installed pressure gauges and temperature gauges on his engines. He sought precise information, because precision meant money. Followers of Weber might say "time wasted is money forgone"; Watt would say "energy wasted equals money lost."

The crux of Watt's innovations lies in the idea of a four-cycle principle. Inject steam in phase one; cut off steam inflow in phase two; condense in stage three; complete the cycle in phase four. You get pumping action that is economically efficient. You are exploiting the temperature differential between steam creator and condensing agent in the most practical way possible. This is basically the idea exploited by Carnot who developed a theoretical model of work generated by a four-stroke engine. It is the First Law of Thermodynamics in embryo. One of the key ideas of nineteenth-century science was forecast in the practical experience of tinkering with steam engines. Industry was driving science; in turn, science was driving industry. The pavement for the road to rapid innovation was put down by practical individuals mucking around in the material arena, mainly concerned with driving down production costs. In turn, they looked eagerly to the growing number of experimental scientists who were putting the machines of industry to work in their laboratories.

Materialism took off in science for other reasons as well. Emblematic of the shift is the development of organic chemistry out of inorganic chemistry. To provide the proper perspective, let us return to alchemy and the Hermetic tradition.

From inorganic to organic chemistry

Let us return to the remarkable story of how chemistry came to supplant alchemy. As noted earlier, alchemy was practiced throughout the Axial Age civilizations of the Eurasian world. The Chinese knew of it. So, apparently, did people in India. Certainly, Islamic thinkers thought it important, though its validity was a matter of healthy debate. Once it made its way into Europe via Islam it became entrenched there. Even if the Church despised it, secular rulers maintained an active interest in it, inviting alchemists to their courts for demonstrations. That rulers had an active interest in it is hardly surprising: turning alloys of metal into pure gold would facilitate issuing of coinage. It would reduce costs. Moreover, proper use of the Philosopher's Stone might well have huge benefits for health and longevity. After all, Aristotle's theory suggested that there were important correspondences between the micro-environment of the human body with its various organs and the macro-environment of the universe.

Given the quasi-religious search for purification central to alchemy, it is hardly surprising that the field could—and actually did—become increasingly wrapped up in mysticism. Indeed, this appears to have been the case in China, where it eventually merged with Taoism and later Neo-Confucianism. It reached a similar dead-end in the Islamic world, fueling philosophical speculation leading on to intellectual cul-de-sacs. Only in Western Europe did alchemy evolve into chemistry, a hard science. Why?

As we have seen, one part of the answer lies in the technology of precision instrument making. A major reason why alchemy shed its mystical skin, transforming itself into a professional field that eventually became respectable enough to be taught in universities in the West but not elsewhere, lies in the decidedly materialist bent of hermetically inspired alchemists. The alchemists were technologists, pure and simple. Ideologically, they were opposed to Scholasticism. Technology was driving science as it has for most of human history, at least up until the mid-nineteenth century, when technology gradually became applied science.[17]

Through repeated experiments—in which elements were decomposed into their constituent parts that were then employed in reversing the process, the various parts being reassembled into the original element in the laboratory—chemistry as a systematic proto-academic field emerged. As Klein and Lefèvre (2007) point out, this program, extended throughout the eighteenth century, yielded the monumental table of chemical nomenclature painstakingly put together and published jointly by Lavoisier and his colleagues in 1787. Behind this massive project were years of advance in material science gradually creating a consensus around the theory of chemical affinity. In their view, Lavoisier was more the heir than the instigator of a new version of chemistry.

To be sure, Lavoisier is justifiably famous for his theory of oxidation (the taking on of oxygen) refuting the older thesis that phlogiston was given off by compounds in chemical processes. However, Klein and Lefèvre (2007) suggest that the biggest breakthroughs in chemistry came after Lavoisier's head was savagely removed from his frame by the chop of the guillotine (not because he was a scientist, rather because under the *ancien régime* he had aggrandized riches as a tax farmer, albeit sowing his opulence into his laboratories). Their thesis is that the breakthroughs in chemistry went hand in hand with an appreciation of the existence of carbon chains. As they pointed out, the focus on carbon chains had nothing to do with Lavoisier. Rather, it was fundamental to the emergence during the nineteenth century of a wholly new field: organic chemistry.

What Lavoisier and his colleagues achieved in the eighteenth century was a detailed breakdown of how to produce and decompose inorganic substances. They did not extend their methodology into the analysis of plants and animals. With the advances achieved during in the 1820s and 1830s mainly by Germans—notably the entrepreneur cum scientist Justus Liebig (famous for the law of the minimum, applied to soil science and the creation of the Oxo bouillon cube) and Friedrich Wöhler who synthesized urea—detailed analysis of carbon compounds jumped by leaps and bounds. The legitimacy of vitalism—the idea that organic life was fundamentally at odds with chemical materialism—was shaken at its core among the ranks of professional scientists. After all philosophical debate over the uniqueness of a vital principle was one thing; synthesizing life forms in a test tube was altogether different. For the first time, it became possible to posit a completely materialistic theory of matter, inorganic as well as organic, an overarching theory for plants, animals, and metals. The separation between animate life and inanimate life was shattered. In principle, chemistry could create life.

Organic chemistry opened the door to a wholly materialistic theory of life itself. This was a door that chemistry was hardly alone in throwing open. A practice originally steeped in mysticism and based on purification—fundamental to religion—was gradually transformed into a totally materialistic theory bereft of otherworldly elements like the Philosopher`s Stone. Not surprisingly, materialistic theories became increasingly popular during the nineteenth centuries, particularly among literate professionals enthusiastic to learn about new advances in knowledge. Witness Darwinian natural selection, Marxism arguing ideology was the superstructure resting on a material substructure informed by technology cum class structure, Social Darwinism, and eugenics.

Technological capitalism was coming into its own. Merged with merchant capitalism, it emerged triumphant during the first industrial revolution. The scientifically informed second industrial revolution—electricity, the internal combustion engine, the germ theory of disease and other marvels taking central stage, driving astounding improvements in material existence—cemented it as a unified ideological system. To be sure, tensions existed within capitalism, which was imagined as a single conceptual framework for spawning new technologies, spreading industrialization worldwide, integrating far-flung lands into a vast checkerboard on which entrepreneurs could display their innovative talents.

What is this emerging capitalism? It is the mobility of capital enhanced by credit creation. It did not take final shape until the first industrial revolution of the eighteenth and early nineteenth centuries. At the core of capitalism is rapid innovation, capital being drawn from declining sectors; capital being pulled in the vortex of expanding sectors; capital seeking the highest rate of return owners of it can realize through investment. Similarly, because capitalism takes two forms—merchant capitalism that feeds on international flows and technological capitalism that feeds on innovation, both domestic and international—the mobility of capital is realized both in the domestic and international arena. Stemming from this mobility are ups and downs in domestic production and domestic employment. The instability of capitalism is an insight Marx had, an insight that remains true for the time he wrote—in the mid-nineteenth century—and in today's twenty-first-century world as well.

If Marx was correct in his pinpointing of the timing of capitalism's emergence and its most salient deficiency—instability—he was wrong in focusing exclusively on material factors. One of the key lessons of this study is that both ideas and material forces matter. Weber, who emphasized the importance of the conceptual environment for the emergence of capitalism in the West, was right about ideology mattering. To be specific, he was correct that some form of ancient thought realized in a newer guise mattered. Where he was wrong was his focus on the wrong type of Axial thought, Christian Augustinian predestination.

Why did the West develop technological capitalism? To borrow Leibnitz's notion of sufficient reason, the answer offered by this book is twofold:

obsession with precision instruments and the pendulum swing advanced by the ancient Greeks. Why was it so deeply engrained in Western Europe, failing to take off in the Byzantine Empire and in the Islamic world, both of which were heirs to ancient Greek thought? Because neither the Byzantine Empire dominated by the emperor, or the Islamic world dominated by caliphs—each exploiting the masking function Axial style religious belief provides—were rocked back and forth by the pendulum swing in material and intellectual affairs. Out of the turmoil of the pendulum swings emerged triumphant Europe, increasingly opulent, increasing powerful.

Notes

1 I write "so-called scientific revolution" because I am convinced the term is misleading. It is misleading because the advances in science made during the seventeenth century were mainly concentrated in the fields of physics and anatomy, not in chemistry was still mired in alchemy. It is also misleading because the key figures—notably Descartes, Newton, Leibnitz, and Boyle—thought of themselves as natural philosophers not scientists. Indeed, common use of the word "scientist" does not gain currency prior to the nineteenth century.

   Shapin (1996: 1) captures the paradox arising from assigning the scientific revolution to the seventeenth century with his bold opening line "There was no such thing as the Scientific Revolution and this is a book about it." Along the same lines, one can argue that the act of putting names on periods of history is itself a historical process, historians working at particular points in time looking for imagined break points upon which they can hang their pet theories about the nature of change.

   For example, Le Goff (2015) convincingly argues that historians obsessed with the idea that the European medieval era constituted a dark period when knowledge and culture atrophied—ancient Greek and Latin culture being almost totally abandoned—created the idea of the Renaissance is a distinct period in history. Believing that the revival of ancient learning was key to moving forward towards modernism they created a unique historical era—unique because it was limited to Europe—during which the straightjacket of the dark period was finally wrenched off, light bursting onto the European stage. Le Goff's thesis is that the medieval period does not really end until the onset of the first industrial revolution of the eighteenth century. I concur, eschewing the use of the term "Renaissance" in this volume.

2 See Landes (1983: 72–75, 80–81, and 86–87). Mokyr (1990) refers to the mechanical clock as a macro-invention, one spawning a myriad of micro-inventions. In particular, Mokyr (1990: 50) emphasizes the fact that the practice of clock-making induced specialist artisans to reach for new standards in the accuracy required to create reliable mechanical devices. In short, manufacturing along precise lines became an indicator of quality, something sought after by elites. For a classic account of mechanical inventions see Usher (1929).

3 White (1978: 126–127).

4 White (1978: 198–199).

5 It is worth noting that Huygens sought a patent for his clock with pendulum as regulator from the government of France. He was turned down because the French government wanted to avoid dealing with protests from the master clock-makers, who used the political clout of their guilds to stifle patent competition. See Turner (2008: 269–270).

6 See Mackenney (1987: Chapter 5).

7 For the use of the term "natural philosophy"—as opposed to science—see foot-note 1 for this chapter.

8 See Hall (1962: 8–9). In my account of natural philosophy, I draw heavily on Chang (2007), Fara (2009), Jacob (1997), Klein and Lefèvre (2007), McClellan III and Dorn (2006), Moran (2005), Pickstone (2000), and Shapin (1996).

9 See Hall (1962: 61). Technically, the sun was not situated at the exact center of the universe in the framework advanced by Copernicus. However, it was very close to the center. Fara (2009: 65) argues that Islamic predecessors to Copernicus had revised the Ptolemaic framework by introducing devices like those introduced by Copernicus.

10 See Hall (1962: 81–90).

11 For a detailed account of the tangled relationships developed between Galileo, Brahe, and Kepler, see Koestler (1959, 1986).

12 For a salutary debunking of heroism in science, dispelling myths from the ancients to Einstein, see Fara (2009).

13 The remainder of this paragraph is based on Fara (2009: 143 ff).

14 For moderate, radical and counter-enlightenment movements see Chapter 12.

15 The American revolutionaries went one step further than the British did in attenuating the political pendulum swing. The Constitutional checks and balances of the United States—power divided between the executive, legislative and judicial branches at the federal level; as well power divided between states and the federal government—was designed to create a mechanical form of government that would not explode into fragments, old constitutions being scrapped in favor of new ones, a practice imbedded in French practice but not in the British tradition.

16 For the discussion of the science of the steam engine and the implications of Watt's experiments with it for the First Law of Thermodynamics I draw heavily upon Chang (2007: 176 ff).

17 For the general argument that this is the case, see McClellan III and Dorn (2006). For an interesting treatment of the relationship between pure intellectual knowledge and applied technology, see Mokyr (2002).

12 Nationalism and imperialism

Nationalism went hand in hand with intellectual and material changes emerging out of natural philosophy. Among intellectuals it was apparent that natural philosophy either led to deism or to materialism. Moreover, it made the promise of unending progress attractive. Moderns had surpassed the ancients.

Enlightenment struggles

The eighteenth-century European Enlightenment movement in philosophy struggled with the problems of materialism, deism, and progress. They did not do so in a vacuum. Practical political leaders did so as well. After all, if the deity was not involved in shaping the back and forth of politics and warfare it—either because he simply wound up the clock and let it run or because he did not exist—it was up to mere humans to solve social and political problems. If there was no god intervening in the world, how could you explain miracles? Better forget that idea. Moreover, was it plausible that kings ruled by divine right? Not likely. If sovereignty did not rest with monarchs and emperors, in what did it rest?

The obvious answer to the question concerning sovereignty is that it rests with the people. This was a truly radical idea. Sovereignty did not rest in royalty. It did not rest in god or within a pantheon of deities. It rested in the citizens occupying a physical territory. A properly constituted state should reflect this reality. A properly constituted state should exist so the people can experience progress: political, economic, and intellectual progress.

Understood in this way, nationalism is modern. To be sure, nations existed during the Axial Age. However, Axial Age thought did not conceive of sovereignty resting with the citizenry as a whole. This conclusion even holds for the ancient Athenians who probably came closest to achieving liberal democracy, one of the variants of modern nationalism. The key reason is that Axial Age societies were dominated by a small coterie of literate elites who sought legitimacy in securing contact with a transcendental world, or by winning ferocious bloody contests upon battlefields.

The spread of the nation–state system

Mosk (2013) develops a theory of modern nationalism, arguing that its practical expression is the nation–state system.[1] He argues the system began with the emergence of England as a nation–state in the seventh century, spreading to the United States with the American Revolution, to France with the French Revolution, and later throughout Europe and into East Asia beginning with the Japan of the Meiji Restoration. I summarize six points key to his argument here.

Nationalism is modern. Nationalism is expressed in a variety of ideologies: for instance, liberal democracy, communism, fascism. In theory, it is devoted to achieving political, military, and economic progress for the great mass of national citizens, for the rest of the world as a potential afterthought.

Nationalism spreads through disruptive violence. Civil or international warfare ushering in control of the state by a group committed to a theory of progress accompanies the establishment of a nationalistic ideology within a state. Ideological branding plays an important role in shaping the history of a nation–state. Once a nation–state branding ideology is firmly established within a population domestic violence rates tend to plummet.

The spread of nationalism since 1600 has created a global nation–state system. As nationalism spreads a system of states containing disparate ethnic and religious groups within the sovereign territories gives way to a system of states each professing some nationalistic ideology. For instance, a world of empires ruled by dynasties that co-exist with city states, nomadic chiefdoms, hunting and gathering tribes, and the like is replaced by a world divided into nation–states. Empires like the Ottoman, Russian, and Austro-Hungarian empires ultimately break up into nation–state entities.

Nationalism emerged in Europe and areas of European settlement like the United States. This is because the theory of progress and its practical application to science and technology first emerged in Europe, shaping the Enlightenment movement of the eighteenth century.

In order to push forward material progress benefitting the masses, nation–state policy makers promote public investment in three major forms of infrastructure: human capital enhancing (education, public health); physical (hydroelectric systems, dams, roads, harbors, railroads); and financial (central banks, equity markets). This spawns growth in improvement in the factors of production, and—depending on the nature of the nationalistic ideology—total factor productivity growth. One important consequence of the economic progress engendered by nationalism is a decline in the relative price of exerting military force (relative to prices prevailing for commodities consumed in the civilian economy). This is one reason—although not the only reason—why nationalism encourages an escalation in war-making capacity.

The reduction in the relative price of exerting military force has ushered in a post-World War II era in which the specter of Total War self-destruction looms over industrialized nation–states, redirecting research and development in military fields from offensive to defensive purposes. At the same time, it has dramatically cut the cost of carrying on guerrilla war in preindustrial regions. The result is a spread of the nation–state system in regions once colonized by the major industrial powers. Increasingly, competition between states has moved from the military field to the field of economic competition.

Moderate enlightenment, radical enlightenment and counter-enlightenment

Regarding the ideological branding of nation–states, Mosk (2013) argues that it falls into three distinct categories: moderate enlightenment; radical enlightenment; and counter-enlightenment. Why was the enlightenment so important, spawning three variants of the nation–state?

When we think of the enlightenment in terms of ideas we usually focus on a handful of key thinkers active in Europe and North America. Notable are philosophers like Spinoza, Locke, Hume, Smith, Kant, Franklin, Jefferson, de Condercet, d'Alembert, Diderot, Helvétius, Holbach, La Mettrie, Rousseau, and Voltaire.

Profoundly influenced by deism, British and American thinkers—Locke, Hume, Smith, and Jefferson—advanced a moderate enlightenment theory designed to create stability by hemming in the political pendulum swing. The emphasis was on unfettered development of empirical enquiry (notably science), freedom of thought, unfettered market outcomes, individualism, the protection of private property (including intellectual property through copyright and patents), and a minimalist approach to state intervention. A key notion was preventing the leaders of the state from unnecessarily interfering in the day to day activities of citizens. After all, power corrupts and absolute power corrupts absolutely. A classic statement of these principles is framed in the first ten amendments to the Constitution of the United States. As well, the system of checks and balances introduced in the Articles of the Constitution are designed to place strong limits on the abuse of power exercised by legislators, members of the executive branch or judges. Note that the American system of checks and balances strongly limits the swath of air the political pendulum swing carves out. It limits rapid change. It has a conservative agenda built into it.

A second wing of the Enlightenment emerged in France. It was profoundly materialist. Emerging out of a country dominated religiously by the Catholic Church, it was decidedly anti-clerical. Dubbed the radical enlightenment in the literature, it has its classical expression in the phase of the French Revolution leading up to the Terror. It highlighted equality and devotion to the republican state. Since most of the radical enlightenment thinkers were atheists or agnostics who believed that religion was humbug, a crucible of superstitions aimed at justifying oppressive rule by dysfunctional elites, it was decidedly secular. Because equality of outcome—not just equality of opportunity as conceived in the American theory—was a crucial goal of political leaders versed in this approach to nation-building was fully prepared to interfere in markets with the aim of securing a "just" price. Struggling to achieve equality for every citizen, maintaining a policy of anti-clericalism in a country where Catholicism is deeply entrenched, has generated considerable instability in France. There are fewer constraints on the swing of the political pendulum.

Together, the moderate and radical enlightenment schools provided the theoretical underpinnings of liberal nationalism.

Debates within liberal nationalism

The debate between the classic moderate enlightenment vision—emphasizing private individual initiative and self-interest as a motivator for disciplining human behavior—and the radical enlightenment principle of maximizing social welfare through redistribution lay at the root of the population theory of Thomas Malthus. Malthus wrote the original pamphlet that morphed into *An Essay on Population* as an attack on William Godwin, British critic of aristocratic privileges, proto-Anarchist hater of oppressive government, and author of *Enquiry concerning Political Justice* (1793). Malthus argued that idealist schemes for obtaining equality of economic outcomes would flounder on materialist realities, in this case the laws of population, the so-called ultimate and immediate laws.

The ultimate law restates the law of diminishing returns. Fix the amount of land, increasing the volume of labor applied to it. The additional product on the margin—the extra contribution to the bounty of corn, wheat, barley, and meat—falls off as the number of labor units is applied. As a result, the average—and marginal product—of the workers drifts downward.

The immediate laws refer to the actual determinants of population growth. Unlike animals hunting one another in the wild, facing possible extinction as a species because their numbers outstrip their ecological environment, humans are blessed with reasoning (as an Anglican minister, Malthus probably attributed this capacity to a benevolent Christian God). Therefore, as individuals participating in households, they have the capacity to limit their population, perhaps through abstinence from intercourse. Moreover, properly devised institutions can act as a brake: imposing restrictions of age of marriage, requiring proof of earning capacity before allowing matrimony, clamping down on prostitution, mandating compulsory work in exchange for poor relief, and so forth. This resulting check is the preventative check. The positive check operating through the aegis of the Grim Reaper takes a variety of forms: famine, war, pestilence, and the like. Combined, these checks slow population growth rates, keeping them far below the maximum potential.

Malthus asserted that the positive and preventative checks operated in inverse relationship one to the other: the more judicious restraint obtained, the lower the prevailing mortality. The reasoning was simple, yet elegant in its simplicity. The standard of living would be higher the fewer the number of people. Restrict growth in human numbers, and less people live off the land. A higher standard of living increases the capacity of people to ward off death from infectious disease.

Strongly convinced that the rate of technological progress and the level of capital accumulation per worker were modest—not unrealistic assumptions for agriculture, but questionable in the case of manufacturing—Malthus argued that the only way to achieve an improvement in the overall standard of living for the masses was through the exercise of the preventative check. According to his view, the iron law of wages held. Improve the standard of living in the short run by enhancing the productivity of workers through improvements, say, by the use of iron ploughs or a semi-mechanized method of threshing. The rise in the productivity of labor would encourage earlier marriage—farm laborers could save more quickly, thereby affording to secure a cottage in which they could raise a family—ultimately driving up population and diminishing the standard of living, which would ultimately fall back to the culturally defined subsistence level (culturally defined in the sense that it reflects the way marriage institutions operated in different regions of the world).

Armed with this reasoning, Malthus advocated restriction on access to marriage. He argued dissuading the poor and indigent from procreating is superior to socialistically inspired redistribution of income and resources. He believed that the poor were destitute because they gave birth to too many children, that poor relief actually encouraged early marriage and excessive reproduction among the less well off. Instead of collecting the dole and being indolent, the poor should be required to labor in workhouses, ultimately earning enough income to support a family and marry. In short, Malthusian reasoning was both positive and normative. In so far as it was normative, it amounted to a strong defense of moderate enlightenment principles, the importance of religion and private property for maintaining a relative high standard of morality. Virtue was more than its own reward. It could and did contribute to material wellbeing. Utopian schemes redistributing income would end up encouraging population increase, lowering the standard of living for everyone.

Malthusian reasoning spread outside the purview of economics. The idea of species competing for scarce resources was implicit in the idea that population growth could run up against limits to food production. It was for this reason that Malthus's theory ended up inspiring Charles Darwin. Species compete for scarce reasons. Some die out, others survive. Random variation in phenotypes spawns adaptations within species; as well, it leads to the creation of new species. A materialistic mechanism generates long-run evolution of animate life on planet earth.

In short, disputes between moderate and radical enlightenment theorists about how to improve society, how to guarantee progress for all citizens, created a heady brew of controversies. As well, it set into motion the complete rejection of both theories.

Counter-enlightenment and religious nationalism

A counter-enlightenment reaction set in. Initially the forces of counter-enlightenment gathered around the defense of state-sponsored religious institutions. This is the variant I call "religious nationalism." In religious nationalism, state law and religious law overlap to a considerable degree. One statement of this vision was made by Voltaire, who believed that religion was essential to social stability. Even if God did not exist, it was a good idea to invent the notion of a transcendental overseer. This smacks of Platonism. A cynic might turn the argument on its head, pointing out that religion was created by elites to keep the masses in check. This was a line of thought embraced by Marxist materialists, championing the slogan that religion was "the opiate of the masses." Another interpretation of the counter-enlightenment doctrine permeated a book penned by Jean-Jacques Rousseau, *The Social Contract*. Rousseau's views gained traction in part because the architects of the French Terror espoused them.

Arguing that "man was born free, but everywhere he is in chains," Rousseau espoused utopianism. He believed the blessings of freedom could only come if society was based upon a set of religious principles (though not Christianity, which he viewed as corrupt). The state should take over capital. It should abolish private property, which was the source of inequality and social strife. Sovereignty should rest in a General Will expressing the views of the masses. The state should carve out a mass line, imposing it on everyone. Dissenters should be punished, in the worst case executed. We can see in this vision a concept institutionalized by twentieth-century communist and fascist states. A single-party propaganda bureau stamps out the mass line. The state, operating with its policing agencies, purges dissent.

Interestingly enough, Rousseau thought his utopian model could exorcise the Malthusian population monster. The state could declare a limit on reproduction, restricting the number of births to two offspring, for instance. The "one child" policy of Communist China is a perfect example of this approach.

The debates of the Enlightenment were hardly limited to intellectuals, public philosophers as it were. One of the hallmarks of the Enlightenment was the creation of a "public sphere" where vigorous debate took place. Literacy was on the rise everywhere in Europe—particularly in the Protestant countries where every adult was expected to be able to read the Bible. Magazines, books, pamphlets, newspapers flourished. French academies— the Academy of Science and the *L'Académie française* that held contests including debates over the rival theories of Newton and Descartes—sponsored debates. Philosophers like Rousseau competed for public prizes, submitting their essays to juries.

All of this went hand in hand with technological capitalism. In advancing his theory of an industrial enlightenment, Mokyr (2002, 2009) stresses the mixing of mechanics, inventors, and scientists in private and publicly subsidized gatherings.

One of the reasons why the nation–state system spread so rapidly in the late-nineteenth century, and subsequently in twentieth century, is imperialism. Imperialism arose out of the clash between merchant capitalism and technological capitalism. Merchant capitalism is international in its orientation, technological capitalism less so. That technological capitalism is less international in its orientation lies in the logic of import substitution. A major reason why innovators innovate is the search for ways to create national products that can effectively compete with imports. Consider England in the eighteenth and nineteenth centuries. Before the middle of the eighteenth century, England imported massive amounts of cotton textiles from India. Because of innovations in cotton textile spinning and weaving—the flying shuttle, the water frame, the jenny, the mule, the power loom—England switched from being a major importer of cotton textiles to a major exporter. The same story took place in the nineteenth century. In the early nineteenth century, best practice technique in England for manufacturing steel involved importing high quality iron from Sweden, re-carbonizing it, thereby creating blister steel. Bessemer converters, later the open-hearth process, allowed English steelmakers to create high quality steel at internationally competitive prices without having to resort to the import of Swedish iron.

Technological capitalism versus merchant capitalism

Technological capitalism and merchant capitalism were not particularly comfortable with each other. Adam Smith in his classic *The Wealth of Nations* pointed out the problem:[2]

> The capital, however, that is acquired to any country by commerce and manufactures, is all a very precarious and uncertain possession, till some part of it has been secured and realized in the cultivation and improvement of its lands. A merchant, it has been said very properly, is not necessarily the citizen of any particular country. It is in a great measure indifferent to him from what place he carries on his trade; and a very trifling disgust will make him remove his capital, and together with it all the industry which it supports, from one country to another.

In short, the problem with mercantilism is that it does not well serve national interests. It bleeds away some portion of the capital that should be used within the nation.

At the same time, the technological progress engendered by technological capitalism facilitates the actual practice of imperialism. The reason is simple: it reduces the relative cost of exerting military force.[3]

Technological capitalism had powerful spinoffs for military combat, and vice-versa; technological advance in the military sub-economy contributed to price reductions and product innovation in the civilian economy. Between the 1830s and the American Civil War, guns had been totally transformed. From muskets loaded through the barrel, gun manufacturing had advanced onto breach-loading rifles, to the Gatling gun able to spew out bullets at a speed never anticipated by militaries of the early nineteenth century. By World War I, troops could move by foot, by horseback, by railroad, or by armored truck. The tank came into use. Germany, unified and heavily industrialized by 1905, was engaged in a Dreadnought race with the United Kingdom. Steel-hulled battleships bristling with heavy duty cannons faced off against each other at Jutland. Aerial warfare came into its own. The next logical step was the aircraft carrier.

Total War was a grim reality. Trench warfare in which machine guns slaughtered advancing troops turned a war supposed to take only six months into the horrific carnage of the Great War. Commerce was prepared to embrace the Grim Reaper. The German manufacturer Krupp licensed the technology of making powerful ammunition to a British company that used it to mass-produce bullets used to kill German soldiers. Ironically, the same bullets were used to send British soldiers to their untimely graves. After the Great War was over, Krupp demanded royalty payments from the British company on the grounds that it had exploited a technology during the conflict without paying for its use. How popular do you think paying royalties was in the United Kingdom?

In short, technological capitalism harbors a dark side. According to the logic of the military power equation, driving down the unit cost of exerting military force increases military potential for the countries benefiting from advances in military technology. Accordingly, the military organizations of the industrial giants of the late-nineteenth century—the United Kingdom, the leading western European countries, and the United States—had within their grasp the power to push around countries in the non-industrial world. Africa was carved up into colonies by European powers beginning in the early 1880s. Germany, France, Belgium, and the United Kingdom were unusually active in this endeavor.

Predatory imperialism

To be sure, religious competition played a role in the political logic of this new imperialism. Stopping the spread of Islam south played a role. Catholic priests from France competed with American and British evangelicals. That said, the primary motive of imperialism was the search for raw materials, the search for new consumer markets, and the search for new investment opportunities, yielding higher rates of return than those accruing from domestic investment. Merchant capitalism was fully prepared to take advantage of higher rates of return on capital flowing from mines dug and exploited, railroad lines constructed, coffee and tea plantations opened, and banana forests planted in colonies.

All of this put Christianity in a bind.[4] On the one hand, imperialism made it easier for missionaries to reach masses of humanity unfamiliar with the truth of Christian doctrine, the salvation offered by belief in Jesus Christ. On the other hand, many missionaries were appalled by the way Europeans exploited their colonial subjects. To be sure, not all missionaries saw a contradiction between European-led commerce and Christianity. For one, David Livingstone, committed to extinguishing the vestiges of the slave trade in Africa, believed promoting alternative forms of trade would accomplish a task the British navy had been unable to stop. With this in mind, he pushed the ideology of "Christianity, commerce, and civilization" onto what he considered to be a benighted Africa.

In the Far East, European and American imperialism unleashed a backlash. Japan is the classic case. After the Opium Wars of the late 1830s and early 1840s forced China to cede treaty ports, shogun and *daimyo* alike were alerted to the fact the West had new military resources at hand that could upset their isolationist policy. Once Commodore Perry's Black Ships forced Japan open in the 1850s, it became completely evident to many *samurai* that the military disparity between *samurai* swords and Western guns and battleships was massive. Something had to be done to protect the homeland: embracing technological capitalism, to be precise.

Having already developed their own form of merchant capitalism, the Japanese were well suited to carry this out. Overthrowing the shogun and abolishing fragmented feudalism was one logical step. Forging national unity through the promotion of the cult of the Emperor was another. Under the logic of this theory, the *samurai* who overthrew the Tokugawa regime, replacing it with nominal rule under the Meiji Emperor, reached back in an atavistic fashion to Shinto while embracing Western technology as the road to progress. The result was creation of an umbrella ideology for the new nation–state: *fukoku kyohei* (wealthy country/strong military).

What proved to be relatively easy to accomplish in Japan proved a huge challenge in China. Mosk (2011) suggests that the difference lies in the nature of the elite. In Japan, the *samurai* elite were landless. Their status was hereditary, based on primogeniture. By the second half of the Tokugawa period, many were involved in managing fief businesses. Merchant capitalism had already flourished for centuries in Japan, so the step to adopting a new form of capitalism based on Western learning did not pose a major threat to elite status. The challenge for the old elites was to figure out how to maneuver themselves into status positions in the new nation–states. Competing for jobs in merchant houses, positions in the imperial bureaucracy, and posts in the new Western inspired army and navy was just the ticket. As a big tent ideology *fukoku kyohei* tied to the cult of the Emperor offered real opportunity to the old elite. To be sure, not all *samurai* were happy about the abolition of their feudal status, and a brief civil war was fought in order to quell their restiveness. The fact is that enough of the old elite managed to grasp onto elite status in the new regime to ensure that the political transformation proceeded relatively smoothly.

In China, the Confucian elite competed for lucrative positions in the imperial bureaucracy through a daunting examination system. Few advanced to the upper echelons of the system, but the landed elite were committed to trying, since the rewards accruing from obtaining a high-level position were vast. The examinations were based on mastering the Neo-Confucian classics. Candidates devoted years to the study of these classics. They were not inclined to embrace commerce, as Confucian thought frowned on it. Only the decision of the Manchu officialdom to reform the examination system—introducing Western science and engineering—could shake the Chinese elite out of their loyalty to the defunct concept of a Confucian empire. Once the imperial regime crossed the Rubicon in 1905, the elite, exasperated by the loss of their skills won over years of arduous study, allowed the regime to collapse. In 1911, China became a republic, though not one enjoying the support of many of the former elites, including military officials.

It was the disparity between Japan and China that roiled diplomacy in the Far East. Japan, emulating the Western powers, embraced imperialism. It carved out an empire in Asia, securing Taiwan from China in the 1890s, and control over Korea regularized diplomatically in 1910. Defeating Russia in the Russo-Japanese War of 1905 gave Japan control over the Manchurian railroads. The road to World War II in the Far East was opened up. Western imperialism had stimulated the rise of imperial Japan. Flexing its military muscle, the Japanese nation–state laid claim to leadership in a new form of imperialism in the Far East. The idea was simple. Drive out the Western powers; initiate a new, non-Western form of empire building, one dominated by industrializing Japan, one committed to extending its imperial umbrella over a gravely weakened China.

Notes

1 The discussion of nationalism given here draws heavily from Chapters 2 and 3 of Mosk (2013).
2 Smith (1937: 395).
3 See Mosk (2013).
4 See the chapters in the volume edited by Etherington (2005) for the British case. See Daughton (2006) for the French case. The French case is interesting because it highlights the conflict between nationalism and religion. In France, republicanism was strongly associated with anti-clerical thinking. This had been the case ever since the French Revolution of the late-eighteenth century. Republican-dominated French governments were not favorably disposed toward the needs of Catholic clergy in the territories they had colonized.

Part IV

Implications

13 Religious nationalism and technological capitalism

Contra Marx, religion did not wither away under communism. Despite the claims of Weber, religion did not disappear as scientific advances ushered in demystification of the world. True, the materialistic orientation of communism has left deep footprints on some countries: notably contemporary China; less so Russia, where the Russian Orthodox faith has grown in the aftermath of the disintegration of one-party Soviet Union Communist Party rule, ushering in the complete collapse of the Soviet state during the late 1980s and 1990s.

To be sure, secularism—evidenced by growing toleration of atheism and agnosticism ushered in by separation of church and state—has gathered force, particularly within the international arena carved out by liberal nationalist states. Attendance in Christian churches has plummeted in Western Europe. Magnificent church buildings stand empty, or are sold as mosques, or are used for daycare centers. Still, Protestant Christianity is spreading by leaps and bounds in Latin America and Africa, and is even making inroads into China. More importantly, religious nationalism has come to the fore as a potent ideological force, spawning, among other things, international terrorism.

The expectation that religion would wither away—a view once solidly entrenched among the chattering classes, among the legions of liberal scholars, journalists, and so-called progressives—has withered away even as religion has not. To say religion is back as a potent political reality is one way of acknowledging the current reality. Another view—consistent with the argument of this book—is that it never disappeared. Indeed, in my view, it has inexorably grown into a powerful barrier to social and economic improvement in many regions of the developing world at the very time liberal nationalism has taken shape in the West. However troubling it is for economic advance in the contemporary world, it is not new. Its roots go back centuries. It emerged in the eighteenth and nineteenth centuries with the counter-enlightenment, eventually morphing into modern religious nationalism.

Not surprisingly, investigating the impact of contemporary religion on economic development has emerged as a vibrant sub-field within sociology and economics. Testimony to this fact is a plethora of writings on the economics of religion.[1] In this chapter, and the next chapter, I hope to contribute to this literature.

Technological capitalism trumps merchant capitalism: the growth in per capita income

Since the onset of the first industrial revolution, per capita income has grown at a phenomenal rate. This fact is immediately apparent from Table 13.1:[2]

The lesson of this table is clear: technological capitalism, unleashed during the first industrial revolution, trumps merchant capitalism. For most of human history, per capita income hovered between $1 and $2 dollars a day, measured in international 1990 Geary-Khamis dollars. With the onset of technological capitalism, it has soared in Western Europe, the Western offshoots, and Japan.

By the term "trumps" I mean overshadows, dominates. By 1820, merchant capitalism had been around for over a millennium. It had spread from the Middle East to Europe, even making significant inroads into the eastern zone of Eurasia, penetrating and flourishing in the island archipelago of Japan. Despite the global diffusion of merchant capitalism, it failed to improve per capita in a significant way. To be sure, under mercantilism Western Europe had experienced a modest improvement in living standards. The Malthusian monster appeared to be held at bay: population grew even as per capita income crawled upward. Predation and comparative advantage trade did succeed in improving somewhat the level of opulence enjoyed by the great cities of the imperial core countries in the West. Favored enclaves carved out in the environs of Amsterdam, London, Paris, and Brussels enjoyed great riches. But did this accumulated wealth exceed what the elites living within the environs of Rome during the heyday of the Roman Empire had managed to cobble together? Comparisons between the

Table 13.1 Per capita income in 1990 International Geary–Khamis Dollars, 1820–1998

Region	1820	1998	Compound annual growth rate, 1820–1998 (%)
World	667	5,709	1.21%
Western Europe	1,232	17,921	1.51
Western offshoots[a]	1,201	26,146	1.75
Japan	1,130	21,470	1.93
Latin America	665	5,795	1.22
Eastern Europe and former USSR	667	4,354	1.06
Asia (excluding Japan)	575	2,936	0.92
Africa	418	1,368	0.67

Note:
(a)   The Western offshoots include the United States, Canada, Australia, and New Zealand.

eighteenth-century basket of commodities consumed by European elites and those enjoyed by Roman elites are tricky. Still, scholars advancing the literature on the Roman economy suggest overall living standards for the eighteenth and early nineteenth century Western imperialist powers—nominal incomes and wages deflated by consumer prices—were remarkably similar to those achieved in the Roman Empire when it reached its economic apex.[3]

All of this changed during the nineteenth century as technological capitalism took hold.

From this cold, hard fact follows a second fact. Mastering applied science—technology—has become increasingly important for economic development. Societies that put a strong emphasis on educating their children in science stand a better chance of innovating. No amount of wishful thinking about the virtues of an education devoid of science can stand up against this conclusion.

This brings us squarely up against the issue of national policy regarding education. How open is education in a country to the teaching of science? The point is this: in so far as religious teaching contradicts science policy, the priorities established for the educational system matter. To be specific, consider a country strictly adhering to religious nationalism. Presumably, its religious theology draws conclusions about the nature of reality. Suppose these views are inconsistent with scientific thinking. A plausible inference is that its educational system is profoundly impacted by religious authorities who have a vested interest in strict interpretation of Axial Age inspired texts (including the Qur'an).

By dint of being less likely to embrace science, is a religious nationalist nation–state less likely to be innovative? Is it less likely to foster sustained growth in economic per capita?

This chapter looks at the question in two ways. It looks at the relationship between attitudes toward the truth of religion and innovation, relating the former variable to national policies. It looks at this relationship in terms of widely utilized concept: secularism. Second, it looks at the relationship between a widely used measure of per capita welfare, the human development index (HDI), and the policies of countries. In both cases, it is possible to show that Axial Age thinking institutionalized in state policy negatively impacts technological capitalism. It deters technical innovation; it reduces the capacity to seize economic opportunities.

To be sure, most of the literature on this question revolves around the so-called opposition of science to religion. Specifically, it revolves around an even more narrowly conceived question: is neo-Darwinian evolutionary thinking valid? Strict fundamentalists who take Axial Age faith-based scriptures literally—for instance, the Hebrew Bible, the New Testament, the Qur'an, the Upanishads, and so forth—may well reject the notion of random variation generating long-run evolution. The stories recounted in Genesis, for instance—God as creator making Adam in his image, the species allowed onto Noah's ark—are clearly incompatible with Darwinian logic.

In my opinion, the controversy engendered by this very specific issue—the Neo-Darwinism synthesis of genetics and Darwinian evolutionary thinking—is excessive. The difference between scientific thinking and Axial Age-inspired thinking resides elsewhere.[4] A person can be a practicing scientist yet still reject Darwinian style evolution. There are plenty of good examples. One instance: the influential nineteenth-century British scientist Lord Kelvin (William Thomson) rejected Darwinism on completely scientific grounds. Based on calculations he made employing the Second Law of Thermodynamics, he concluded that the earth was not old enough to allow evolution from highly simplified forms of life—for instance, a cell with a nucleus—to anatomically complex creatures like humans.

I think the fundamental difference has to do with the presence or absence of critical thinking. Modern science emerged out of natural philosophy. The intellectual pendulum swing was so vigorous within the field of natural philosophy that any result—theoretical or empirical—was immediately questioned, probed for inconsistencies, subjected to further analysis. Axial Age thinking is rooted in faith. Faith can and does ignore hard facts. As often as not, authors of religious texts made up "facts" in order to justify their social and political prominence. A good example is the writing and successful promulgation of the Hebrew Bible by political and religious elites holding sway over the Jewish communities of antiquity.

That said, attitudes concerning neo-Darwinian thinking do tell us something. Most lay persons—as opposed to specialists enjoying a detailed understanding of the genetics underlying Neo-Darwinism—tend to think in terms of the validity or non-validity of materialistic evolution as an explanation for the life forms we observe on the earth. For this very reason, attitudes about the past existence of dinosaurs matter: if you believe dinosaurs existed eons ago, becoming extinct 65 million years ago, it is difficult to believe the earth is the age stated by the Book of Genesis.

For want of a better name, I will call the person who gives priority to scientific thinking a secularist. This is not a perfect definition, by any means. Still, we will have to live with it.

Secularism

For the purposes of this statistical endeavor, we define the secular proportion as those individuals within a population who are either self-declared agnostic or atheist.[5] There are good reasons for thinking this is an underestimate of the proportion secular. For one thing, many individuals classify themselves as belonging to a religion because they participate in the rituals of that religion, at least on an occasional basis. This does not make them true believers in that faith. As an illustration of the fact that religious identity is on the decline, the fact that 45% of marriages in the United States during the first decade of the twenty-first century were interfaith marriages suggests people are taking religion less and less seriously.[6]

That secularism measured as we calibrate here is less pervasive than we might anticipate based on the arguments advanced above is apparent from Table 13.2.

If we are seeking places where secularism is deeply entrenched, it is apparent that former Communist Asia and Europe are the strongest candidates. The table also suggests that populations residing in monarchies and countries espousing an official religion are more likely to be religious than countries lacking these institutions, and that countries with poor governance (as calibrated by adherence to law and the efficiency of government) are likely to not be secular. For instance, in Africa where governance tends to be deeply flawed in the vast majority of countries, belief in some religion—animism and ancestor worship in some, Christianity and Islam in others—is solidly grounded.[7] Perhaps people seek out churches or mosques out of desire for security. In lawless environments, families threatened by violence are naturally attracted to sanctuaries. In addition, in countries where government services are lacking, there is little if any public education. Many are illiterate. How can an illiterate child know much if anything about science and the scientific method? Why would we expect pride in one's nation to be strong? In so far as humans hunger for some belief system to make sense of the sufferings of life on earth and the brevity of life itself, what option is there outside of religion?

Even in Europe secularism is not as entrenched as one might suspect, given the fact that natural philosophy and the Enlightenment emerged out of Europe. One line of argument is that the Enlightenment was actually a failure, that in its wake came two brutal Total Wars (World War I and II), the Holocaust, the collapse of communism as a progressive system, and, most recently, genocide in Yugoslavia. This seems to be the position taken by one of the most influential schools of philosophy in Europe, the German Frankfurt School. That the rationality of Kant could usher in the madness and horrors of the twentieth century suggests that Enlightenment rationality was fundamentally flawed, ultimately a failure, at worst benighted.[8]

To delve deeper into this problem, let us return to the argument involving identity and possible conflicts over identity. Recall we argued that individuals feel less loss of identity-driven utility if the various belief systems they subscribe to are in line with one another. Taking a cue from this argument, we introduce a new variable into our analysis, one capturing the attitude of the nation–state regarding religion. This is **GIR**, government regulation of religion.[9] The idea is that in a state highly supportive of religion, people are more likely to be religious; when the state is hostile toward faith, people tend to lean toward secularism. An individual identifies with his or her nation–state and its branding particularly when the state's governance is considered adequate (nationalism is more muted when the state is viewed as failing its people). Thus, we expect **GIR** to be positively associated with religious attachment.

Table 13.2 Agnosticism and atheism

	All countries		Non-communist countries								Communist or former communist (Com)	
			Govlaw < 15				Govlaw > 16					
			Offchmon = 0		Offchmon > 1		Offchmon = 0		Offchmon > 1			
	Athagn%	Govlaw	Athagn%	Govlaw	Athagn%	Govlaw	Athagn%	Govlaw	Athagn%	Govlaw	Athagn%	Govlaw
Africa[b]	0.75%	9.9	0.50%	7.78	0.90%	6.7	1.40%	19	–	–	0.80%	13.6
Americas and the Caribbean[c]	2.51%	13.8	2.50%	13.8	4.22%	15	11.6%	24	11.2%	24.4	13.0%	16.3
Asia (including Russia 536.307 pt)[d]	1.86%	14.6	1.46%	8.39	0.78%	9.0	1.53%	18	12.6%	24.8	34.2%	3.51
Europe[e]	17.0%	25.9	–	–	–	–	19.5%	25	13.5%	26.1	11.1%	18.2
Pacific Ocean (including Philippines and Oceania)[f]	6.12%	16.0	0.91%	12	–	–	2.2%	22	19.1%	26.1	–	–

Percentage of population agnostic and/or atheist (**Athagn%**) and sum of measure for government functioning and rule of law (**Govlaw**) for regions of the world and for groups of non-communist countries according to **Govlaw** levels (sub-classified by whether a country is a monarchy and/or has an official religion (**Offchmon**), and for (former) communist or communist (**Com**) countries (population weighted averages for groups) [a]

Source: The Association of Religion Data Archives online website www.thearda.com/internationalData/ accessed in October and November 2012; the Association of Religion Data Archives is at the Department of Sociology, the Pennsylvania State University, 211 Oswald Tower, College Park, PA.

Notes:

A The variable **Govlaw** is defined as the sum of the government functioning variable (ranging from 0 to 12 where 12 is the best functioning) and the rule of law variable (ranging from 0 to 16 where 16 is the most law abiding). The **Offchmon** variable refers to whether a country has a monarch or an official church (**Offchmon** = 0 means no monarchy or official church; **Offchmon** = 1 means an official church or a monarch; and **Offchmon** = 2 means both. Only data for countries with figures for **Govlaw** values are used in making the calculations (these are likely to be countries with low values for **Govlaw**).

B Former communist countries are Botswana, Congo (Republic of), Namibia, and Niger; non-former communist countries with **Govlaw** less than or equal to 15 and **Offchmon** = 0 are: Angola, Burkino Faso, Burundi, Cameron, Central African Republic, Chad, Congo (Democratic Republic), Cote d'Ivoire, Eritrea, Gabon, Gambia, Guinea, Guinea–Bissau, Kenya, Liberia, Malawi, Mozambique, Nigeria, Rwanda, Sierra Leone, Uganda, Western Sahara, and Zimbabwe; non-former communist countries with **Govlaw** less than or equal to 15 and **Offchmon** greater than 0 are Algeria, Comoros, Djibouti, Egypt, Togo, Tunisia, and Zambia; non-former communist countries with **Govlaw** greater than or equal to 16 are Benin, Botswana, Cape Verde, Ghana, Mauritius, Sao Tome and Principe, Senegal, Seychelles, South Africa, and Tanzania.

C (Former) communist countries are Chile, Cuba, and Nicaragua; non-former communist countries with **Govlaw** less than or equal to 15 and **Offchmon** = 0 are Bolivia, Brazil, Columbia, Ecuador, El Salvador, Guatemala, Guyana, Haiti, Honduras, Mexico, Paraguay, Peru, and Venezuela; a non-former communist country with **Govlaw** less than or equal to 15 and **Offchmon** greater than 0 is Jamaica; non-former communist countries with **Govlaw** greater than or equal to 16 and **Offchmon** = 0 are Argentina, Dominica, Panama, Puerto Rico, the United States, and Uruguay; non-former communist countries with **Govlaw** greater than or equal to 16 and **Offchmon** greater than 0 are Antigua and Barbuda, Bahamas, Barbados, Belize, Canada, Costa Rica, Dominica Republic, Grenada, Saint Kitts and Nevis, Saint Lucia, and Saint Vincent and the Grenadines.

D (Former) communist countries are Afghanistan, Armenia, Cambodia, China, Kazakhstan, Korea (North), Kyrgyzstan, Laos, Mongolia, Russia, Tajikistan, Turkmenistan, Uzbekistan, and Vietnam; non-former communist countries with **Govlaw** less than or equal to 15 and **Offchmon** = 0 are Burma, Lebanon, Nepal, Singapore, Syria, and Turkey; non-former communist countries with **Govlaw** less than or equal to 15 and **Offchmon** greater than 0 are Bahrain, Bangladesh, Bhutan, Brunei, Indonesia, Iran, Iraq, Jordan, Kuwait, Malaysia, Oman, Pakistan, Palestine, Qatar, Saudi Arabia, Sri Lanka, UAE, and Yemen; countries with **Govlaw** greater than or equal to 16 and **Offchmon** = 0 are Cyprus, Hong Kong, India, Korea (South), and Taiwan; non-former communist countries with **Govlaw** greater than or equal to 16 and **Offchmon** greater than 0 are Israel and Japan.

E (Former) communist countries are Albania, Belarus, Bosnia/Herzegovina, Bulgaria, Croatia, Czech Republic, Estonia, Georgia, Hungary, Kosovo, Latvia, Lithuania, Macedonia, Moldava, Montenegro, Poland, Romania, Serbia, Slovakia, Slovenia, and Ukraine; non-former communist countries with **Govlaw** greater than 15 and **Offchmon** = 0 are Austria, France, Germany, Ireland, Italy, Portugal, San Marino, and Switzerland; non-former communist countries with **Govlaw** greater than 15 and **Offchmon** greater than 0 are Belgium, Denmark, Finland, Greece, Iceland, Liechtenstein, Luxembourg, Malta, Monaco, the Netherlands, Norway, Sweden, and the United Kingdom.

F There are no former communist countries in this group. Countries with **Govlaw** less than or equal to 15 and **Offchmon** = 0 are Papua New Guinea, the Philippines, and Tonga; Countries with **Govlaw** greater than or equal to 16 and **Offchmon** = 0 are Kiribati, Marshall Islands, Micronesia Federation, Narau, Tuvalu, and Vanuatu; countries with **Govlaw** greater than or equal to 16 and **Offchmon** greater than 0 are Australia and New Zealand.

Table 13.3 Determinants of secularism

Dependent variable:	(Athagn%)	
	Athagn%	ln (Athagn%)
Regressors		
Intercept	7.8430	0.3556
	(3.2063)	(0.2918)
Govlaw	0.1588	0.0638
	(0.1299)	(0.0131)
GIR	−0.1773	−0.0210
	(0.0598)	(0.0054)
R²	0.1780	0.2502
n	164	164

Ordinary least squares regression: secularism measured by percentage atheistic and agnostic

Notes:
a White's (1980) heteroskedasticity-consistent standard errors appear in parentheses.
b n = sample size.
c A log–log model is not considered as **GIR** includes some negative values.

Evidence consistent with this hypothesis appears in Table 13.3. To be sure, statistical significance is not the only criterion one would want to apply in evaluating these regressions. But getting solid results is not a bad thing. These results are solid; they have real bite.[10]

Secularism is intimately tied up with the governance or lack of governance provided by nation–states and the attitudes of the states toward religion. This means states branding themselves in terms of religion—religious nationalism states—are less likely to be secular.

Innovation and secularism

Consider innovation. In Table 13.4, population weighted averages for governance, income per capita, growth in income per capita between 1990–2 and 2008–10 are presented for groups of countries classified by ranges for the global innovation index (**gii**).

In general, the more innovative a country the more likely it is to be secular. Moreover, important from an economic development perspective are the results concerning countries having values of the **gii** between 40 and 49. These are principally developing countries. Yet the values for their innovativeness are extremely close to those prevailing in the high income per capita countries where we would expect innovation to be pervasive since—other things equal—higher income per capita countries can invest more in research and development. For the group of countries with the innovation index between 40 and 49, secularism is unusually strong. For instance, China is in this group; post-Maoist China is very secular and very innovative.[11]

Table 13.4 Innovation, good governance, and income per capita

Gii	Athagn%	Govlaw	ypce[a]	ratylye[a]
50 < gii[b]				
56.15	14.52	25.36	27,346	1.36
40 < gii < 50 [c]				
45.25	34.73	6.09	4,083	3.53
30 < gii < 40 [d]				
35.49	3.54	15.30	3,354	1.94
gii < 30 [e]				
25.66	1.11	9.62	1,997	1.55

Countries classified by four levels of the global innovation index (**gii**): population weighted group averages for: the percentage of population agnostic or atheist (**Athagn%**), the sum of a measure of government functioning and rule of law (**Govlaw**), per capita income circa 1990–02 (**ypce**), and the ratio of per capita income circa 2008–10 relative to per capita income circa 1990–02 (**ratylye**)

Sources for Table 1 4.2; Center for International Comparisons of Production, Income and Prices, Penn World Tables (Version 7.1), downloaded from website https://pwt.sas.upenn.edu on February 16, 2013; and www.globalinnovationindex.rg/gii downloaded from website on March 6, 2013.

Notes:
A Based on Penn World Table data in international dollars.
B In order of descending values of the gii variable, highest to lowest: Switzerland, Sweden, Singapore, Finland, United Kingdom, Netherlands, Denmark, Hong Kong, Ireland, Luxembourg, United States, Canada, New Zealand, Norway, Germany, Malta, Israel, Iceland, Estonia, Belgium, South Korea, Australia, France, and Japan.
C In order of descending values of the gii variable, highest to lowest: Slovenia, Czech Republic, Cyprus, Spain, Latvia, Hungary, Malaysia, Qatar, China, Portugal, Italy, United Arab Emirates, Lithuania, Chile, Bulgaria, Slovakia, Bahrain, Croatia, Poland, Serbia, and Montenegro.
D In order of descending values of the gii variable, highest to lowest: Saudi Arabia, Mauritius, Moldova, Russia, Romania, Brunei, South Africa, Kuwait, Jordan, Thailand, Brazil, Tunisia, Costa Rica, Lebanon, Macedonia, Ukraine, India, Columbia, Greece, Uruguay, Mongolia, Armenia, Argentina, Georgia, Bosnia/Herzegovina, Namibia, Peru, Turkey, Guyana, Belarus, Mexico, Belize, Trinidad & Tobago, Swaziland, Kazakhstan, Vietnam, Paraguay, Botswana, Dominican Republic, Panama, Morocco, Albania, Azerbaijan, and Jamaica.
E In order of descending values of the gii variable, highest to lowest: El Salvador, Sri Lanka, Philippines, Kenya, Senegal, Ecuador, Guatemala, Indonesia, Egypt, Rwanda, Iran, Nicaragua, Gabon, Kyrgyzstan, Tajikistan, Zambia, Honduras, Mozambique, Uganda, Malawi, Mali, Bolivia, Zimbabwe, Uganda, Mali, Venezuela, Cameron, Burkina Faso, Nigeria, Algeria, Benin, Tanzania, Uzbekistan, Cambodia, Gambia, Pakistan, Syria, Cote d'Ivoire, Angola, Burundi, Togo, Laos, Yemen, Niger and Sudan.

Secularism matters because it generates economic growth, because it is dynamic, because it encourages innovation, because it is friendly towards science. This can be clearly seen in the regressions reported in Table 13.5

Here again standard statistical criteria suggest the results are robust. It is encouraging that a very simple model can generate such a compelling result. To be sure, establishing this does not prove the thesis is true. Still it gives credibility to someone trying to make the case that there is a positive relationship between secularism and innovation.

Table 13.5 Secularism, innovation, and the economic growth rate

Panel A: The Determinants of gii

Dependent variable:	gii	ln(gii)	ln(gii)
Regressors			
Intercept	27.4868	3.3154	0.9899
	(0.8012)	(0.0249)	(0.2613)
Athagn%	0.4026	0.0107	
	(0.0827)	(0.0020)	
ypce	0.0007	$1.6*10^{-5}$	
	(0.0001)	(0.0000)	
ln (Athagn%)			0.0729
			(0.0235)
ln(ypce)			−0.0748
			(0.0309)
R^2	0.6297	0.5983	0.0951
n	137	137	137

Panel B: The determinants of the ratio of per capita income (circa 2008–10) to per capita income (circa 1990–92)

Dependent variable:	ratylye	ln(ratylye)	ln(ratylye)
Regressors			
Intercept	1.6308	0.4286	0.9899
	(0.0729)	(0.0417)	(0.2613)
Athagn%	0.0144	0.0079	
	(0.0070)	(0.0031)	
ypce	$-1.14*10^{-5}$	$-5.82*10^{-6}$	
	(0.0000)	(0.0000)	
ln (Athagn%)			0.0729
			(0.0235)
ln(ypce)			−0.0748
			(0.0309)
R^2	0.0798	0.0735	0.0951
n	137	137	137

Secularism drives innovation (**gii**) and the rate of growth in per capita income (ratylye) ordinary least Squares Regression

Notes
a White's (1980) heteroskedasticity-consistent standard errors appear in parentheses.
b n = sample size.

Fine and well, you might say. But what is the role of science in all this? Using survey data for Europe alone (Turkey is included in the sample as it was applying to enter the European Union at the time the survey was under-taken)—albeit a limitation, since Europe tends to be secular—we can relate attitudes toward, and knowledge of, science to our measures of innovation and secularism. Grouped averages appear in Table 13.6.

The overlap between embracing innovation, secularism, and scientific thinking is apparent from the averages given in the table.

Table 13.6 Innovation, economic growth, and attitudes regarding Evolution

| Secularism and attitudes toward evolution[a] | | | Per capita income circa 2010 (y) and **ratylye** | | | |
athagn%	accev1	accev2	y	ratyle	govlaw	gii
60 <gii						
17.6%	75.5%	22.2%	36,474	1.44	26.5	62.0
50 <gii < 60						
20.7	73.9	16.2	35,384	1.28	26.5	54.6
40 < gii < 50						
12.0	65.6	28.1	24,289	1.51	23.7	44.6
gii < 40						
2.0	35.3	36.6	14,640	1.55	16.7	35.0

Sources: Eurobarometer data for 2005 given in Dawkins (2009: pp. 432–5).

Innovation (**gii**), income growth (**ratylye**) and European attitudes regarding evolution (circa 2005): population weighted averages for groups of european countries

Notes:
a **accev1** defined as the percentage of persons interviewed who answered "true" to the question as to whether human beings as we know them today are developed from an earlier species of animals; **accev2** defined as the percentage of persons interviewed who answered "true" to the question as to whether the earliest humans lived at the same time as the dinosaurs.
b Group consists of Switzerland, Sweden, Finland, the United Kingdom, and the Netherlands (listed in terms of descending values of **gii**).
c Group consists of Denmark, Ireland, Luxembourg, Norway, Germany, Malta, Iceland, Estonia, Belgium, and France (listed in terms of descending values of **gii**).
d Group consists of Slovenia, Czech Republic, Cyprus, Spain, Latvia, Hungary, Portugal, Italy, Lithuania, Bulgaria, Slovakia, Croatia, and Poland (listed in terms of descending values of **gii**).
e Group consists of Romania, Greece, and Turkey (listed in terms of descending values of **gii**).

In sum innovation is tied to secularism and secularism is tied to state policy. Countries that hew to a religious nationalist agenda are less likely to be secular; less likely to be innovative.

The human development index as a measure of secular welfare

To many economists, per capita income is a remarkably misleading, an impoverished, measure of welfare. Many assert it is nothing more than a measure of opulence. Opulence is not welfare. From the account penned in this book it is apparent many humans derive great satisfaction—their hearts consoled in times of tribulation, their spirits healed after personal losses, their dreams emboldened—from religion. If nothing else, religion offers negative freedom: it succors those wounded from inequities endured and personal failures that lay strewn across the walkways of their lives.

The human development index offers a secular equivalent to what religion has traditionally brought to the table. It measures welfare as a weighted sum of an index of per capita income, an index of life expectancy, and an index of educational achievement. The idea is to arrive at a comprehensive measurement of opportunity, including proxies for the freedom to make choices about one's personal future, inclusive of economic and political progress as experienced by a typical individual within a country. Freedom in this sense is positive freedom, an indicator of the capacity to grasp opportunities for advancement.

The human development index can be viewed as an indicator of the standard of living. As well it can be viewed as an input into raising the standard of living. The idea is that a populace generously endowed with human development is well equipped to take advantage of innovations, either generated at home or abroad. Since it is an index of secular welfare it would hardly be surprising to find that religious nationalist states have lower levels of the human development index than liberal nationalist states. This would be a reasonable *a priori* starting point for analysis.

Does religious nationalism diminish the human development index? Does it matter that religious nationalism may limit options that are more abundant in liberal nationalist countries? The approach I take here in addressing this question is to make a stark comparison between religious nationalism and liberal nationalism. To set up this contrast, I have chosen to measure religious nationalism in terms of liberal nationalism. What is the logic behind this approach?

The end of the Cold War ushered in an ideological clash pitting liberal nationalism against religious nationalism

In the post-Cold War period, the deepest ideological chasm is between extreme liberal nationalism—espousing the view that the best government is one guaranteeing freedom of opportunity and belief for its citizenry, restricting its activity to protecting individuals from encroachments on their liberty—and extreme religious nationalism, theocracy. As argued, earlier neither ideal type exists in the real world. What does exist is a spectrum, exemplified in this paper by the variable **LIBRELIN**, ranging from values near 1 (relatively liberal) and values near 0 (relatively religious).

Armed with these definitions, I establish three points: (1) there is a positive association between **LIBRELIN** and the human development index; (2) the association between **LIBRELIN** and the human development index is principally but not exclusively the result of nation–state policies reflecting the ideology of the nation–state. A secondary factor is the standard of living that is shaped by human agency and natural resource endowments; (3) the International cross-sectional associations between secularism and the human development index are best understood in terms of where a country places on the **LIBRELIN** spectrum. However, causation may flow in the other direction as well: from human development to secular orientation. These findings are consistent with the *a priori* assumptions we made.

I have argued that no nation–state is an unblemished example of liberal or religious nationalism. All are hybrids. The reason is simple: heterogeneity within populations. Still, ideology stated in terms of starkly stated principle is important. This is especially true because nation–state propaganda—and even its formal diplomacy—involves choosing ideological friends and criticizing ideological foes. To be sure, propaganda can be a hollow shell. The Cold War illustrates this point. Communism preached an international revolution of the working classes ushering in a marvelous utopian world where states would ultimately be extinguished. In no way did this ideological position deter the Soviet Union or Communist China from pursuing state goals. Indeed, it did not prevent the two communist states from moving toward the brink of all-out war with one another. War between China and Vietnam is a classic example.

To a geopolitical realist, this is not necessarily a bad thing. If one assumes national leaders really make decisions—or at least should make decisions—along the lines of stark military, economic, and power realities alone, denigrating ideological principles, one might say that nation–state branding is irrelevant, and thank goodness for that. The problem with this view is that economic performance—hence the capacity to throw resources into military equipment and personnel—does depend on ideology. Moreover, it is not obvious that ideology is as irrelevant in international diplomacy and the geopolitical machinations of states as coldblooded geopolitical analysis suggests.

In short, while it is important to acknowledge that nation–state ideological branding is imperfect, it is equally important to not dismiss it out of hand. Indeed, the argument of this paper is that in the post-1990 world, adhering to liberal nationalism or religious nationalism matters. In particular, it matters for human development, and hence for long-run economic performance.

In the aftermath of the Cold War, religious nationalism emerged as an increasingly visible form of nationalism opposed to liberal nationalism. That said, the ideological conflict between religious nationalists and their opponents commenced much earlier, during the Cold War itself. The end of the Cold War simply reshaped the identity of some of the opposing parties.

While it is true that the collapse of European Communism refashioned ideological divisions worldwide, the Cold War itself set the stage for the conflict between liberal nationalism and religious nationalism. One reason it did so was because the Cold War promoted the rights revolution in the United States and Western Europe, setting the stage for growing distrust of Western influence in those parts of the world where religious nationalist ideology enjoyed a strong political base.

A second reason it did so during the Cold War was due to deep-seeded political divisions in the developing world. Typical of the divisions was a political contest between adherents to communism or leftist socialism, most

of whom were attracted to materialism and the anti-colonialist ideology
of the Communist bloc—we can call them anti-colonial secularists—and
their opponents, most of whom rejected secularism, embracing religion as
a defining characteristic of idealized national identity. With the collapse
of the Communist bloc, many developing world former Communist Party
adherents jumped from one form of counter-enlightenment nationalism to
its antithesis, namely, religious nationalism. In effect, they were jettisoning
one form of counter-enlightenment nationalism for another form of counter-enlightenment nationalism.[12] Often as not, dictatorial rulers in these
countries, realizing the potential for suppressing political dissent by masking their despotic rule with the trappings of religious rectitude, promoted
religious nationalism as a coherent state-building strategy.

The rights revolution taking place within the world of liberal nationalism certainly played a decisive role. One of the most important consequences of the Cold War was the promotion of the rights revolution
in the United States and Europe. In the ideological tussle between the
United States and the Soviet Union, a common criticism advanced by
the Soviets was for the mistreatment of African-Americans in the United
States. Opposing totalitarian one-party rule in the Communist bloc,
American propaganda claimed the West guaranteed freedom. So why
weren't African-Americans free in the Jim Crow southern states? African-
American leaders like Martin Luther King realized this, shaping his message for civil rights in terms of progress toward greater freedom. Once
the rights revolution got under way for African-Americans, arguments
for women's rights, children's rights, gay rights, and ultimately animal
rights established a strong foothold in the United States. Pinker (2011)
devotes an entire chapter (Chapter 7) to the rights revolution. In it he provides compelling evidence for the United States that a "rights revolution"
swept across the American landscape, especially after 1960. Use of terms
like "civil rights," "women's rights," and "gay rights" gained currency in
publications; hate-crime murders of African-Americans plummeted; disapproval of interracial marriage among whites (98% in 1955) dropped to
around 27% by 1995; rape levels fell along a steep trend line; and assaults
by intimate partners (per 100,000 women) dropped from around 1,000 in
1993 to around 500 in 2005.

Those clinging to the traditional values of the world's major religions—generally but not uniformly patriarchal—did not necessarily view
these trends with equanimity. Indeed, in the United States, where religious
orientation was given a strong fillip by the so-called war against godless
communism, the rights revolution encouraged a strong religious backlash
among so-called fundamentalist Christians. During the 1970s and 1980s,
opposition to abortion—the right to make use of one's body as a woman
chooses being one tenet of the women's rights movement—and gay marriage
was increasingly politicized in the United States. The backlash was hardly
restricted to the United States. Ominously, it became a growing source of

discontent directed against the American push for expansion of rights within the group of countries allied with the United States during the Cold War. To be sure, in Western Europe—committed to the rights revolution partly due to guilt over its horrific record on human rights during World War II—the spinoff of the American rights revolution did not raise hackles. But in the Central Eastern Treaty Organization (CENTO) bloc of United States allies (Iran, Iraq, Pakistan, and Turkey), where religious nationalist sentiment vigorously contended with secularism, the rights revolution—notably the promotion of women's rights—was not welcomed, and was viewed unfavorably by political elites and opponents of secularism.

Without a doubt, resistance to the rights revolution in the West did play a role in fomenting religious nationalism. Still, religious nationalist sentiment was on the rise during the Cold War in two groups of countries for wholly domestic reasons as well.

Ironically, one group consisted of the Communist bloc itself. In Eastern Europe and the Soviet Union, opponents of totalitarianism often flocked to the churches. As De George and Scanlan (1974) and Ramet (1989) point out, the churches were officially tolerated but bureaucratically controlled by communist regimes ostensibly committed to Marxist-inspired atheism. Indeed, they offered a model for national identification alternative to communist-defined nationalism in countries like Czechoslovakia, Hungary, Poland, Romania, and the Soviet Union. Indeed, Stalin himself encouraged allegiance to the Russian Orthodox Church during World War II, due to the church's nationalistic appeal.

A second group consisted of non-communist countries that were not committed to liberal nationalism. A substantial number of these countries were governed by secular personality cults backed up by the military. This was because nation–state building during the Cold War was strongly influenced by the retreat of European and Japanese imperialism after 1945 leaving a power vacuum that charismatic military figures could exploit. To be sure, depending on the colony involved, colonizing governments left a legacy that newly independent nation–states could draw upon: notably, legal systems and physical infrastructure. Typically, the secular liberal nationalist model was promoted by the colonizer as an ideal type. Rejecting this form of government were two types of resistance movements: one revolutionary, the other religious.

With the collapse of colonialism, it was not unusual for the secularists, exploiting the operational advantages of well-disciplined revolutionary parties or military cliques, to seize power. Finding the rhetoric of, or the financial largess offered by, the Soviet Union persuasive, they often leaned toward communism. After all, building on Lenin's theory of imperialism as the highest stage of capitalism, the Soviet Union formulated its foreign policy in Africa, Southeast Asia, and the Middle East around an anti-colonialist theme. As a result, strongly anti-religious but also deeply anti-liberal movements sprang up in many of the freshly minted nation–states freed of colonial interference. Resisting these movements were religious nationalists who viewed with trepidation attempts by communist-leaning secular elites to suppress religion. In the typical case, religious nationalists rejected all forms of secular rule: liberal and Marxist–Leninist single party versions alike.

Given this background, it is not surprising that the collapse of the Soviet Union and the sweeping away of communist regimes in Eastern Europe ushered in a global wave of religious nationalism. The Soviet Union dissolved and Soviet communism repudiated and dismantled, Eastern Europe liberated from on-going Russian military threats, and Germany reunified, thus strengthening Western Europe: all of this set the stage for a resurgence of religion in Eastern Europe and Russia. Particularly in former regions of the Soviet Union heavily populated with Muslims, religious nationalism flourished. As well, Catholic Poland emerged as a bulwark of Christian nationalism in Central Europe. As communist insurgencies in Southeast Asia and the Middle East lost steam, advocates of religious nationalism became increasingly emboldened, bolstering religion as a vehicle for national unification across the Eurasian land mass from the shores of Thailand to the borders of Germany.

To some scholars, this state of affairs has thrown open the gates to a new Cold War, a global battle between liberal nationalism and religious nationalism.[13] To other scholars, the resurgence of religion in the public sphere called into question the validity of the secularization hypothesis, the sociological theory that links economic and political modernization to secular thinking and a falloff in performance of religious ritual including church attendance. That the public sphere—political and economic affairs in particular—has been increasingly informed by religious argument goes hand in hand with the fact that the world appears to be becoming increasingly religious, a conclusion that can be culled from comparing figures on religious affiliation for 1970 with those for 2010. Has secularization been reversed? Is the entire issue of the meaning of secularization leaving the realm of sociological theory and moving increasingly into the field of political economy? How important is the revival of religious fervor and religious state branding for economic development?

Measuring religious nationalism in terms of liberal nationalism

To probe statistically the question of how religious nationalism has impacted economic development, we need to come up with a metric for religious nationalism. It turns out this is most easily accomplished by calibrating religious nationalism as the degree of deviation away from liberal nationalism.

While the index of liberal nationalism—**LIBRELIN**—is imperfect, it does capture characteristics that can be employed in constructing proxies useful for measuring the range of nation–state branding. These proxies serve as indicators of how liberal a state appears to be, or, the flipside, how religious of a state it is.

In constructing the indices I use here, I assume that protecting freedom is inseparable from guaranteeing rule of law, transparency, and administrative efficiency, and that the capacity to realize nation–state building through infrastructure investment matters.

The **LIBRELIN** variable is constructed as follows. There are two components both normalized to one, averaged together yielding a range for **LIBRELIN** running between 0 and 1. That is:

(13.1) **LIBRELIN** = ½ (SECIN) + ½ (GOVLAW).

The first component, **SECIN**, captures secular orientation in government. Using data from the Association of Religion Data Archives (2013, 2014), **SECIN** is calculated from four measures of secular orientation:

(13.2) **SECIN** = ¼ (FRS) + ¼ (LAWR) + ¼ (FEXB) + ¼ (CONFR)

Where[14]

FRS = Freedom of expression of beliefs (normalized to one); **LAWR** = is the legal system largely based on religious law (normalized to one); **FEXB** = a measure of freedom of expression of beliefs (normalized to one); and **CONFR** = does the constitution and/or the legal system guarantee freedom of religion?

The second component of **LIBRELIN** captures government efficiency and rule of law. Its acronym is **GOVLAW**. **GOVLAW** is computed as follows[15]:

(13.3) **GOVLAW** = ½ (GOVFUN) + ½ (LAW)

where **GOVFUN** = indicator of the quality of government functioning; and **LAW** = indicator of the rule of law. As with the measure **SECIN** the underlying data is from the Association of Religion Data Archives (2013, 2014).

In the tabulations relating **LIBRELIN** to the human development index, I prefer using the non-income human development index value (**HDIny**), not the standard human development index (**HDI**). In tabulations involving the overall human development index, I use an adjusted version of the **LIBRELIN**, namely:[16]

(13.4) **LIBRELINAD** = 2/3 (LIBRELIN) + 1/3 (ENGIN)

where **ENGIN** = index of per capita efficiency adjusted energy consumption. The idea is to adjust a nation–state's level of **LIBRELIN** by the capacity of the country to secure energy resources. I am assuming much of this energy is used to fuel infrastructure construction and the flow of transport, communication, and educational services utilizing the infrastructure.

Human development in liberal nationalist states trumps human development in religious nationalist states

Our principal task in this section is to document an association between the liberal-religious index **LIBRELIN** and the non-income human development index **HDIny**; and, further, to extend the analysis to the relationship between the adjusted liberal-religious index **LIBRELINAD** and the human development index (**HDI**). Establishing causation—as opposed to association—is another matter altogether. While I eschew a formal attempt to capture cause and effect, my approach does provide evidence suggesting causation runs from the nature of nationalism to the level of the human development index. My main focus is on the cross-section for the year 2010; the values for all variables involved are for 2010 or thereabouts. Reference to trends leading up to the year 2010 is made occasionally.

Cross-tabulations appear in Tables 13.7.

Several points jump out from perusal of the figures. There is a positive relationship between **LIBRELIN** and both the **HDI** and the **HDIny** (the relationship between the liberal-religious nationalism index and the non-income human development index does not appear to be a strong as the association between the energy adjusted **LIBRELIN** and the **HDI**). In short, command over material resources—for instance, per capita income—matters. Still, as a group, countries enjoying the highest level of **LIBRELIN** (**LIBRELIN** greater than or equal to .9) enjoy higher ranking for the **HDI** than they do for gross national income (**GNI**). Indeed, this group is the only group enjoying this characteristic. One possible reason why this is the case is the positive relationship between **LIBRELIN** and the percentage of the population satisfied with their freedom of choice (**SAT**) observed in the cross-tabulations. In the group of countries with the lowest levels of **LIBRELIN**, levels of **SAT** are low, as are levels of safety (**SAFE**).

According to standard liberal reasoning, freedom of choice in establishing a career, managing a business, and exercising voice in the public sphere matter for shaping the level of output per worker. People work harder when they find their employment gratifying as well as remunerative. Forcing individuals into jobs they despise is not conducive to encouraging diligence, responsibility, and dedication to duty. The results concerning **SAT** suggest this view is valid.

As well, feeling safe is important. If an individual fears being robbed, violated sexually, arrested without recourse to due legal process, he or she is likely to avoid taking risks, a key element fostering innovation.

The importance of nation–state branding for human development is corroborated by Figures 13.1 and 13.2. Especially convincing is the tight scatter diagram fit captured in Figure 13.2.

Religious nationalism and technological capitalism 181

Table 13.7 Liberal nationalism, religious nationalism, and the human development index (A)

Panel A: LIBRELIN Variables, Circa 2010[a]

Range for LIBRELIN	LIBRELIN	Adjusted LIBRELIN	Energy per capita (ENGpc)	% Muslim
LIBRELIN > .9 [b]	.932	.786	5382.6	2.3%
.9 > LIBRELIN > .7[c]	.721	.511	996.1	10.9
.7 > LIBRELIN > .5[d]	.577	.415	971.2	37.5
.5 > LIBRELIN > .3[e]	.369	.303	1838.0	18.4
.3 > LIBRELIN [f]	.182	.163	1368.9	82.6

Part B: Human development index (HDI) variables, circa 2010)[g]

Range for LIBRELIN	HDI	HDIny	HDI Rank– GNI Rank	SAT	SAFE
LIBRELIN > .9[b]	.888	.913	+7.1	85.3%	71.7%
.9> LIBRELIN > .7[c]	.580	.612	-3.6	77.4	62.5
.7 > LIBRELIN > .5[d]	.593	.639	-2.5	77.5	57.7
.5 > LIBRELIN > .3[e]	.642	.688	-2.6	71.4	72.4
.3 > LIBRELIN [f]	.545	.578	-3.9	47.8	54.7

Population weighted averages of human development measures classified by the liberal-religious nationalism index (LIBRELIN), values of LIBRELIN near 1 indicating strong adherence to liberal nationalism and values under .3 indicating strong adherence to religious nationalism.

Sources: Association of Religion Data Archives (2013, 2014), United Nations Development Programme (2010, 2013) and World Bank (2014).

Notes:
a LIBRELIN is calculated by weighting together with equal weights of ½ an index of secular values and an index of government effectiveness/rule of law combined. See text for discussion. The adjusted value of LIBRELIN is computed by adding together the LIBRELIN (weighted two-thirds) to an index of energy per capita (based on the figures for energy per capita measured in kilograms of oil equivalents per capita net of imports and exports), ENGIN.
b This group consists of 16 countries: listed in descending values of LIBRELIN they are Norway, Sweden, Estonia, Ireland, Austria, Chile, the United States, Portugal, Australia, Denmark, Spain, Canada, France, Germany, Belgium, and Japan.
c This group consists of 19 countries: listed in descending values of LIBERLIN they are Lithuania, Italy, Botswana, Mongolia, Slovakia, South Africa, Namibia, Latvia, Hungary, Israel, Senegal, Romania, Bulgaria, Brazil, Greece, Argentina, Ukraine, Peru, and India.
d This group consists of 19 countries: listed in descending values of LIBRELIN they are Ecuador, Mexico, Macedonia, Philippines, Turkey, Nicaragua, Columbia, Kenya, Guatemala, Moldova, Georgia, Tanzania, Thailand, Nigeria, Nepal, Venezuela, Kyrgyzstan, Armenia, and Indonesia.
e This group consists of 18 countries: listed in descending values of LIBRELIN they are Russia, Malaysia, Kuwait, Sri Lanka, Jordan, Azerbaijan, Morocco, Kazakhstan, Cameroon, Tajikistan, Vietnam, Bangladesh, Algeria, Bahrain, Belarus, Zimbabwe, and Egypt.
f This group consists of nine countries: listed in descending values of LIBRELIN they are Tunisia, Turkmenistan, Uzbekistan, Syria, Sudan, Pakistan, Iran, Burma (Myanmar), and Saudi Arabia.
g The HDIny is the non-income HDI; SAT is the percentage of the people during the period 2007-2011 satisfied with their freedom of choice; and SAFE is the percentage of the population reporting that they feel safe. For some of the countries, notably those likely to have low percentages SAT and SAFE, estimates for SAT and SAFE are not available.

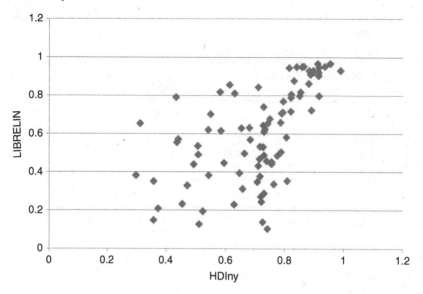

Figure 13.1 Non-income HDI (HDIny) and liberal-religious nationalism index (LIBRELIN).

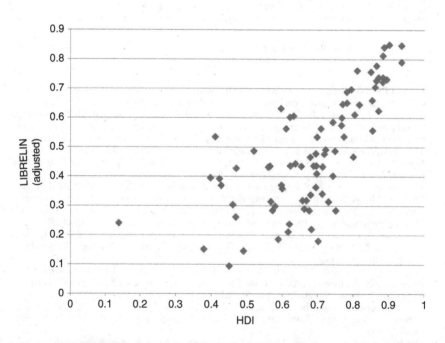

Figure 13.2 HDI and adjusted liberal-religious nationalism index [LIBRELIN (adjusted)].

In this figure, values for the adjusted liberal-religious nationalism index are plotted against values for the overall human development index (not just the non-income human development index). Recall the view of successful nation–state building I espouse makes actually implementing a nationalism agenda through infrastructure essential.

Within the literature on religious nationalism, much attention has been devoted to Islam. It is often argued that adherence to Islamic beliefs in government raises conceptual problems with the promoting human rights, even where *sharia* is not the law of the land, even where Salafist-jihadists are not strongly entrenched. The tabulations in Table 13.7 do suggest that the percentage Muslim is unusually high in the group where **LIBRELIN** is the lowest. Does this mean that human development is unusually low in predominantly Muslim countries? No. As can be seen from Table 13.8, countries with the lowest level of non-income human development are not predominantly Muslim.

Nor can it be said that predominantly Muslim countries eschew democracy. According to recent tabulations made by Freedom House, there are 117 democracies in the world as of the year 2012, up dramatically from 1990 when communism collapsed (there were 69 democracies at that time). Of these, a substantial number exist in the Muslim world. As can be seen from Table 13.9, Turkey, Indonesia, Malaysia, Kuwait, Morocco, Tunisia, and Syria are all classified as democracies.

That said, what is true is that democracy in Islamic countries is not high-quality democracy (at least as measured by Freedom House). This leads to an important point: being a democracy is not equivalent to adhering to liberal nationalism. Democracy is majority rule exercised through elections. Liberal nationalism is about protecting individual rights, including the rights of minority groups. The agendas differ. Majorities can trample upon individual liberty; majorities can make a mockery of minority group rights. One does not have to cite conditions in Tehran or Cairo to make this case. Consider Germany in 1933, the year Adolf Hitler became Reich Chancellor on the heels of a strong vote for the Nazi party. Or, again, recall how the United States prior to the passage of the thirteenth, fourteenth, and fifteenth amendments to the Constitution trampled on the rights of slaves, and later on former slaves in the American south, during the heyday of Jim Crow.

What does appear to be true of human development in predominantly Muslim countries is the following: at any given level of per capita income, human development is lower in Muslim countries than it is in countries adhering more closely to liberal nationalist values. This conclusion can be inferred from Table 13.7 (the group with the lowest level of **LIBRELIN** has the largest negative gap between the rank of the **HDI** and the rank of the **GNI**). Table 13.10 provides corroborating evidence: it shows that South Korea was able to achieve a far higher level of human development than predominantly Muslim countries enjoying far higher levels of per capita income than South Korea did prior to the year 2000.

Table 13.8 Liberal nationalism, religious nationalism, and the human development
index (B)

Panel A: LIBRELIN Variables, Circa 2010

Range for HDIny	LIBRELIN	Adjusted LIBRELIN	ENGpc	% Muslim
HDIny> .9[b]	.930	.789	5516.3	2.5%
.9 > HDIny> .8[c]	.824	.627	2552.3	2.1
.8 > HDIny> .7[d]	.434	.351	2006.5	11.7
.7 > HDIny> .6[e]	.476	.349	1035.2	61.8
.6 > HDIny> .5[f]	.595	.415	598.7	30.1
.5 > HDIny[g]	.496	.348	576.6	45.6

Panel B: Human development indices, circa 2010

Range for HDIny	HDI	HDIny	HDI Rank–GNI Rank	SAT	SAFE
HDIny > .9[b]	.893	.917	+7.5	88.3%	75.0%
.9 > HDIny > .8[c]	.811	.849	+6.3	71.2	58.4
.8 > HDIny > .7[d]	.679	.722	−2.3	74.5	67.0
.7 > HDIny > .6[e]	.614	.662	−4.3	80.8	82.7
.6 > HDIny > .5[f]	.510	.546	−3.4	79.1	72.7
.5 > HDIny[g]	.403	.432	−10.6	58.5	51.4

Population weighted averages for human development related variables and the liberal-religious
nationalism index (**LIBRELIN**) classified by values of the non-income human development
index (**HDIny**), values near 1 indicating high human development and values under .5 indicating
low human development [a]

Sources: See sources for Table 13.7.

Notes:
a For definition of variables see Notes to Table 13.7.
b This group consists of 11 countries: listed in descending values of **HDIny**, they are Australia,
   Norway, Ireland, the United States, Israel, Germany, Japan, Canada, Sweden, France and
   Spain.
c This group consists of 17 countries: listed in descending values of **HDIny**, they are Greece,
   Belgium, Denmark, Italy, Estonia, Austria, Slovakia, Hungary, Chile, Lithuania, Latvia,
   Argentina, Romania, Portugal, Bahrain, Georgia, and Bulgaria.
d This group consists of 29 countries: listed in descending order of **HDIny**, they are Ukraine,
   Peru, Armenia, Mexico, Malaysia, Belarus, Azerbaijan, Kazakhstan, Jordan, Ecuador,
   Macedonia, Saudi Arabia, Sri Lanka, Columbia, Moldova, Russia, Tunisia, Brazil,
   Kyrgyzstan, Philippines, Iran, Uzbekistan, Turkmenistan, Algeria, Venezuela, Kuwait,
   Mongolia, Tajikistan, and China.
e This group consists of nine countries: listed in descending order of **HDIny**, they are Thailand,
   Turkey, Indonesia, Egypt, Nicaragua, Vietnam, Syria, and Botswana.
f This group consists of nine countries: listed in descending order of **HDIny**, they are Morocco,
   Guatemala, South Africa, India, Bangladesh, Kenya, Pakistan, Burma (Myanmar), and
   Nepal.
g This group consists of six countries: listed in descending order of **HDIny**, they are Cameroon,
   Zimbabwe, Tanzania, Nigeria, Senegal, and Sudan.

Table 13.9 Liberal nationalism is not identical to democracy

Range of LIBRELIN	HDIny	LIBRELIN	DEMIN
LIBRELIN > .9 [a]	.915	.931	78.3
.9 > LIBRELIN > .8 [b]	.764	.835	63.9
.8 > LIBRELIN > .7 [c]	.598	.710	52.8
.7 > LIBRELIN > .6 [d]	.698	.642	53.1
.6 > LIBRELIN > .5 [e]	.585	.531	46.3
.5 > LIBRELIN [f]	.705	.362	37.7

Liberal nationalism is not democracy; but liberal nationalism is correlated with the quality of democracy (the Democracy Index): population weighted averages for **HDIny** and the Democracy Index (**DEMIN**) classified by levels of the LIBRELIN Variable, 2010

Sources: Global democracy ranking (2014) and sources for Table 13.7.

Notes:
a In descending order of **HDIny**, the countries in this group are: Norway, Sweden, Estonia, Ireland, Austria, the United States, Portugal, Australia, Denmark, Spain, Canada, France, Germany, Belgium, and Japan.
b In descending order of **HDIny**, the countries in this group are: Lithuania, Italy, Botswana, Mongolia, Slovakia, South Africa, Namibia, Latvia, Hungary, and Israel.
c In descending order of **HDIny**, the countries in this group are: Senegal, Romania, Bulgaria, Brazil, Greece, Argentina, Ukraine, Peru, and India.
d In descending order of **HDIny**, the countries in this group are: Ecuador, Mexico, Macedonia, Mali, Philippines, Turkey, Nicaragua, Columbia, Kenya, Guatemala, and Moldova.
e In descending order of **HDIny**, the countries in this group are: Georgia, Tanzania, Thailand, Nigeria, Nepal, Venezuela, Armenia, and Indonesia.
f In descending order of **HDIny**, the countries in this group are: Russia, Malaysia, Kuwait, Sri Lanka, Morocco, China, Egypt, Tunisia, and Syria.

Table 13.10 also suggests two additional points: in some Muslim countries, human development is quite high (notably Bahrain) despite a relatively poor level of defending human rights (suggesting a high level of human development does not guarantee secularism); and human development has been improving in many countries throughout the Muslim world, notably Iran, which has is a hybrid theocracy–democracy.

Does that mean one should be optimistic about human development in the world of religious nationalism? No. Comparison with the South Korean record is a warning that improving human development should never be neglected by nationalists aspiring to successful long-run growth in national per capita income. The Table 13.10 figures—admittedly scanty—imply there is an upper limit to human development in countries under the grasp of religious-nationalism. Using that logic, one can infer that the long-run fate of the oil-producing Persian Gulf region may be dire, especially if the terms of trade it currently enjoys turn sharply against it. After all, international prices for petroleum could well plummet as non-petroleum energy sources gain market share in the coming decades.[17]

The cross-sectional associations we have explored imply religious nationalism diminishes—and liberal nationalism promotes—human development. To be sure, establishing associations is not tantamount to demonstrating

Table 13.10 Per capita income in South Korea and in five Muslim countries

Country	Income per capita[a]			Human development index			LIBRELIN
	1990	2000	2010	Non-Income HDI	HDI	HDI growth rate[b]	
Bahrain	17,909	20,783	23,101	.809	.801	0.72%	.354
Iran	5,810	7,355	9,432	.702	.721	1.35	.138
Kuwait	22,695	37,232	41,240	.771	.714	n.e.	.469
Saudi Arabia	15,515	17,030	20,189	.752	.742	0.96	.103
South Korea	11,643	18,729	26,609	.918	.877	0.95	n.e.

Real income per capita in purchasing power parity adjusted 2005 international dollars and the human development index for five predominantly Muslim countries and South Korea, 1990–2010

Sources: Heston, Summers, and Aten (2012) and sources for Table 13.7.

Notes:
a Based on a chained index.
b Annual compounded growth rate for the HDI between 1990 and 2010.
   n.e. not estimated.

causation: the observed relationship between **LIBRELIN** and human development could be the result of human development promoting liberal values. Not the reverse. Along these lines, assume liberal nationalism is basically secularism, relatively anemic attachment to religion. Human development being substantial, human flourishing—meeting material needs—is enhanced; insecurity stemming from compromised medical services, famine and starvation, extreme poverty, and malnutrition is banished. In the terminology of Norris and Inglehart (2004) where there is "existential security," the demand for religious intervention is muted. Pursuing this logic, Norris and Inglehart (2004: pg. 60 ff) regress "aggregate-level strength of participation in services of religious worship" against a variety of development variables, including the **HDI** and the Gini coefficient measuring the degree of income inequality.[18] Their study finds that almost 50% of the variance in the dependent variable—a proxy for secularism—is explained by two variables, the human development index and the Gini coefficient.

In short, should the human development index be treated as an independent or dependent variable in regression analysis?

In my opinion, the strongest causation runs from norms captured in nation–state branding to human development and material outcomes, not the reverse. For instance, in most major oil-producing states of the Muslim world, per capita incomes are substantial—in principle there is no major "existential security" problem. But human development is truncated. Moreover, human development changes relatively slowly—over generations, really, as older individuals, generally less educated than their younger colleagues, die off—but regime change can be rapid. Witness Iran, where an Islamic revolution ousted the Shah, or Afghanistan, where a communist government gave way to an Islamic state.[19] When religious nationalism gains ascendency, religious participation soars—not necessarily because citizens become more religious in their deeply held personal values, but simply because political pressure is applied root and branch throughout the society. Outspoken dissidents—atheists and agnostics—may be sent to prison. Ignoring religion in both public and private spheres becomes dangerous. The fact that religious nationalism is unlikely to take hold in the bloc of liberal nationalist countries means religiosity is a matter of personal choice, not a concomitant of public coercion. In this bloc of countries where human development is high, hence per capita substantial, religiosity may be either muted or magnified depending on the situation (low in Western Europe but high in the United States).

However, if causation does run both ways—from human development to religiosity and from religiosity to human development—falling into a religion trap is a real possibility. In long-run international equilibrium one could have a liberal nationalist group enjoying substantial human development facing off against an entrenched religious nationalist group in which low to moderate human development prevails. There are other reasons for thinking a modern religious trap is a possibility. These reasons revolve around civil war, a topic to which we now turn.

Notes

1 See *inter alia* Barro (2005), Barro and McCleary (2003), Breyer (1994), Iannaccone (1991), and Fox (2008).
2 For the measurement of per capita income expressed in 1990 international Geary-Khamis dollars, see Mosk (2013).
3 See Temin (2013).
4 For a particularly clear discussion of the problem see Coyne (2015). Coyne's chief agenda is combating "accommodationalism," by which he means arguing that scientific investigation through rigorous argument and experiment and religious faith are fully consistent with one another. "Accomodationalist" reasoning has been defended by some scientists and philosophers alike, for instance, by Gould (2003) on the scientific side and by Plantinga (2011) in philosophy.
5 This definition is mine, mine alone. Other definitions have been advanced. Indeed, the literature on "secularism" is huge. See, for example, Calhoun, Jeurgensmeyer, and Van Antwerpen (2011), Casanova (2009), Joas and Wiegandt (2009), Mandieta and Vanantwerpen (2011), Norris and Inglehart (2004), Taylor (2007), and Warner, Vanantwerpen, and Calhoun (2010).
6 See Riley (2013).
7 On the weakness of African states, see Migdal (1988).
8 On the Frankfurt School, see Connerton (1980), Friedman (1981), Habermas (2002, 2012), and Tar (1977). The Frankfurt School attempted to forge an amalgam of Freudian-inspired psychoanalysis with Marxism. As a result, writers associated with the Frankfurt School tend to be skeptical about the value of religion, or at least about the appropriateness of religious argumentation in the public sphere, including the fashioning of laws. Both Marxism and Freudian psychology are pessimistic about the long-run viability of religion, seeing it as something

that will ultimately be transcended through progress, and in the case of Freud's theoretical framework by arising above neurotic fears. For Freud's hostility to religion—fueled by his belief that religion was akin to a primitive neurosis that would eventually wither away as civilization advanced—see Freud (1946, 1973).

9 I take the values of **GIR** from Fox (2008) which provides a global set of values. For countries where Fox characterizes a nation-state's attitude as hostile to religion—as is the case with China, Cuba, France, and North Korea for instance—I multiply the **GIR** value Fox obtains by minus 1. In this way, the range of values varies between high positive values (for Saudi Arabia) to low negative values (as in the case of China). For other global studies of religion, see Bellah (1965, 1970), Breyer (1994), and Merriman (2009).

10 I am indebted to David Giles, who carried out the regressions reported in this table and in Table 13.5. I must confess to being somewhat suspicious of claims made by practitioners of conventional classical econometrics, with its emphasis on accepting or rejecting hypotheses based on statistical significance. I am convinced by arguments stressing the fact that statistically significant regression results do not necessarily prove anything, that economic significance is different from statistical significance. As well, I share the view of some Bayesian statisticians that in the long-run empirical knowledge is gained through a *de facto* Bayesian process, results obtained by a scholar only making sense in the context of the already existing literature. For instance, my results in this paper differ from those secured by Barro and McCleary (2003); I do not find that being religious promotes economic growth. However, it is worth admitting I am testing my framework using data on "negative religiosity." By contrast, the Barro and McCleary analysis is based on data and proxies for "religiosity." To a Bayesian, the fact that the results differ suggests setting up a more complex statistical framework—not attempted here—for running a simultaneous "horse race" between the two views.

11 China under the cult of Mao was a different matter altogether. On the transition from Maoist utopian communism to market socialism in the post-1978 period, see Mosk (2011).

12 See Buzalka (2006), Michel (1988), Ramet (1989), and Van der Veer and Lehmann (1999).

13 See Jeurgensmeyer (1993, 2003, 2008).

14 In the data source for **FRS**, a low score indicates freedom and a high score lack of freedom (the scores range from 0 to 7). I subtracted the numbers given from 7, then normalized the resulting scores to a range running from 0 to 1; for **LAWR**, I assigned a value of 1 if no laws are religious, .9 if some laws are religious, .1 if most laws are religious, and 0 if all laws are religious; for **FEXB** I took the original scores ranging from 0 to 16, normalizing them to a range running from 0 to 1; and for **CONFR** I assigned a value of 1 if the constitution or the legal system guaranteed freedom of religion, 0 otherwise.

15 In the original data source, the values for **GOVFUN** run from 0 to 12 and the values for **LAW** run from 0 to 16. I normalized the values to one in making my estimates of **GOVLAW**.

16 The data on per capita energy consumption adjusted for imports and exports is taken from the World Bank (2014). The source figures are in kilograms of oil equivalent. To convert these to an index I took the highest value of energy consumption per capita for the group of countries I examine in this study—for Kuwait—adjusting it by multiplying the value for Kuwait (10893) by the efficiency with which Kuwait converts this energy to income (.39833). This provided the upper level for the index that was normalized to run from 0 to 1, where 1 is the value for Kuwait.

17 Bahrain is a country those most optimistic about the prospects of human development in the Islamic world often point to. It boasts the first major "post-oil" economy in the Persian Gulf. But it is small—consisting of an archipelago of 33 islands—with a populace of only 1.2 million persons. It is increasingly becoming a major financial hub for the Muslim world, making strides in Islamic banking. Its record on human rights is abysmal. Whether it can remain politically stable in the future is a major concern, as the ruling family is Sunni and the bulk of the populace Shi'a.

   While this book takes the position that religious nationalism is a general problem, hardly limited to the Islamic world, it is worth mentioning that there is a literature emphasizing legal or religious barriers preventing Muslim societies from developing modern commerce, from taking full advantage of opportunities in globally viable investment. For instance, see the discussion in Diner (2009) and Kuran (2011), tracing these problems back to the practices put into place during the Golden Age of Islam (from the seventeenth through the thirteenth centuries).

   For a contrary view arguing that intellectual elites in Islamic countries were prepared to embrace Western Enlightenment principles during the late-nineteenth and early-twentieth century, only to see their ideas pushed aside, marginalized, by Islamic nationalists, see Elshakry (2013) and Moaddel (2005).

18 The cross-sectional regressions they run are for date collected over the period from 1981 to 2001.

19 Beyer (1994: pp. 166 ff) attributes the overthrow of the Shah of Iran and the instituting of a theocratic state to the strength of the Islamic clergy in the lives of most Iranians at the local level. The Shah's attempts to weaken the hold of the clergy over the populace by promoting secular education and controlling the theological faculties in both seminaries and secular universities ran into opposition at the local level. It was not particularly successful.

14 Religious civil war and the religion trap

Religion traps

In Chapter 4, I argued that the Hasmonean Jewish state fell into a religion trap. Civil war broke out, leading to root and branch takeover by Roman armies. Judaism itself survived, but only as a religion flourishing in Diaspora communities. It is only in the twentieth century that Jews have managed to carve out a state in the Holy Land, Israel. The modern state is in no way akin to the ancient state. For one thing, it is a democracy committed to the pendulum swing informing liberal nationalism. To be sure, there are extremist sub-communities in Israel committed to violent solutions, to assassination, to terrorism. However, the existence of violent extremists in populations adhering to the political pendulum swing through regular election cycles occurs in most, if not all, liberal nationalist states.

That said, religious terrorism is not an impediment to economic advance in liberal nationalist states. To be sure, combating it is costly. Maintaining security comes with a price tag, including surrendering some rights to privacy, a fact I personally find deplorable. Liberalism has suffered as a result. However, none of the liberal nationalist states have fallen into religious traps like that which left the Jewish state of the ancient world in dismal ruins.

However, religious traps do exist in the post-Cold War world. Unfortunately, these traps have impeded economic advance among many low income per capita states struggling with impediments to economic development. In turn, these religiously driven crises have spawned massive outflows of refugees, attempting to escape their lot in rapidly deteriorating military conditions, seeking safer havens in the world of liberal nationalist states. Most of these refugees are fleeing religious nationalist states. Why?

The argument is simple. It consists of four steps:

Step one: Religious nationalism empowers those who speak for God, the guardians of the Truth. Garnering a monopoly over public discourse concerning laws and policies—enjoying virtual immunity from dissent, wielding the weapon of slander, branding one's critics heretics—the guardians of public virtue aggrandize power. Power corrupts. Despite its claim to channel virtue, the rulers of religious nationalistic states encourage naked plunder by opportunists lurking in their inner circles.

Step two: The corruption of rulers and their opportunistic lackeys and henchmen in religious nationalist states undermines their credibility among the largely disenfranchised true-believers of the faith. In turn, true believers gather together—often in secrecy—spearheading religious reform movements aimed at purifying the rituals, ideologies, and social norms of the faith. To purify their religious practices, they turn to the distant past, to the texts and oral traditions of the founders of their faith. In so doing, they turn their back on ideas and norms emerging in generations subsequent to that of the founders. Embracing militant revivalism, their movement ultimately walks a knife-edge between dissent and outright dissidence.

Step three: Conflict between the official guardians of the Truth and the dissidents tears apart the social fabric. In the worst cases it spawns civil war, destroying infrastructure, squashing national unity, dismantling government institutions, destroying trust. Economic development languishes.

Step four: Revivalism feasts off economic failure. Knowing one is one of the blessed, secure in one's knowledge of Truth (in some religions enjoying a guarantee of an afterlife in Paradise) offers comfort for the starved, oppressed, outcast masses. The hold of religion over the populace is strengthened. Getting the state to better represent the tenets of its faith becomes more—not less—attractive. The religious trap slams shut.

An important corollary of this analysis is democracy is unlikely to change outcomes. Democracy is not equivalent to human rights. Democracy is majority rule. If the majority is committed to a particular faith—and in states where religious nationalism prevails, this is inevitably the case, if for no other reason than repression of anti-religious expression by the state—elections will strengthen, not weaken the credibility of religious nationalist ideology. Reformist religious parties contesting any one particular menu of religious nationalistic policies put in place by the government through elections may well change the complexion of policy making. But it will not move the government into the liberal nationalist camp.

To make the case that religious traps do exist and have retarded economic advance in the developing world, I proceed as follows. Armed with the distinction between liberal nationalist and religious nationalist states, I demonstrate liberal nationalist states are relatively free of corruption while religious nationalist states tend to be corrupt. Next, I demonstrate that revivalism is characteristic of post-Cold War religion, that it has grown rapidly in regions, most of which have failed to grow rapidly in terms of per capita income, and it has deepened social fissures there. Examples are drawn from Africa, where the spread of Pentecostal Christianity is especially dramatic; the Middle East, where adherence to Salafist Islam has jumped by leaps and bounds; and India, where Hindu Nationalism has gone hand-in-hand with the promotion of the Hindutva ideology. I go on to show that social fissures unleashed by religious nationalism have caused deep seated political conflicts and civil wars resulting in humanitarian refugee crises.

Corruption in religious nationalist states

One of the themes of this book is the overlap between corruption and religious gift exchange.

Employing the index **LIBRELIN,** we can verify that corruption accompanies religious nationalism. As an indicator of corruption, we use the **cpi**—the corruption perceptions index—constructed by Transparency International (2014). The index measures perception of public sector corruption. To be sure, this index does not capture all the corruption rampant in a country. Still, we can be fairly confident if officials are on the take, then so are private citizens.

Figure 14.1 provides graphical evidence. While I would be the last to deny that beauty is in the eye of the beholder, I feel fairly confident in concluding that corruption and religious nationalism go hand in hand.

Corruption is hardly the only problem that assertion of divine authority by the state engenders. Organize education around studying and memorizing the Vedas, or the Qur'an; or the Torah and the Talmud; or the New Testament; or the Analects of Confucius. Ignore those achievements in natural philosophy and science spawning technological capitalism. Make certain schoolchildren do not know about Newton's theory of gravitation; in your textbooks, disparage Maxwell's equations for electricity and magnetism; instruct your professors to ignore the laws of entropy; follow Nazi science

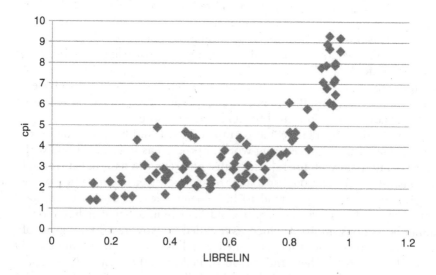

Figure 14.1 The public sector corruption perceptions index (cpi) and the liberal-religious nationalism index (LIBRELIN).

Note: Values for the LIBRELIN variable lie between 0 and 1, those close to 0 indicating strong adherence to religious nationalism, those near 1 corresponding to strong commitment to liberal nationalism. The cpi varies between 0 and 10, values close to 0 indicating corruption in public service is endemic, values close to 1 indicating relatively honest public service.

in dispensing with Einstein's "Jewish" special and general theory of relativity; ignore Schrodinger's wave equation; reject the theory of the Big Bang; claim that Darwin's theory of natural selection had no evidence supporting it; argue Mendel inspired genetics is too materialistic; and so forth. Ignore the notion of progress in scientific endeavor, older theories giving way to newer theories, debate and critical theory driving forward knowledge. Shut yourself off. Draw comfort from closure. Be complacent. Fall behind other countries in innovation and creativity. Reject technological capitalism, repudiating the notion of rational discourse and acceptance of the pendulum swing. Dedicate yourself to the miraculous, to faith healing, to Christian Science teachings suspicious of mainstream Western medicine, or to personal purification through violence, hitching your fate to jihadist holy war and suicide bombing martyrdom.

The cold, hard fact is rote learning and unquestioning obedience to dogma breeds more than complacency. Black and white thinking puts a premium on conflict, eschewing political consensus building. It is the path to internecine conflict. It does not respect the pendulum swing in ideas, political decision making, and technological innovation.

Cycles of religious revival purifications divide communities

Proceed back to the supposed practices of the Apostles as related in the New Testament; back to the Qur'an, the *hadith*, the Prophet's *sunnah*; back to the Vedas. Celebrate Christianity as the ecstatic religious experience it might have been prior to its becoming the official religion of the Roman Empire. Celebrate Islam as it was practiced during the first three generations of its existence, a time when pious caliphs ruled Islamic lands and *jihad* was bringing far flung lands to heel; focus on the texts of the Brahmins, avoiding mention of the caste system that has given Hinduism a decidedly negative reputation internationally. In short, purify through revival.

These are the keystones of the current generation of religious revivalists among the adherents of the world's most important and most rapidly growing faiths: Pentecostalism within Christianity; Salafists within Islam; and Hindutva adherents in Hinduism.

Unlike Islam and Hinduism, whose engines of rapid expansion lie in the natural rate of increase due to protracted birth rates, Christianity has rapidly spread outside of its traditional base—Europe—where it is actually in decline to the developing world. Churches have sprung up in Latin America, Africa, and Asia at a dizzying pace. Many of these churches are evangelical, specifically Pentecostal.

Pentecostalism is an international movement with its origins in the United States. Following earlier American revivalist movements—the First Great Awakening of the eighteenth century spearheaded by charismatic preachers like George Whitefield and the Second Great Awakening of the early nineteenth century that spread like wildfire in the African-American slave communities—was the Pentecostal movement in racially mixed churches in Southern California in the early 1900s. [1] Relatively bereft of sophisticated theology, Pentecostalism is a religion of pure experience. Three characteristics—experience of the spirit represented by speaking in tongues (glossolalia); being born again in Christ, experiencing a complete transformation of human nature, purification; and a starkly dualistic world view, a heightened awareness of Satanic forces that must be battled against through commitment to Jesus Christ—are generally associated with the sect, though practice varies from community to community. [2]

What is especially remarkable about Pentecostalism is its ability to compete successfully with Catholicism and traditional Protestant churches. Consider Africa, where Catholicism, Lutheranism, Calvinism, and other Protestant denominations successfully converted millions during the late-nineteenth century, particularly in the wake of the Berlin Conference of the mid-1880s that carved up Africa among the contending European powers. [3] Drawing upon the financial and volunteer assistance of African-Americans, Pentecostalism took off in the post-World War period, growing especially fast in the 1970s and 1980s as Africans struggled with corruption, dismal records of economic growth, and ethnically driven social discord.

In many ways, the success of African Pentecostalism lies in its ability to appropriate pre-Christian tribal practices and beliefs. Fear witchcraft? Join a Pentecostal church where "born-again witches" (former witches converted to Christ) will advise you on how to combat Satanic forces. Terrified of infectious and parasitic diseases rampant in sub-Saharan Africa? Be healed by the hand of God. Beaten down by malnutrition and poverty? Experience the richness of life in Christ through the prosperity gospel. [4]

Open up to the power of Christ's healing powers. Likewise, reject modern science, especially the theory of evolution. Accept the Bible as the "inspired" word of God. Modernism is evil.[5] Likewise, reject Islam; fight against the imposition of *sharia* law on national populations. In short, be militant in faith; contest Islam in an African religious space caught between militant Islam and militant Pentecostalism; contest modern medicine and technology.

Without doubt, the spread of Pentecostalism in Africa is both cause and consequence of Africa's anemic economic advance. It fosters conflict with Islam; it fosters rejection of science and Enlightenment ideas tied to liberal nationalism; it consoles followers with the knowledge that true prosperity lies in incorporating Christ within. To be sure, the prosperity gospel associated with Pentecostalism does argue that accumulating material riches is not a sacrilege. Still, it is difficult to see how its program encourages secular progress. To boot, corruption has reared its ugly head, as a sizable number of Pentecostal preachers have been caught operating scams.[6]

Spearheading the purification of Islam is the Salafi movement. Basing itself on the view of Muhammad that "the people of my own generation are the best, then those who come after them, and then those of the next generation", the movement advocates living according to the principles of the *salaf*, the first three generations of Muslims.

Among other things, this means eschewing the great Islamic tradition of recasting ancient Greek philosophy, reviving the works of Plato, Aristotle, and Greek mathematics. In short, it means turning ones back on the glories of the golden age of Islam. Mimicking the literalism of fundamentalist Christianity and Pentecostalism, it advocates the imposition of a strict form of *sharia* law. In effect, it advocates setting up governments along the lines of religious nationalism. To be sure, it draws from some of the most peace-inducing aspects of Islam: espousing charity for the poor, encouraging honesty in commercial dealings (but eschewing formal interest on loans), providing hospitals and *madrassas* that are open to the poor. At the same time, it promotes anti-Enlightenment doctrines and, in the hands of militant jihadists, cruel punishments directed at thieves, adulterers, and apostates: stoning, crucifying, beheading, amputating of limbs, wanton destruction of the religious shrines and temples of competing faiths, making sure women are illiterate and obedient by driving them from schools, and so forth. [7]

Like Salafism, the Hindutva movement in India aims at reviving ancient practices as recorded in ancient texts: namely the Vedas. Like Salafism, it has strong political overtones, embracing a militant form of Hindu nationalism that brings it in conflict with the Indian Muslim community. [8] One example among others will suffice. Sharing sacred space is a festering issue dividing the two communities. Hindus claim that Ayodhya in Uttar Pradesh is the birthplace of Rama, asserting that a Mughal official, Babar, committed sacrilege by smashing into ruins a temple dedicated to Rama and replacing it with the Babri Mosque (from the Muslim perspective, he was simply demonstrating his devotion to Islam by destroying impious icons). In the late 1980s, Hindu groups began fashioning bricks, transporting them to Ayodhya, using them to rebuild the temple to Rama at the site of the mosque. Riots between Hindus and Muslims broke out in 1989. Scores were killed. The backwash from the riots reshaped Indian politics. Formed in protest over government handling of the affair, a Hindu nationalist party, the Bharatiya Janata Party (BJP) emerged. BJP leaders argued that the attempt of the national government to settle the dispute in an even-handed manner was actually discrimination, pure and simple. In their eyes, it convincingly proved the ruling Congress Party was only too willing to stomp upon the rights and interests of the Hindu majority in order to garner Muslim votes. Perhaps to their lights it was nothing more than cynical "divide and rule" politics, reminiscent of British Raj rule.

The Hindutva movement has had a chilling effect on freedom of speech and publishing in India. Invoking Article 295a of the Indian Penal Code, advocates of a "pure" Vedic form of Hinduism have prevented the dissemination of books on Hinduism that discuss a wide variety of practices within the faith. The argument made by the opponents of freedom of the press is that writing on Hinduism that strays from the "Hindutva" party line denigrates their followers, insults them, subjecting them to possible ridicule and psychological pain. To be sure, many of the folk myths of Hinduism are provocative, off-color, lascivious, and sensual. Not puritanical. But so what? All religious movements have their off-color sides, emerging from their gritty folk movements where the profane intermixes with the pure. Despite this fact, because the Indian code is supposed to insure there is no injury to any one religious community within the country, the Hindutva advocates have found a legal mechanism for banning books whose accounts of folk traditions and caste discrimination they consider denigrating to Hinduism. It is ironic that a group that has attacked Muslim communities in waves of pogrom-like riots feels comfortable invoking a "negative freedom" inspired law crafted to prevent the exercise of religious freedom according to any one faith from disparaging the practice of other faiths. In short, the Hindutva movement is no friend of liberal nationalism as applied in India. Some critics of the politics of the movement have gone as far as accusing it of being fascistic.

The thrust of this section is that the cutting edge of the world's major religions in the post-Cold War world lie in the hands of atavistic groups bent on purifying their faiths. This feeds religious nationalism, bringing it into open opposition to liberal nationalism. Armed with this insight, we turn to the ramifications of this fact for civil peace, harmony, and material prosperity in the developing world.

Exile, voice, and loyalty: the spawning of refugee humanitarian crises in the post-Cold War world

The close of the Cold War failed to usher in an age of peace. True, the Hemoclysm, the blood flood of 1914–1975 marred by two major global wars and internal conflicts over national ideology as the number of nation–states proliferated, is over.[9] Indeed, according to the United Nations High Commissioner for Refugees (UNHCR) the number of refugees displaced by conflicts has once again soared to levels experienced in the immediate aftermath of World War II. Exile—forced exit—has re-emerged as a grim, angry reminder of the inability of groups to co-exist, to forge long-lasting compromise, to carve out viable political consensus.

While it is not true that all these crises are the upshots of religious cleavage, the fact is most of the world's refugees—those accounting for a majority of the number of refugee-years generated in the post-Cold War era—are the victims of ethno-religious disputes. By ethno-religious is meant the overlap of ethnicity and religion. The term captures the common-sense notion that ethnicity and religious affiliation often go together, because members of a particular faith, a specific sect, intermarry. Over time, the tendency of ethnic groups to restrict marriage and reproduction to their group goes hand in hand with the tendency of religious sects to differentiate themselves from one another.

With this in mind, consider Table 14.1.

Table 14.1 Corruption and religion

Panel A: Percentage of world refugee-years between 1990–2012 (Refyear%), percentage of world population (Pop%) and ratio of Refyear% divided by Pop% (RATIO)[b]

Group	Refyear%	Pop%	RATIO
RELrefr > 1000[c]	58.6%	1.7%	34.25
1000 > RELrefr > 100[d]	19.6	6.1	3.21
100 > RELrefr > 50[e]	4.6	5.1	0.89
50 > RELrefr > 10[f]	2.2	7.1	0.31
10 > RELrefr > 1[g]	2.1	38.3	0.06
1 > RELrefr[h]	0.2	28.7	0.01

Panel B: Corruption, religiosity and per capita income growth

Group	Refugee-year variables[b]	cpi	athagn%	raty	RATIO
	Avgrefr	RELrefr	CONrefr		
1000 >RELrefr > 100[d]	5,124	320.66	.408	2.36	180.8
100 >RELrefr > 50[e]	1,171	73.30	.471	3.05	146.4
50 >RELrefr > 10[f]	461	28.87	.415	3.01	153.7
10 >RELrefr > 1[g]	74	4.61	.378	3.14	383.7
1 >RELrefr[h]	5	0.34	.482	3.99	195.8

Corruption, religiosity, and per capita income growth for countries cross-classified by five-year relative refugee-years per million persons, 1990–2012 (RELrefr); population weighted averages for the public-sector corruption perceptions index (cpi), Percentage Atheist and Agnostic (athagn%), and the Ratio of Per Capita Income in 2010 divided by per capita income in 1990 (raty)[a].

Sources: Association of Religion Data Archives (2014); Heston, Summers, and Atten Penn World 7.1Table 7.1 (2012); Transparency International (2014) and United Nations High Commissioner for Refugees (2014).

continued

Table 14.1 Continued

Notes:

a The refugee data are for countries of origin, not country of settlement. Countries in which the number of refugee-years per capita in any year between 1990 and 2012 is less than 1000 are excluded from the sample of countries. The variables for corruption and atheism/agnosticism are for 2010. For some countries in the sample, data on per capita income was unavailable for 1990, in which case figures for the first year for which data is available was used to compute the ratio of income per capita.

b The variable **avgrefr** is the average for the five-year refugee-years for the periods 1990–94, 1995–1999, 2000–2004, 2005–2009, and 2010–2012 (the average computed by weighting the figure for 2010–2012 by .6). The variable **RELrefr** is the relative level of the **avgrefr** compared to the value of the **avgrefr** for the world as a whole (the latter set equal to 100). The variable **CONrefr** measures the concentration of refugee-years over the entire period 1990–2012 by computing the percentage (in decimal terms) of the highest value—highest of the values for the five periods—relative to the total number of refugee-years accumulated between 1990 and 2012.

c In descending order of **RELrefr**, the countries in this group are: Liberia, Afghanistan, Bhutan, Bosnia/Herzegovina, Somalia, Eritrea, Timor-Leste, Burundi, Rwanda, Sierra Leone, Croatia, Iraq, Azerbaijan, Armenia, and Mauritania.

d In descending order of **RELrefr**, the countries in this group are: Mozambique, Togo, Serbia, Sudan, Chad, Tajikistan, Laos, Central African Republic, Sri Lanka, Djibouti, Vietnam, Congo (Democratic Republic), Congo (Republic), Nicaragua, Myanmar (Burma), Slovenia, Mali, Lebanon, Georgia, Cambodia, Syria, Macedonia, El Salvador, Suriname, Guatemala, Albania, and Guinea-Bissau.

e In descending order of **RELrefr**, the countries in this group are: Ethiopia, Senegal, St. Vincent and Grenadines, Columbia, Cuba, Iran, Haiti, Uganda, Côte d'Ivoire, and Turkey.

f In descending order of **RELrefr**, the countries in this group are: Moldova, Russia, Uzbekistan, Fiji, Kyrgyzstan, Ghana, Niger, Romania, Gambia, Kazakhstan, Chile, Ukraine, Namibia, Zimbabwe, Latvia, Estonia, Bulgaria, Kuwait, Poland, Czech Republic, Cameroon, Belarus, Hungary, and Libya.

g In descending order of **RELrefr**, the countries in this group are: Algeria, Jordan, Peru, Turkmenistan, Bangladesh, Kenya, Philippines, Honduras, Mongolia, Tunisia, Israel, China, Jamaica, Pakistan, Yemen, Nigeria, Uruguay, South Africa, Venezuela, Papua New Guinea, Nepal, Indonesia, Egypt, Ecuador, Burkino Faso, Zambia, and Morocco.

h In descending order of **RELrefr**, the countries in this group are: Mexico, Tanzania, Argentina, India, Thailand, Korea (Republic of), United States, and Brazil.

The table analyzes the number of refugees given on an annual basis by the United Nations High Commissioner for Refugees, hence the number of refugee-years between 1990 and 2012. To be specific, the averages for refugee-years are totals for four five-year periods—1990–4, 1995–9, 2000–4, 2005–9, and 2010–12—and one three-year period.

In appraising the statistics presented in the table, one must recognize that the High Commissioner figures are underestimates of the actual number of persons displaced, dispatched to exile.

The first point evident in the table is the fact that almost 60% of all refugee-years occurred in small number of countries (to be precise fourteen in number). In terms of population, 59% of the refugee-years generated between 1990 and 2012 occurred in countries with less than 2% of the world's population.

The second point established by the table is that countries in which refugee crises are substantial are corrupt and awash in religiosity. It should be emphasized that the sample of countries used in computing the group averages in the table is restricted to countries for which the number of refugees exceeds 1,000 in at least one year between 1990 and 2012. As a result, data for most of the world's least corrupt countries—in Western Europe, Canada, Australia, New Zealand, Japan, and so forth—are not used to generate averages for the table. If these countries were included, the level of corruption (the **cpi**) for the group with the lowest level of refugee-years per capita would be close to 0.9. Not surprisingly, this group would enjoy the most elevated level for the liberal-religious nationalism index (**LIBRELIN**), an average close to one.

The third conclusion evident from Table 14.1 is that experiencing a refugee crisis deters economic growth. This is hardly surprising. While some refugee crises are due to adverse weather events or geological disturbances—typhoons, hurricanes, tsunamis—most are the result of civil conflicts. These conflicts are often protracted, as attested by the low level of the **CONrefr** variable that acts as a proxy for the concentration of the crisis within a single five-year (or three year) period. For instance, the **CONrefr** average is considerably higher for the group with the lowest level of refugee-years per capita.

With Table 14.2 we can look at the problem of why and where refugee crises break out in terms of the liberal religious-nationalism variable **LIBRELIN**.

As the cross-classification shows countries that score low on the index—countries in which religious nationalistic tendencies are deeply entrenched—are countries having a strong propensity to fall into refugee generating political and military crises. Figure 14.2 covers the same ground in another format, graphical. It shows the association between religious orientation in nationalism and tendency to generate crises exists, albeit displaying a scatter-diagram with less "tightness of fit" than that appearing in Figure 14.1.

Table 14.2 Refugee crises, corruption, and religiosity

Group	Refugee-year variables			cpi	athagn %	Raty	LIBRELIN
	avgrefr	RELrefr	CONrefr				
.3 > LIBRELIN[b]	8,785.16	549.76	.432	2.07	1.54%	144.30	.184
.5 > LIBRELIN > .3[c]	493.99	30.91	.334	3.19	28.01	444.19	.371
.7 > LIBRELIN > .5[d]	445.28	27.87	.504	2.88	2.27	156.32	.572
LIBRELIN > .7[e]	38.82	2.43	.468	4.03	4.15	196.97	.756

Population weighted averages for refugee-year variables, corruption, religiosity, and per capita income growth: countries classified by the liberal-religious nationalism index for 2010 (**LIBRELIN**) [a]

Sources: Sources to Table 14.1 and Chapter 13.

Notes:
a See Table 15.1 for definitions of variables and the text for discussion of the **LIBRELIN** variable.
b In ascending order of the **LIBRELIN**, the countries in this group are: Myanmar, Iran, Afghanistan, Pakistan, Sudan, Syria, Mauritania, Uzbekistan, Kuwait, Turkmenistan, and Tunisia.
c In ascending order of the **LIBRELIN**, the countries in this group are: Egypt, Zimbabwe, Bhutan, China, Ethiopia, Algeria, Belarus, Chad, Vietnam, Tajikistan, Cameroon, Morocco, Bangladesh, Jordan, Sri Lanka, and Russia.
d In ascending order of the **LIBRELIN**, the countries in this group are: Indonesia, Azerbaijan, Kyrgyzstan, Venezuela, Nepal, Nigeria, Thailand, Tanzania, Georgia, Moldova, Guinea-Bissau, Kazakhstan, Colombia, Nicaragua, Turkey, Philippines, Mexico, Mali, Macedonia, and Ecuador.
e In ascending order of the **LIBRELIN**, the countries in this group are: India, Peru, Argentina, Ukraine, Brazil, Bulgaria, Romania, Senegal, Israel, Hungary, Latvia, Namibia, South Africa, Mongolia, United States, Chile, and Estonia.

    To shed more light on the role of ethnic-religious divisiveness in generating crises spawning refugees, it is useful to examine the circumstances surrounding the humanitarian crises erupting in each of the fourteen countries in the group with the highest level of refugee-years per capita. Table 14.3 sets the stage for this discussion.
    The table provides two sets of ethno-cultural fractionalization/diversity proxies, as well as estimates of the religious makeup of the national populations. Per capita income advance (or decline in the case of indices for 2010 failing short of 100) is also recorded for these countries.
    All the refugee crises involved stem from civil wars. One of these wars is a pure war of secession (East Timor/Timor-Leste), several are many ethnic in nature (Liberia, Sierra Leone, Burundi and Rwanda). The remainder definitely involve religious differences as—it turns out—does Timor-Leste. The discussion of the cases is organized in the following order: Timor-Leste first, then the African ethnic wars, then the remainder according to geographical region (Africa first followed by Asia, Eastern Europe/Former Soviet Union, and finally the Middle East).

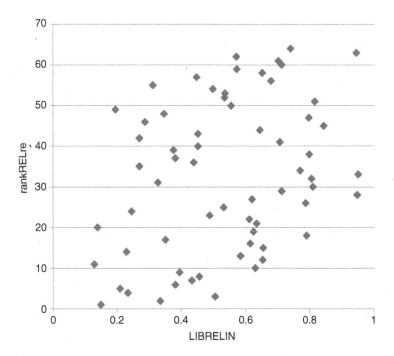

Figure 14.2 Rank number for the relative level of refugee-years per capita (rankRELre) and the liberal-religious nationalism index (LIBRELIN)

Note: The rank for the country with the highest level for RELrefr is 1; countries with the highest ranks have the lowest levels of RELrefr.

A former Portuguese colony, East Timor was slotted to gain independence in the mid-1970s, opening the door for invasion by Indonesia whose district West Timor bordered on East Timor. Successfully invading East Timor, Indonesia ruled the land with an iron fist, suppressing secessionist rebellion with extrajudicial executions, torture, and politically generated famines. From a religious perspective, the Indonesian occupation that persisted from 1975 until 1999 forced the East Timor population—many of whom were animists—to embrace Catholicism, with the Catholic population jumping from around a third to about 80%. The reason lies in the religious nationalistic feature of the Indonesian constitution, the principle of *pancasila*. The first principle of *pancasila* is belief in one God (had the majority Muslim population had their way, the first principle would have stated "belief in Allah"). In practice, Islam, Catholicism, Protestantism, Confucianism, Buddhism, and Hinduism are recognized as officially sanctioned faiths. Animism, Judaism, atheism, and agnosticism are suppressed. [10]

Four of the African nation–state refugee crises come in pairs: Liberia/ Sierra Leone and Burundi/Rwanda. As Panel B of Table 14.3 shows, three

Table 14.3 Ethnic diversity, religious adherence, and corruption

Panel A: Ethno-linguistic fragmentation (Ethlin), cultural diversity (Culdiv), ethnic fractionalization (Ethfrac), linguistic fractionalization (Linfrac), religious fractionalization (Relfrac), and religious adherence

Country/Region	Fearon estimates		Alesina et al. estimates			Religious adherence
	Ethlin	Culdiv	Ethfrac	Linfrac	Relfrac	
Africa						
Liberia	.899	.644	.9084	.9038	.4883	Christian (41.5%); Muslim (18–20%)
Somalia	.812	.290	.8117	.0326	.0028	Muslim (99.8%)
Eritrea	.647	.380	.6524	.6530	.4253	Christian (47.9%); Muslim (50.1%)
Sierra Leone	.764	.534	.8191	.7634	.5395	Christian (20–30%); Muslim (64.6%)
Mauritania	.625	.272	.6150	.3260	.0149	Muslim (99.1%)
Burundi	.328	.040	.2951	.2977	.5158	Catholic (62%); Ethno-religious (5.5%); Muslim (2–10%)
Rwanda	.180	.000	.3238	.0000	0.5066	Catholic (57%); Protestant (26%) Muslim (4.8%)
Asia						
Bhutan	.605	.518	.6050	.6056	.3787	Buddhist (84%); Hindu (11.4%)
Timor-Leste	n.a.	n.a.	n.a.	n.a.	n.a.	Catholic (85.5%); Muslim (3.6%)
Eastern Europe/Former Soviet Union						
Bosnia/Herzegovina	.681	.146	.6300	.6751	.6851	Serbian Orthodox Christian (36%); Catholic (15%); Muslim (47.5%)
Croatia	.375	.185	.3690	.0763	0.4447	Catholic (85%); Serbian Orthodox Christian (6%); Muslim (1.9%)
Armenia	.134	.124	.1272	.1291	.4576	Armenian Christian (93.5%)
Azerbaijan	.188	.187	.2047	.2054	.4899	Sunni Muslim (33.6%); Shi'a Muslim (62.4%); Christian (3.3%)
Middle East						
Afghanistan	.751	.679	.7693	.6141	.2717	Sunni Muslim (80%); Shi'a Muslim (19%)
Iraq	.549	.355	.3689	.3694	.4844	Sunni Muslim (29.4%); Shi'a Muslim (69.7%)

Panel B: Average relative number of refugee-years; religiosity; corruption; per capita income growth; and liberal-religious nationalism index

Country/Region	RELrefr	athagn%	cpi	Raty	LIBRELIN
Africa					
Liberia	8,619.9	1.6 %	3.3	89.4	n.a.
Somalia	4,022.1	0.2	1.1	66.9	n.a.
Eritrea	3,301.0	3.0	2.6	71.5	n.a.
Sierra Leone	2,466.2	1.3	2.4	96.6	n.a.
Mauritania	1,037.6	0.2	2.3	117.9	.234
Burundi	2,782.4	0.2	1.8	66.8	n.a.
Rwanda	2,570.3	0.3	4.0	139.4	n.a.
Asia					
Bhutan	6,658.2	0.1	5.7	244.5	.335
Timor-Leste	3,053.0	0.4	2.5	85.2	n.a.
Eastern Europe/Former Soviet Union					
Bosnia/Herzegovina	5,543.9	3.6	3.2	492.8	n.a.
Croatia	2,133.0	6.3	4.1	111.6	n.a.
Armenia	1,365.8	12.7	2.6	262.3	n.a.
Azerbaijan	1,395.7	8.9	2.4	492.5	.505
Middle East					
Afghanistan	7,701.8	0.2	1.4	95.5	.149
Iraq	1,735.9	0.6	1.5	120.6	n.a.

Ethnic and cultural diversity, religious adherence, corruption, and per capita income growth for the fourteen countries with the highest levels of average refugee-years, 1990–2012

Sources: See Table 14.1 and en.wikipedia.org (2014).

Note:
See Table 14.1 for definition of variables appearing in Panel B.

of the four countries involved experienced declines in per capita income as an outcome of internecine conflict.[11] All four wars resulted from contested elections or coups, one faction—typically an ethnic group or coalition of ethnic groups—seized control of the government, channeling largess to their own faction at the expense of rivals.

Spillover from Liberian conflicts—Liberian leader Charles Taylor assembled a rebel army consisting mainly of Gio and Mano tribes who moved into sanctuaries in the country's neighbors as it retreated—created chaos in Sierra Leone. Refugees from the Liberian wars—mainly children—were recruited by Taylor as soldiers buttressing his effort to build a rebel base in Sierra Leone. The fact that diamond mining was a major economic activity in Sierra Leone allowed both government and rebel forces to sustain their bloody conflict.

The Burundi/Rwanda turmoil followed a fairly similar trajectory. Hutus and Tutsis were at each other's throats in both states that had been carved out a former Belgian colony (height differentiates the two groups, the average Tutsi being significantly taller than the typical Hutu). Genocide was a horrifying characteristic of both civil wars: in Rwanda, it reached a peak in the bloodletting aimed at Tutsis during 1994; in Burundi, it had been an ongoing problem from the early 1970s as a Tutsi-dominated army ravaged Hutu villages. There is little evidence of religious cleavage in these four wars. For instance, both Hutus and Tutsis are Christians. To boot, both tribal groups worship a second god, *Imaana*, who operates in a shadow world populated by spirits of dead relatives, posing potential harm to innocent victims unless properly assuaged with gifts and incantations.

In general, in sub-Saharan Africa, nationalism is fairly weak (South Africa is an exception): tribal identity often trumps national identity. Not surprisingly, spillover of bloodletting from one state to its neighbors is a constant problem for all states. Religious divisions only intensify this dynamic. For instance, Salafist Muslim groups operating in Nigeria wreak havoc in Cameroon; the spread of Pentecostalism south of the Sahara pits activist Christians against Islamic dominated governments.

North of the Sahara, religion plays a more decisive role in the destabilization of states. True, in Mauritania, where virtually all citizens are adherents of Sunni Islam, cleavage per se is not an issue; rather, ethnic difference—between blacks and Arabs—created ongoing tension. Still, a campaign of political Islamism during the 1970s, the promotion of *sharia* law, and the spread of schools, charities, and Muslim centers—driven partly by generous funding from Saudi Arabia and the Sunni Gulf states—was a lightning rod unleashing invidious civil war.

Again, on the horn of Africa—in Somalia and Eritrea—religious nationalism is a major instigator of conflict. To be sure, the Eritrean crisis was the outcome of a three-decade long secessionist war in which Eritrea eventually broke free from Ethiopia. Once independent, its human rights record deteriorated, with Shi'a Islamic communities and many Christian sects finding themselves victims of persecution. Indeed, gaining religious freedom is considered a major reason for emigration from the land.

In Somalia, civil war broke out in the early 1990s as a group of *sharia* courts—the Islamic Courts Union—united to form a rival authority contesting the official government's rule over the country. As the Islamic Courts Union fell apart due to internecine squabbling, Salafist groups like Al-Shabaab and Hixbul Islam emerged with a decided jihadist agenda, carrying on guerrilla warfare. Complicated by the machinations of warlords and the resort to piracy as a money-making activity, the country descended into chaos. Not surprisingly, Somalia's per capita income plummeted. A once prosperous entrepôt region accessing Red Sea trading opportunity became an economic train wreck as religious nationalist conflict ran rampant.

For those who believe Buddhism is a religion of non-violence, abstaining from killing birds, lizards, and the smallest insects, the ethnic cleansing carried out in Bhutan should serve to correct illusions (Sri Lanka and Myanmar are also prominent in the annals of Buddhist tormenting of their religious rivals). During the 1990s, Bhutan expelled about a fifth of its populace in order to preserve the purity of its Tibetan Mahayana Buddhist culture. The government claimed it was mainly disbanding Nepalese who by all rights should return to Nepal where they belonged. Many of these unfortunate victims of religious nationalist cleansing became stateless. Enough said about the much-vaunted claim of Buddhism to embody pacifism; so much for the claim that any religion has an unblemished record of eschewing violence.

The conflicts set off by the dismemberment of the former Soviet Union and former Yugoslavia illustrate with a vengeance the truism that atheistic communist ideology was completely powerless in suppressing deep seated religious differences. In the case of the Armenia/Azerbaijan conflict, bloodletting was generated by interstate conflict over the Nagorno-Karabakh region that Armenia was ultimately able to wrest away from Azerbaijan. As important as territory is in explaining the violence, the bottom line is that Armenia is heavily Christian; Azerbaijan Muslim. The fact that civilian massacres were a major factor in the military confrontation between two freshly minted states spun out of the Soviet Union is testimony to the ethnoreligious hatred and distrust that stymied a diplomatic solution to the competing territorial claims. Similarly, the collapse of Yugoslavia in the early 1990s explains why the Bosnia/Herzegovina and Croatian conflicts broke out. In Bosnia/Herzegovina, Muslim Bosniaks fought mainly Orthodox Christian Serbs and Catholic Croatians in a conflict punctuated by terrible genocides. In the Croatian conflict, Serbs attempted to separate off territory from Croatia, bringing it under the aegis of Serbian authority.

The two Middle Eastern refugee crises arose as a direct result of religious nationalism. In the Afghanistan case, a militant faction within a specific ethnic group (Pashtuns) committed itself to a Salafist agenda that put down deep roots in neighboring Pakistan (Deobandi fundamentalism, a revivalist movement in Sunni Islam influenced by Saudi Wahhabism). The Taliban, infamous for their destruction of ancient Buddhist monuments that graced the ancient Silk Route, grew out of this turmoil. Secretly funded by Pakistan's Inter-Services Intelligence agency (ISI), the Taliban joined up with al Qaeda to jointly wage war against the Northern Front, headed by a Sufi mystic ostensibly fighting for democracy. In Iraq, internecine fighting between Sunni Kurds, Sunni Arabs and Shi'a has torn the country into shreds.[12]

In sum, ethno-religious conflict explains virtually every major refugee crisis occurring during the 1990–2012 period.

The thesis of this chapter is simple: in the post-Cold War period, ethno-religious cleavages have spawned the vast majority of the world's humanitarian crises.

Let me go further. Increasingly religious cleavage is accounting for—and in the future, will account for—the majority of the globe's refugee crises. The reason lies in a crucial difference between ethnicity and religious affiliation. True, as argued they often tend to go together at the local level. But, as the Burundi/Rwanda crises establishes, they do not have to overlap. More to the point, the world's major and fastest growing faiths—Christianity, Islam, and Hinduism—are global in their outreach. They encompass many ethnicities.

Conflicts that start out locally can rapidly spin out into international conflicts as the vast human and financial resources that can be tapped within global religious communities are channeled into national conflicts, the dominos falling one after another. Consider Islam: Salafist *jihad* operates under global umbrellas, notably al Qaeda and its regional and national franchises. Saudi Arabia and the Gulf states fund Sunni programs throughout the Middle East and Northern Africa, some falling into the hands of militant jihadist groups. At the same time, *jihad* organizes and operates locally. Shi'a dominated Iran funds Hezbollah in Lebanon. Before it was suppressed by the Egyptian government, the Muslim Brotherhood sponsored militant Hamas in Gaza. Funded by Saudi oil sales, Pakistani *madrassas* have served as training grounds for the Afghani Taliban.

From an economic development perspective, refugee crises riding the whirlwind of warfare deter growth. They undermine trust, entrammeling trade and cooperation; they slam the brakes on infrastructure construction; they complicate governing; dealing with them draws upon fiscal resources that could be better used elsewhere. Worst of all, they can end up generating traps that are self-reinforcing barriers to economic progress. Religious traps are a particular variant of such a trap, which appear to be growing by leaps and bounds during the post-1990 period.

According to the logic of my argument, religious traps are intimately tied up with religious atavism, with revivalism, with the veneration of a so-called first generation religious purity that has been sullied by corruption over time. Hence, movements like Pentecostalism, Salafism, the Hindutva movement emerge, aimed at the purification of faith. Channeled into individual piety, there is no problem. Politicized, harnessed to religious nationalism, there are dangers aplenty. Elevating the archaic in the classroom is a barrier to progress. Moreover, it throws up walls, immense looming barriers to the spread of knowledge, barriers to reasoned public debate over ideas and policies.

Worse yet, religious atavism discourages communication between distinct religious traditions. It is arrogant in the extreme: my god channels the Truth; your god is spurious. I am blessed; you are cursed. In short, it sets the stage for dehumanizing the Other. Once dehumanized—once outcast as a pariah—the Other becomes a prime target for genocide or the local pogrom. Rather than embracing the pendulum swing of liberal nationalism, benefiting from technological capitalism, countries caught in religion traps find themselves barred from sustained economic development. This is a heavy price to pay.

Notes

1 For histories of Pentecostalism, see Anderson (2010, 2014) and Hollenweger (1972). For the First and Second Great Awakenings, see Evans (2013). It is said that the founders of the Azusa Street church in Los Angeles aimed at purifying a Christianity stumbling along with empty rituals and desiccated creeds. Celebrating the "original fire from Heaven" on the Day of Pentecost, members of the faith would feel the "latter rain" promised by God. Miracles would be performed; the dead could be brought back to life from their coffins; the sick could be healed; all owing to faith.
2 On speaking in tongues, see Christie-Murray (1978). Anderson (2014) provides a useful discussion of Pentecostal theology, including disputes with American fundamentalism.
3 See Akinwumi (2008).
4 See Gerloff (2008), Kalu (2008), Kroesbergen (2014), Mwaura (2008), Paris (2009), Shoko (2009), and Ukah and Echtler (2009).
5 See Hollenweger (1972: 292–3).
6 See Kalu (2008) for some notable examples.
7 For a discussion of the adverse impact of Islam—especially Salafist Islam—on economic development, see Diner (2009), Kuran (2011), Hefner (2005b), Moaddel (2005), Omer and Springs (2013), and my own discussion in Chapter 7.
8 See Van der Veer (1998).
9 On the Hemocycslm, see Mosk (2013: 231–7).
10 For discussions of *pansacila* and the efforts of Indonesia Muslims to influence state policy in Indonesia, see Feillard (1997), Hefner (1997), and Horvatich (1997),
11 See Easterly (2001) for a penetrating discussion of the adverse effects of ethnolinguistic fractionalization upon economic growth in Africa.
12 As discussed in Chapter 7—see especially footnote 7 in that chapter—the origins of the Shi'a–Sunni conflict go back to the seventh century, ultimately turning on how to govern Islamic communities (the Sunni view supports a king–sage model with the Caliphate at its core; the Shi'a view falls basically into a sage–king pattern, the supreme religious leader, the leading Ayatollah, channelling divine knowledge, trumping secular political leaders). In countries heavily Sunni, Shi'a are not considered to be Muslims. They are assumed to be heretics. For recent survey data illustrating this point, see Pew Research, Religion and Public Life Project (2012).

15 Conclusions

As humans, we are simultaneously idealists and materialists. Our perception of reality is cluttered with symbols wrestled into symbolic systems—ideologies—and with so-called factual observations, the product of our senses aided by instruments. Some of us are inherently more materialistic; some of us live primarily within a universe bristling with abstract concepts. We are diverse; we are heterogeneous at both individual and societal levels. That said, none of us can escape the fact that we are influenced by ideologies which shape our materialist behavior, our actions as technicians, our scientific innovations

Ideologies can be classified in a general way, or they can be described in increasingly precise ways. Consider religion, which I define as purification buttressed by faith. Christianity is a specific religion. Within the grand tent are sub-religions: for instance, Catholicism, Lutheranism, Anglicanism, Methodism, Unitarianism, Baptism, the Fellowship of Friends, and so forth. At a very concrete local level, Christianity is the community gathered in a neighborhood church just down the street you live on. As the concept of being Christian is usually understood, it carries intellectual heft. It means giving special attention to the ideas, the life and the death of Jesus of Nazareth. In a negative sense, it means not being Muslim, Jewish, Buddhist, Confucian, and so forth. To be sure, an individual can muddy the ideological waters by claiming multiple religious identities. Normally, however, a religious person is first and foremost affiliated with only one variant. In short, affiliation with a faith has consequences in the worlds of ideas and material reality.

In a materialist sense, a religion consists of humans and physical assets used in the rituals of the religion. It consists of persons marshalling resources—for instance, money and time—to make sure their belief system, their faith, is supported, is advertised. Symbols help them achieve this goal: the cross on a church structure for instance. Their faith exists in their ideals, their doctrines, their chosen scriptures; as well, it exists in the physical world of flesh and blood individuals, in buildings, in billboards exhorting others to join their community, in solemn gatherings in a wooded grove, in outreach ventures promoting good works, in online websites.

As ideologies go, religions are very old. Indeed, they owe their origins to the purifying rituals, heroic myths, and ceremonies of hunting and gathering tribes. Hunters and gatherers are predators: they kill animals; they fight other tribes over territory; they attempt to protect their ecological niches. Not surprisingly, the aboriginal myths of all major religions involve warrior gods invoked by priestly rituals, providing sustenance and vigor to their fellow warriors. Warriors and priests gradually emerged as elites in populations that managed to defeat their rivals, or at least keep their rivals at bay through political arrangements.

On the steppes of Central Asia, gods were often as not storm gods, encouraged through ritual sacrifices to provide rainfall, dispensers of lightning bolts and the awe-inspiring crackle of thunder. How were these gods brought on board? From what we know about the distant past, human sacrifice was one option; another was animal sacrifice. Horses, sheep, and cattle were offered up as gifts to a transcendental world where death, disease, and starvation were unknown. The key to the transcendental world was its purity. It was ideal.

Heroes interacted with the transcendental: prophets listened to divine voices; David-like figures dispatched ferocious Goliaths with mere stones; participants in Orphic cults worked themselves up into frenzies, tearing apart terrified victims in bloody, trance-like rituals.

In regions conducive to developing settled agriculture with domesticated plants and animals, it proved possible to expand the carrying capacity of the environment, stimulating population growth and the specialization and division of labor. To sustain specialization—hence exchange—substantial cooperation was a prerequisite. Was the transition of heroic religions into social control ideologies a necessary or sufficient condition for this level of cooperation? It is possible causation goes both ways: groups transforming heroic religion into social control systems were able to successfully move to settled agriculture due to their heightened level of cooperation; or the converse, cooperation leading to some kind of consensus around cooperation-enhancing ideology? This is a challenging question spawning much speculation, but unfortunately without a definitive answer.

What we do know is that a variety of social control religions developed in the great agrarian civilizations of Eurasia during the so-called Axial Age, sometime between 1500 BCE and 1 CE: Hinduism, Jainism, and Buddhism in India; Confucianism and Taoism in China; Zoroaster worship in Persia; Judaism and Christianity in the Near East. Characteristic of all these faiths is three-pronged purification: ritual purification, ethical purification, and political purification. By ritual purification, I mean alimentary rules, dictates around burial of the dead and sexual intercourse, and rules about the conduct of animal—or human—sacrifice. By ethical purification, I mean rules like the golden rule, prohibitions against killing or stealing from members of your community. By political purification, I mean the drawing of lines between different members of a community based on their role in purifying the community, for instance, the assignment to the Brahmin caste of elevated social status. As well, political purification may mean drawing lines between one community and another, for instance, between my tribe and your tribe.

Cemented by a common religious ideology, cooperation develops within the ranks of a successful agrarian civilization. However, this does not mean cooperation is enhanced *between* groups adhering to different faiths. Nor does it rule out social strife between sub-groups within a group worshipping—carrying out gift exchange towards—a common transcendental world. Purification taking different forms, factions may develop around each type of purification. Officially sanctioned priests—those enjoying the favor of kings for instance—are likely to promote elaborate rituals and the construction of temples. Prophets seized by utopian mystical visions are likely to question the legitimacy of corrupt priests aggrandizing riches through their control of tithes and donations collected for temple ritual. Obsessed by guaranteeing territorial security, it is natural military elites favor religiously sanctioned policies bolstering the military prowess of the national community.

One of the remarkable aspects of the Axial Age is the diversity of solutions to cementing social control. In China, a draconian legalist ideology aimed at maximizing military potential appears to have trumped ritual-oriented Confucianism and mystical Taoism. Ironically, Chinese emperors learned to mask their harsh legal practices with Confucianism. Ostensibly benevolent toward the masses, Confucianism served to inculcate a relatively homogenous class of elite bureaucrats devoted to maintaining the political integrity of the imperial center. In India, caste definitions ultimately based on levels of purity—or impurity, depending on your viewpoint—emerged as a powerful device holding together diverse communities. Military conquests and migration helped spread the concept from northwest to south and east, from the Indus River basin to the Ganges, fostering a kind of social unity. According to this form of unity Brahmins from one district were inclined to share and interact more intensely with Brahmins from another district than they would with their immediate neighbors whom they treated as social inferiors. In the Levant, Judaism emerged as a polytheistic faith—like Hinduism—gradually morphing into monotheism. The fact that geopolitical, materialistic, reality shaped this process—the Hebrew peoples being continually defeated by more powerful neighbors, sent as slaves and prisoners into exile, their temple left in ruins, their kings overthrown—illustrates the point central to this book. Material forces and ideas interact.

Of the major Axial Age solutions, the Greek is of paramount importance to the themes of this volume. The key point I draw from a discussion of Greek Axial Age ritual, thought ,and drama is the crucial importance of the pendulum swing. Acceptance of the pendulum swing—in politics, in art, in philosophy—lies at the core of the Greek achievement. Underlying the pendulum swing concept is the acceptance of diversity, particularly diversity of thought. Remarkably for an Axial Age civilization, the golden age of Greek civilization engendered vigorous competitive debate. Was materialistic science preferable to mystical Platonism? Was democracy preferable to oligarchy? Did war debase peoples, even those who triumphed in battle? Should secular political rule in the hands of a multitude of citizen groups trump control by a dictatorship legitimating its control through promotion of one officially sanctioned religion? As it turns out, embracing the pendulum swing explains why two forms of capitalism—merchant and technological—flourished in Western Europe.

Given the dramatic differences between the particular institutions Axial Age religions fostered in settling into relatively stable social control mechanisms, is it surprising that the advocates of any one of these faiths felt deep emotional turmoil when brought in contact with the possible benefits promised by a competitor doctrine? No. Emblematic is the turmoil—leading to all out civil war—visited on the Jewish community in the final centuries BCE as their faith clashed with Greek thought-inspired Hellenism.

Like religion, capitalism is a powerful ideology evoking strong emotions. It is a general concept. I define it as capital mobility buttressed by credit creation. Having defined it this way, I reject the notion that capitalism is mere price-taking, market-oriented behavior. Markets have been around for a long time. As I construe it, capitalism is the exact opposite. It is decidedly modern, not ancient.

Capitalism did not emerge until the seventh century. It was an outgrowth of a religion developed among merchant tribes active in Mecca: Islam. In that guise, it was merchant capitalism, celebrating the benevolent graces a powerful god, Allah, visited upon a community of warring traders active in the hustle and bustle of the material world. Invoking a transcendental presence providing a common ideological umbrella encompassing a diverse community of squabbling merchant groups, faith in Islam brought relative peace and civility to communities trading along the Silk Road. This Islamic version of capitalism was a first step on the road to an increasingly complex, increasingly formidable ideology that integrated markets across a huge empire carved out by Islamic armies, ushering in the use of the bill of exchange and partnerships as practical vehicles for creating credit.

Why did religion as I define it—and capitalism as I define it—emerge at very different points in human history? The answer is simple: Axial Age thought disparaged usury, the private amassing of wealth, particularly monetized assets. Why? The answer is both materialist and idealist.

From a materialist perspective, predation overshadowed economic exchange in the ancient world. For instance, the Roman Empire flourished because its armies were highly efficient predators. Unlike commerce, in principle win–win—voluntary self-interested exchange taking place because both parties expect to benefit—predation is win–lose. It feeds on itself. Lose a war, you want revenge; successful generals jockey for power, engendering civil war. Operating armies and navies requires considerable resources material and human: taxes, requisitions, monopoly over booty captured in warfare campaigns must go into sustaining predation. It demands strict rigid cooperation among the rank and file soldiers who often as not were abused by their superiors, leading to rebellions that had to be quelled. Not surprisingly, in a predation-dominated world of empire building, predators sought and secured a lion's share of the loot.

As well, the resources absorbed into predation cut into the resources available for gift exchange, to the performance of rituals and the building of temples devoted to a community's interaction with the transcendental world. Secondary to military elites were religious elites. By dint of their role in ritual, priests amassed wealth ostensibly for performing their religious rituals. This wealth they could and did loan out to borrowers. And wealth flowed their way. Donations by wealthy patrons seeking social status, tithes on the community of believers, gifts by political elites or generals competing for legitimacy all flowed into their coffers. From the point of view of ethical purifiers, the amassing of priestly wealth corrupted gift exchange devoted to the transcendental world. It sullied purity.

In short, accumulation of wealth encouraged predation—hence, warfare—and it encouraged corruption among the ranks of the religious elite. In many eyes—including those of the masses—it undermined the legitimacy of the cooperation inducing ideology. Allowing those most capable of aggrandizing wealth—priests, generals, kings—to acquire even more wealth by loaning out their riches at interest corrupted society. For this reason, unbridled usury was anathema to the founders and proponents of Axial Age religions.

Once pioneered under Islam, however, the benefits of credit creation—through mechanisms like the bill of exchange and partnerships—were too attractive to disparage. From the Islamic world, credit creation spread into Europe. Remarkably, in Europe merchant capitalism took flight, becoming far more potent and innovative than it had been in the Muslim world. Why?

This is where the pendulum swing endemic to Europe comes to its fore. Western Europe, pummeled by chiefdoms swirling out of central Asia (perhaps driven by increasingly inclement cold weather), collapsed into decentralized feudalism, the Roman Empire dissolving in the wake of these predatory invasions. In their wake, Christianity emerged as a masking religion designed to hold together the political unity of the empire. This was a feat Confucianism successfully managed to achieve through most of Chinese history. Contrary to the solution achieved in China, the masking achieved in the disintegrating Roman Empire made a strong distinction between the secular and the religious sphere. Feudal completion wedded to the deep divide between secular and religious—church and state feuding over control of resources, feudal estates and princes dueling with one another in internecine warfare—carved out a world of niches in which merchants could function, precious few constraints being imposed by religious authority.

To be sure, the intellectual legacy of Greek thought may have played a role in keeping the pendulum swing in constant motion within the West.

Perhaps this is true. But in my view, this conclusion is unlikely. The fact Greek learning failed to achieve similar results in the Byzantine world; and later on in the Islamic world that made much of Greek thought (the Muslims taking control of Alexandria where many Greek texts were preserved in libraries) raises difficulties. Added to this argument is the fact Christian scripture dominated intellectual life in Western Europe, Greek learning atrophying there until the Crusades brought Islamic translations of Greek texts into the West. These arguments suggest it was the overlap of material and ideological pendulum swings, rather than the mere legacy of ideas pioneered in the Greek Axial Age, that mattered in the long run.

Additional evidence supporting my view comes from a seemingly completely foreign direction: Japan. As in Western Europe, the secular was separate from the sacred. An emperor, head of the Shinto cult, was the embodiment of an ancient belief system involving descent from a sun divinity; a shogun, titular head of a confederation-style government overseeing three hundred or so squabbling feudal fiefs was the secular ruler. To hammer a consensus out of a potentially fragile balance of power system and to acquire material resources, the shogun and his officials were forced to devise a series of "divide and rule" policies. Forcing the restive *samurai* warrior class to live in castle towns under the supervision of their overlords; requiring the feudal overlords to journey to Edo, the shogun's capital, on an oscillating schedule where they would attend to courtly rituals; closing the country off to Christianity and all foreign contact, the one prominent exception being a small group of Dutch merchants residing off the coast of a shogun controlled settlement, Nagasaki: all of these policies stemmed from a calculated effort to limit accumulation of power by factions of overlords hostile to the shogun, potentially favorable to the emperor. In short, the policies were designed to stave off a pendulum swing away from the shogun's rule. Ultimately, the policies failed, as they collapsed under Western pressure, ushering in the Meiji Restoration of 1868. That the system was doomed to eventual failure lay in its highly competitive feudal fragmentation, with some fiefs able to grow their economies faster than others.

Perhaps intrigued by the presence of Dutch trading companies active in the trade monopolized by the shogun, merchant houses began to flourish in Japan after the sixteenth century. Most got their start handling the internal rice market, servicing the interests of feudal overlords who wished to either sell rice (if they enjoyed fief surpluses) or buy rice (if their rice crop was deficient). Over time, they moved into mining, into the dry goods business, into proto-banking. In short, Japan—sharing the pendulum swing logic of Europe—embraced merchant capitalism a few centuries after Western Europe absorbed it, lock, stock, and barrel, from the Muslims.

In short, fragmentation coupled with the separation of secular and sacred encouraged the spread of merchant capitalism globally. As well, it laid the groundwork for technological capitalism. Technological capitalism took off in Europe for two reasons: materialist fascination with precision instruments and machinery, and the pendulum swing in ideas. Building upon improvements in measuring time, weight, chemical processes, speed, planetary motion, air pressure, blood circulation, and the like, natural philosophy completely swept away Catholic Church-sanctioned Scholasticism during the seventeenth century. Advances were made at a remarkably swift pace, precisely because natural philosophers built their reputations by attacking one another. The dispute between followers of Descartes and Newton is a classical illustration of this severe competition.

Emergent states—notably Spain, Portugal, England, France, and the Netherlands—also pushed the pendulum swing: in the fields of international trade; in military confrontation; in the domestic political arena. By aggrandizing resources hitherto captured by local guilds, diverting them to use by national level governments, mercantilism encouraged the growth of scientific knowledge. Aggrandizing financial resources—selling charters to mercantilist companies and taxing burgeoning trade—added to the amount of funding available to royal houses for assembling armies and navies; at the same time, encouraging research in cannon making, ballistics, and navigation equipment yielded beneficial returns in terms of declining prices for weapons, ships, and siege machinery useful in exerting military force. Competition between bitter rivals helps explain why European national governments underwrote scientific research through direct patronage, patents, and the establishment of learned societies.

In short, mercantilism was an engine of trade expansion; it was an engine of scientific advance; it was an engine of incipient nationalism. Indeed, the first states to burst out of the state mold in which sovereignty rested in the hands of kings, embracing a philosophy in which sovereignty rested in the hands of the people, the citizens, were precisely the heavyweights of mercantilism: England, France, and the Netherlands.

With the idea of the pendulum swing firmly established in scientific matters, it infused political discourse. What was the best form of government? What was the best way to maximize the welfare of the citizens of a country? What is the best way to set the masses free of invidious social constraints imposed by elites? Out of the debates of the eighteenth-century enlightenment emerged three distinct forms of nationalism: moderate enlightenment (English); radical enlightenment (France); and counter-enlightenment (rule by one party, hence the grandfather of communism, fascism, and religious nationalism). While the first two forms of nationalism differ in their slant—moderate enlightenment nationalism tends to be more individualistic and oriented to religious freedom; radical enlightenment tends to be more collectivist and anti-clerical—the two forms of very close. Together, they form the foundation of contemporary liberal nationalism.

In the contemporary world—after communism, the arch-enemy of liberal nationalism collapsed—liberal nationalism faces a new opponent: religious nationalism. Unfortunately for religious nationalist countries, their embrace of faith in the school system undermines their innovative capacity, their ability to absorb and further the refinement of technological capitalism. As a result, they struggle economically. Their human development suffers; so does their rate of per capita income growth. In the worst cases, they may fall into religion traps hindering their advance over the long run.

Unfortunately for the peace of the world today, a second group of states are also teetering on the brink of religious traps: countries whose citizens are deeply divided by religion. These nation–states tend to be highly unstable. They tend to wallow in conflict traps, peace between squabbling factions being tentative at best. Like the religious nationalist countries, they pay a huge price for their unresolved religious confrontations: their economic growth rates are anemic.

Capitalism has proven to be a remarkable engine for economic improvement. However, riding the capitalist tiger is not a game for the timid and the insipid. Capitalism generates instability as some sectors fade and other sectors blossom. In so far as the growth poles of capitalism are based on scientific advance, adherence to ancient religious faiths may suffer, challenging the interests of religious elites. As well, merchant capitalism is driven by logic that is not always consonant with technological capitalism. It seeks the highest rate of return on capital regardless of where the investment in plant and equipment take place. Its orientation is global, not national. As a result, jobs may be shifted from the home market of capital-rich countries to markets developing in countries where wages are lower than they are in the home market. Draining capital out of the nation does tend to breed unemployment, hence instability.

A world caught between liberal nationalism and religious nationalism and a world rankled by the instability of capitalism—encouraging political division and engendering calls for protectionism in capital-rich countries—is a world facing daunting challenges. This is the bracing conclusion of this study. A study drawing its initial focus from the ancient world, the Axial Age, concludes as it does here with a sobering statement regarding our highly uncertain future. Fittingly, our conclusion recalls the image of Janus, looking backward, looking forward. However, as mere humans—not gods like Janus—our view of the future is unclear, fogged in the mist of the unpredictable, the unknowable.

Appendices

Military power equation

Military potential **M** depends upon the size of the economy from which military leaders extract resources, the degree to which they are able to secure a piece of the economic pie (the ratio of military expenditure to total economic output m), and the relative prices of exerting military force. Relative prices (compared to the average price level for all goods and services generated within an economy) for exerting military force depend upon a number of variables: the costs of acquiring and outfitting soldiers; the unit cost of lethality for the weapons their soldiers brandish; the efficiency of transport methods they harness (like chariots, horses, tanks); the burden of upkeep for the roads their armies march over; the challenges for mobility of forces imposed by geographic impediments; and the like. Putting up all this together in a simple equation Mosk (2013) captures the logic of military potential:

$$(A.1) \quad (M = (mY)/p_{mf}$$

p_{mf} being the relative price of exerting military force and **Y** is total output or income. Note that Y is equal to per capita income y multiplied by population size P so:

$$(A.2) \quad (M = (myP)/p_{mf}$$

In short population size is a determinant of potential military capacity. It should be emphasized that this refers to potential capacity. It is not equal to success in warfare. History is replete with examples of cases in which understaffed armies defeated larger threatening forces.

Technological progress in the military sector tends to reduce the relative price of exerting military force. This is one reason states subsidize professionals involved in developing new weapons or devising new methods for organizing armies and navies. Basic to warfare of all types is combining methods for shooting projectiles (including fire) or engaging in killing or maiming enemy through person to person contact.

From a long-run historical perspective warfare has advanced through three major phases. The first was an early era when hand to hand conflict prevailed.

Using rocks, swords, the phalanx, horse drawn siege machinery, chariots, the bow and arrow was characteristic of this method of engaging in battle. Technological advances occurring as Stone Age civilization evolved—through the Bronze Age—into the Iron Age precipitated slow declines in the relative price of exerting military force. In this phase population size matters a great deal.

As late as the era of the Mongolian Conquests in the thirteenth century, slow improvements in the manufacture of weaponry improving lethal capacity had not advanced the science of warfare far past this point. A case in point: the Mongols were unusually successful because they possessed a large percentage of the Eurasian horse population and were unusually adept at employing all means of fighting, including launching plague infested bodies into cities, an early form of biological warfare.

The use of gunpowder ushered in a second phase. Technological progress increasingly focused on creating more accurate guns, more potent shells, and more prodigious cannons. Front loaded flintlock guns gave way to muzzle loaded rifles in the nineteenth century, finally to Gatling guns and automatic weapons. During this phase industrialization became increasingly important for mobilizing military force. The importance of population size begins to fall off during this phase. An industrial power advanced country like England was able to defeat the Chinese in the first Opium War fought between 1839 and 1841.

A third phase was ushered in during the late nineteenth century. This is the era of technological warfare. Declining prices of steel during the nineteenth century paved the way for increasingly formidable battleships. The Dreadnaught race of the late nineteenth century pitched England against Germany. Tanks and aerial warfare came into their own during World War I. Poisonous gases were employed. Eventually atomic weapons were developed. During this phase science has become increasingly important for devising state of the art methods of carrying on combat. Today warfare is being carried on with drones in the aerial sphere; nuclear powered submarines ply the oceans; and a completely technology driven style of fighting—cyber warfare using computer hacking – has taken off.

It is now possible for a relatively small country—North Korea—to develop weapons of mass destruction, allowing it to punch way above its population size in the military arena. The same conclusion holds for Israel that is overshadowed in terms of human numbers by Egypt. This is ultimately the reason why the relative price of exerting military force matters.

An augmented production function dividing knowledge into two forms: knowledge embodied in the qualities of labor, land and capital; and disembodied general purpose knowledge taking the form of ideas

The idea here is to express output generating by a population residing in a politically defined jurisdiction into the product of a function of three factors of production—labor, land, and physical capital—each augmented by knowledge multiplied by a second variable, total factor productivity (**A**) that is a function of general purpose knowledge (ideas), economic structure (the composition of the labor force divided into three sectors, agriculture, manufacturing, and service sector, each sector being further divided into subsectors) and scale economies.

In formulating this equation I draw upon Mosk (2013) that uses it in explaining why nationalism spreads in the post-seventeenth century world. The exact equation appearing in Mosk (2013) differs slightly from the one I develop below but the idea is the same.

Following standard Cobb-Douglas expressions of output used by economists, I write per capita output (q) as:

$$(\text{A.3}) \quad q = A * f(l^a, k^a, la^a) = A * \{(la)^{\alpha*}(k^a)^{\beta*}(la^a)^{\{1-(\alpha+\beta)\}}\}$$

A being the index of total factor productivity; **la** being labor input per capita adjusted for hours worked h and the efficiency of an hours worked (that depends on the diffusion of knowledge concerning production); **ka** being per capita capital adjusted for the quality of capital (that depends on the knowledge embodied in the physical machines and structures); and **laa** being land adjusted for the quality of land (e.g.: irrigated fertilized land enjoying a warm climate being superior to parched dry fields left to grow weeds).

Using a little symbolism to tidy up this presentation I write:

(A.4) $la = h*e(h)*w$, w being the proportion of the population in the labor force (the proportion of the populace who are workers), h being hours worked per worker, and e(h) being the efficiency with which people toil at their tasks;

(A.5) $ka = q_k*k$, q_k being the quality of capital (a function of the embodying of knowledge in machinery, structures and transport vehicles and the extent to which physical capital is devoted to production); and

(A.6) $laa = q_{la} * la$, q_{la} being the quality of land (e.g.: expressing its inherent capacity to produce crops consumed both by animals domesticated by farmers and crops consumed by human consumers.

One of the pleasant features of this presentation is the fact it can be easily turned into a statement about growth rates $G(x) = дx/x$, $дx = x_2 - x_1$, being the change of a variable x on its base.

$$(\text{A.7}) \quad G(q) = G(A) + \alpha*[G(h) + G\{e(h)\} + G(w)] + \beta*[G(q_k) + G(k)]$$
$$+ [1-(\alpha+\beta)] * [G(q_{la})+G(la)]$$

Another benefit offered up by this formulation is the fact that **α** is simply the share of income enjoyed by owners of labor; **β** is the share of income secured by owners of capital; and the term $[1-(\alpha + \beta)]$ is the share of income secured by land-owners.

Actually as it turns out this austere formula is akin to a fruit tree its branches loaded down with considerable fruit. To start with the low hanging plum we can derive some important conclusions about the nature of capitalism. (1) Capitalism is a system in which $G(A)$, $G[e(h)]$, $G(q_k)$ and $G(q_{la})$ are large relative to the growth rates of the other variables. (2) Because $G(A)$ is relatively large, structural change is rapid, capital moving at a feverish pace from one sector to another sector, and from the home market to foreign markets.

Nor is this all: some more plums fall from this tree. Consider the debate between followers of Marx and followers of Weber. Both schools of thought argue that a speed-up of capital growth $G(k)$ is crucial to capitalism. Agreement ends at this point.

Weber emphasized the growth in hours worked, h, and the efficiency with which people worked $e(h)$, and science impacting the growth in total factor productivity $G(A)$. Bundled together these constitute the so-called "iron cage" brought in through the spread of the capitalist spirit.

By contrast Marx emphasized the growth in quality of capital $G(q_k)$. Let me start by discussing this concept in terms I believe Marx himself would find agreeable. His concern was with the organic composition of capital, the substitution of fixed capital—think steam engines, railroads, power looms and lathes—for variable capital, raw materials like cotton fiber and coal. He viewed increases in the second kind of capital bolstering the demand for labor, while the second kind of capital automated workers out of their jobs. His famous thesis was that forces of capitalist accumulation would lead to fixed capital forcing out variable capital, throwing workers out of their employment, undermining their skills, rendering them redundant. In terms of the formulation I use here Marx saw q_k rising as fixed capital displaced variable capital.

In short Marx conceived of capitalism a two-sector system, a capital goods sector co-existing with a consumer goods sector (a luxury goods sector is a possible third, less important sector). Herein lay the source of capitalist instability. Workers made redundant by fixed capital accumulation cannot consume products thrust onto the market by the consumer goods sector. Moreover those persons still able to hang onto their positions as factory workers live in a precarious world. The ranks of the unemployed threaten their standards of living because the so-called labor elite know full well that capitalists can fire them, bringing in unemployed or underemployed substitutes from the growing pool of displaced employees. Wages fail to rise: why should they? Strikes will fail: why should they succeed when potential scabs are circling factory districts? So even those not pushed to the margins of society face difficulties purchasing the growing array of mass produced goods—clothing, processed foods, ceramics—spewed out by the consumer goods sector.

In the second volume of *Capital* Marx played with a simple linear two sector model of a capitalist economy. His aim was to demonstrate its great instability. The multiplier implicit in the fact that a falloff in demand for consumer goods depresses the demand for capital goods, spreading misery like a wildfire, is the keystone of his thesis. Because downturns in the consumer goods sector translate into reduced demand for capital goods, the economy taken as a whole falls further and further way from full employment. Thrown out of work, dispensed with, facing starvation, workers see the handwriting on the wall. They overthrow the system, establishing socialist rule.

Following Marx, later Marxist theorists argued that under worker managed socialism, state ownership of key industries counteracting the octopus like control of capitalists over production—eventually to be done away with under communism in which the state allocates all capital through systematic planning—stability could be won.

I agree with Marx that instability is a characteristic of capitalism. I agree that capital quality is crucial. However I part company with his argument regarding the nature of capital quality. For me the most important aspect of capital quality is its embodying technological change. Interacting with disembodied technological change captured in the total factor productivity parameter, improvements in capital quality do tend to automate workers out of jobs. Employees are deskilled, striping older workers of their advantage over younger workers. In this I follow the reasoning of Schumpeter (1939, 1964) in his remarkable account of the long-run Kondratieff wave—prices rising during innovation, falling during subsequent busts; profits growing at a fevered pace as new technologies are brought to bear, driving down production costs, only to be followed by unhappy squeezes on returns; employment opportunities soaring during the upswing phase, then crashing as bankruptcies spread during a protracted downturn—over the course of half century long periods. At the heart of this mechanism of capitalist production are waves of innovation upon which ride new technologies that once incorporated into state of the art production render impotent those firms clinging to out of date production methods, to fall by the wayside during merciless "creative destruction" phase.

Since the mobility of capital is crucial to capitalism as I conceive it one of the salutary stabilizing factors in this story is the migration of financing from dying to growing sectors. Still this is not enough. In competing against communism which did offer stability through State Capitalistic centralized planning, guaranteeing employment—albeit in inefficient enterprises—capitalism had to change. To survive ideologically it had to abandoning its callous treatment of marginalized groups. In the long-run demand management operating through monetary and fiscal policies (so-called Keynesianism), bailouts of failing firms by government, and the redistributive actions of the welfare state providing some kind of safety net to those relentlessly sidelined by creative destruction came to the fore to save capitalism from its most odious consequences. This story, however, that illustrates the pendulum swing approach I develop in this paper, will not occupy us here.

In conclusion I would like to note that I chose sides with Weber regarding the importance of "demystification." I view advances in science as crucial drivers of the innovation waves emphasized by Schumpeter.

References

A: Books and articles

Adams, C. (2012). "Transport," in Scheidel (2012a): 218–240.

Adogame, A.; Gerloff, R.; and Hock, K. (eds.) (2008) *Christianity in Africa and the African Diaspora: The Appropriation of a Scattered Heritage*, New York: Continuum International Publishing Group.

Akerlof, G. (1984). *An Economic Theorist's Books of Tales*, New York: Cambridge University Press.

Akerlof, G and Kranton, R. (2010). *Identity Economics: How Our Incentives Shape Our Work, Wages, and Well Being*, Princeton, NJ: Princeton University Press.

Akinwumi, O. (2008). "Political or spiritual partition: The impact of the 1884/85 Berlin Conference on Christian missions in Africa," in Adogame, Gerloff, and Hock (2008): 9–19.

Anderson, A. (2010). "Varieties, taxonomies, and definitions," in Allan Anderson, Michael Bergundeer, Andre F. Droogers, and Cornelis van der Laan (2010): 13–29.

Anderson, A. (2014). *An Introduction to Pentecostalism. Second Edition*, New York: Cambridge University Press.

Anderson, A; Bergunder, M.; Droogers, A.; and van der Laan, C. (eds.) *Studying Global Pentecostalism: Theories and Methods*, Berkeley and Los Angeles, CA: University of California Press.

Anderson, R.; Bennett, J.; and Ryan, F. (eds.). (1993). *Making Instruments Count: Essays of Historical Scientific Instruments presented to Gerald L'Estrange Turner*, Aldershot, Hampshire, UK: Variorum.

Anthony, D. (2007). *The Horse the Wheel and Language: How Bronze-Age Riders from the Eurasian Steppes Shaped the Modern World*, Princeton, NJ: Princeton University Press.

Aranson, J; Eisenstadt, S.; and Wittrock, B. (2005). *Axial Civilizations and World History*, Leiden: Brill.

Armstrong, K. (2006). *The Great Transformation: The Beginnings of Our Religious Traditions*, New York: Alfred A. Knopf.

Bang, P. (2012a). "A forum on trade," in Scheidel: 296–303.

Bang, P. (2012b). "Predation," in Scheidel: 197–217.

Barro, R. (2005). "Which countries have state religions?" *Quarterly Journal of Economics*, 104 (4): 1331–70.

Barro, R. and McCleary, R. (2003). "Religion and economic growth across countries," *American Sociological Review*, 68 (5): 760–81.

Becker, E. (1973). *The Denial of Death*, New York: Simon & Schuster.

Beckwith, C. (2009). *Empires of the Silk Road: A History of Central Eurasia from the Bronze Age to the Present*, Princeton, NJ: Princeton University Press.

Bellah, R. (1965). *Religion and Progress in Modern Asia*, New York: The Free Press.

Bellah, R. (1970). *Beyond Belief: Essays on Religion in a Post-Traditional World*, New York: Harper & Row.

Bellah, R. (2011). *Religion in Human Evolution: From the Paleolithic to the Axial Age*, Cambridge, MA: Harvard University Press.

Bellah, R. and Joas, H. (eds.). (2012). *The Axial Age and Its Consequences*, Cambridge, MA: Harvard University Press.

Berling, J. (1980). *The Syncretic Religion of Lin Chao-en*, New York: Columbia University Press.

Blanning, T. (ed.). (2000). *The Short Oxford History of Europe, Volume VIII: The Eighteenth Century, Europe 1688–1815*, New York: Oxford University Press.

Boardman, J.; Griffin, J.; Murray, O. (eds.). (1986). *The Oxford History of the Classical World*, New York: Oxford University Press.

Botticini, M. and Eckstein, Z. (2012). *The Chosen Few: How Education Shaped Jewish History, 70–1492*, Princeton, NJ: Princeton University Press.

Brady Jr., T. (1991). "The rise of merchant empires, 1400–1700: A European counterpoint," in J. Tracy (1990): 117–160.

Bresson, A. (2014). "Capitalism in the ancient Greek economy," in Neal and Williamson (2014): 43–74.

Breyer, P. (1994). *Religion and Globalization*, Thousand Oaks, CA: SAGE Publications.

Brown, P. (2015). *The Ransom of the Soul: Afterlife and Wealth in Early Western Christianity*, Cambridge, MA: Harvard University Press.

Buzalka, J. (2006). *Nation and Religion: The Politics of Commemoration in South-East Poland*, Piscataway, NJ: Transactions Publishers.

Calhoun, C.; Juergensmeyer, M.; and van Antwerpen, J. (eds.). (2011). *Rethinking Secularism*, New York: Oxford University Press.

Cassanova, J. (2009). "The religious situation in Europe," in Joas and Weigandt (2009): 206–228.

Chang, H. (2007). *Inventing Temperature: Measurement and Scientific Progress*, New York: Oxford University Press.

Chi'en, E. (1986). *Chiao Hung and the Restructuring of Neo-Confucianism in the Late Ming*, New York: Columbia University Press.

Chiswick, C. (2014). *Judaism in Transition: How Economic Choices Shape Religious Tradition*, Stanford, CA: Stanford University Press.

Christie-Murray, D. (1978). *Voices from the Gods: Speaking with Tongues*, London: Routledge & Kegan Paul.

Clark, G. (2007). *A Farewell to Alms: A Brief Economic History of the World*, Princeton, NJ: Princeton University Press.

Connerton, P. (1980). *The Tragedy of Enlightenment: An Essay on the Frankfurt School*, Cambridge, UK: Cambridge University Press.

Coulton, G. (1925, 1989). *The Medieval Village*, New York: Dover Publications [Reprint of original published by Cambridge University Press].

Coyne, J. (2015). *Faith vs. Fact: Why Science and Religion Are Incompatible*, New York: Viking.

Daughton, J. (2006). *An Empire Divided: Religion, Republicanism, and the Making of French Colonialism*, New York: Oxford University Press.

Daumas, M. (M. Holbrook, trans.) (1972). *Scientific Instruments of the Seventeenth and Eighteenth Centuries and Their Makers*, London: B. T. Batsford.

Dawkins, R. (1982). *The Extended Phenotype: The Long Reach of the Gene*, New York: Oxford University Press.

Dawkins, R. (1986). *The Blind Watchmaker*, Harlow, UK: Longman.

Dawkins, R. (1989). *The Selfish Gene*, New York: Oxford University Press.

Dawkins, R. (1996). *Climbing Mount Improbable*, New York: W.W. Norton.

Dawkins, R. (1998). *Unweaving the Rainbow: Science, Delusion and the Appetite for Wonder*, Boston, MA: Houghton Mifflin Company.

Dawkins, R. (2008). *The God Delusion*, New York: Houghton Mifflin Harcourt.

Dawkins, R. (2009). *The Greatest Show on Earth: The Evidence for Evolution*, New York: Free Press.

De George, R. and Scanlan, J. (1974). *Marxism and Religion in Eastern Europe: Papers Presented at the Banff International Slavic Conference, September 4–7, 1974*, Boston, MA: D. Reidel Publishing Company.

Deacon, T. (1997). *The Symbolic Species: The Co-evolution of Language and the Brain*, New York: W.W. Norton & Company.

Décarreaux, J. (1964). *Monks and Civilizations: From the Barbarian Invasions to the Reign of Charlemagne*, London: George Allen & Unwin.

Diamond, J. (1997). *Guns, Germs, and Steel: The Fates of Human Societies*, New York: W. W. Norton & Company.

Diner, D. (S. Rendall, trans.) (2009). *Lost in the Sacred: Why the Muslim World Stood Still*, Princeton: Princeton University Press.

Doniger, W. (2009). *The Hindus: An Alternative History*, New York: Penguin Press.

Durkheim, É (C. Cosmon, Trans.) (2001). *The Elementary Forms of Religious Life*, New York: Oxford University Press.

Dutt, R. (1910, 1953). *The Ramayana & The Mahabharata*, New York: E. P. Dutton & Co. Inc.

Dworkin, R. (2013). *Religion Without God*, Cambridge, MA: Harvard University Press.

Easterly, W. (2001). *The Elusive Quest for Growth: Economist's Adventures and Misadventures in the Tropics*, Cambridge, MA: The MIT Press.

Eisenman, R. and Wise, M. (1992). *The Dead Sea Scrolls Uncovered: The First Complete Translation and Interpretation of 50 Key Documents Withheld for Over 35 Years*, Rockport, MA: Element Books Limited.

Eisenstadt, S. (1986). *The Origins and Diversity of Axial Age Civilizations*, Albany, NY: State University of New York Press.

Elshakry, M. (2013). *Reading Darwin in Arabic, 1860–1950*, Chicago, IL: University of Chicago Press.

Epstein, S. and Prak, M. (eds.). (2008). *Guilds, Innovation, and the European Economy, 1400–1800*, New York: Cambridge University Press.

Etherington, N. [ed.] (2005). *Missions and Empire*, New York: Oxford University Press.

Evans, C. (2013). *Histories of American Christianity: An Introduction*, Waco, TX: Baylor University Press.

Fara, P. (2009). *Science: A Four Thousand Year History*, New York: Oxford University Press.

Feillard, A. (1997). "Traditionalist Islam and the state in Indonesia: The road to legitimacy and renewal," in Robert W. Hefner and Patricia Horvatich (1997): 129–155.

Findlay, R. and O'Rourke, K. (2007). *Power and Plenty: Trade, War, and the World Economy in the Second Failure: Why Science is so Successful*, New York: Oxford University Press.

Fox, J. (2008). *A World Survey of Religion and the State*, New York: Cambridge University Press.

Freud, S. (J. Riviere, trans.) (1946). *Civilization and Its Discontents*, London: Hogarth Press.

Freud, S. (W. Robson-Scott, trans.). (1973). *The Future of an Illusion*, London: The Hogarth Press.

Fried, J. (P. Lewis, trans.). (2015). *The Middle Ages*, Cambridge, MA: Harvard University Press.

Friedman, G. (1981) *The Political Philosophy of the Frankfurt School*, Ithaca, NY: Cornell University Press.

Gerloff, R. (2008) "Churches of the spirit: The Pentecostal/Charismatic Movement and Africa's contribution to the renewal of Christianity," in Adogame, A.; Gerloff, R.; and Hock, K. (eds). (2008). *Christianity in Africa and the African Diaspora: The Appropriation of a Scattered Heritage*, New York: Continuum International Publishing Group: pp. 208–220.

Gibbon, E. (no date). *The Decline and Fall of the Roman Empire*, [in Three Volumes] New York: The Modern Library.

Golb, N. (1995). *Who Wrote the Dead Sea Scrolls? The Search for the Secret of Qumran*, New York: Simon and Schuster.

Gould, S. (2003). *The Hedgehog, the Fox, and the Magister's Pox: Mending the Gap Between Science and the Humanities*, New York: Harmony Books.

Graves, R. (1955) *The Greek Myths: The Complete and Definitive Edition*, New York: Penguin Books.

Greif, A. (2006). *Institutions and the Path to the Modern Economy: Lessons from Medieval Trade*, New York: Cambridge University Press.

Habermas, J. (2002). *Religion and Rationality: Essays on Reason, God, and Modernity*, Cambridge, MA: The MIT Press.

Habermas, J. (2012). *An Awareness of What Is Missing: Faith and Reason in a Post-Secular Age*, Cambridge, MA: Polity Press.

Hall, A. (1962). *The Scientific Revolution 1500–1800: The Formation of the Modern Scientific Attitude; Second Edition*, Boston, MA: Beacon Press.

Hawkes, N. (1981). *Early Scientific Instruments*, New York: Abbeville Press.

Hawkins, C. (2012). "Manufacturing," in Scheidel (2012a): 175–194.

Hayami, A. (2009). *Population, Family and Society in Pre-Modern Japan*, Kent, UK: Global Oriental.

Hayami, A. (2015). *Japan's Industrious Revolution: Economic and Social Transformations in the Early Modern Period*, New York: Springer.

Heckscher, E. (M. Shapiro, trans.; E. Söderlund ed.). (1955). *Mercantilism, Volume One*, New York: The Macmillan Company.

Hefner, R. (1997) "Islamization and democratization in Indonesia," in Robert W. Hefner and Patricia Horvatich (1997): 75–128.

Hefner, R. (ed.) (2005a). *Remaking Muslim Practices: Politics, Pluralism, Contestation, Democratization*, Princeton, NJ: Princeton University Press.

Hefner, R (2005b). "Introduction: Modernity and the remaking of Muslim politics," in Robert W. Hefner (2005a): 1–36.

Heston, A. Summers, R. and Aten, B. (2012). World Table 7.1, Center for International Comparison of Production, Income, and Prices at the University of Pennsylvania (July), accessed at http://pwt.sas.upenn.edu/php site/pwt form.php (Penn World Tables)

Hirschman, A. (1977). *The Passions and the Interests: Political Arguments for Capitalism Before Its Triumph*, Princeton, NJ: Princeton University Press.

Hitchens, C. (2007). *God Is not Great: How Religion Poisons Everything*, Toronto: McClelland & Stewart.

Hollenweger, W. (1972). *The Pentecostals*, London: SCM Press.

Horvatich, R. (1997). "The Ahmadiyya movement in Simunil: Islamic reform in one remote and unlikely place," in Robert W. Hefner and Patricia Horvatich (1997): 183–206.

Jacob, M. (1997). *Scientific Culture and the Making of the Industrial West*, New York: Oxford University Press.

Jewish Publication Society of America. (1955). *The Holy Scriptures According to the Masoretic Text* [in Two Volumes], Philadelphia, PA: The Jewish Publication Society of America.

Joas, H. and Wiegandt, K. (eds). (2009). *Secularization and the World's Religions*, Liverpool: Liverpool University Press.

Johns, J. (1990). "Christianity and Islam," in J. McManners (ed.). (1990): 163–195.

Johnson, D. (2016). *God is Watching You: How the Fear of God Makes Us Human*, New York: Oxford University Press.

Johnson, T. and Grim, B. (2013). *The World's Religions in Figures*, Malden, MA: Wiley-Blackwell.

Jones, E. (2003). *The European Miracle: Environments, Economies, and Geopolitics in the History of Europe and Asia*, 3rd Edition. New York: Cambridge University Press.

Jongman, W. (2014). "Reconstructing the Roman Economy," in Larry Neal and Jeffrey G.Williamson (2014): 75–100.

Juergesmeyer, M. (1993). *The New Cold War? Religious Nationalism Confronts the Secular State*, Berkeley and Los Angeles, CA: University of California Press.

Juergesmeyer, M. (2003). *Terror in the Mind of God: The Global Rise of Religious Violence*, Berkeley and Los Angeles, CA: University of California Press.

Juergesmeyer, M. (2008). *Global Rebellion: Religious Challenges to the Secular State from Christian Militias to al Qaeda*, Berkeley and Los Angeles, CA: University of California Press.

Jurca, M. (2014). "Babylonia in the first millennium era BCE – economic growth in times of empire," in Neal and Williamson (2014): 24–42.

Kalu, O. (2008). *African Pentecostalism: An Introduction*, New York: Oxford University Press.

Klein, U. and Lefèvre, W. (2007). *Materials in Eighteenth-Century Science: A Historical Ontology*, Cambridge, MA: The MIT Press.

Koestler, A. (1959, 1986). *The Sleepwalkers: A History of Man's Changing Vision of the Universe*, New York: Penguin Books.

Kroesbergen, H. (ed.). *In Search of Health and Welfare: The Prosperity Gospel in African, Reformed Perspective*, Eugene, OR: Wipf & Stock.

Kuhn, P. (1990). *Soulstealers: The Chinese Sorcery Scare of 1768*, Cambridge, MA: Harvard University Press.

Kuran, T. (2011). *The Long Divergence: How Islamic Law Held Back the Middle East*, Princeton, NJ: Princeton University Press.

Labib, S. (1969). "Capitalism in Medieval Islam," *The Journal of Economic History*, 29, 1: 79–96.

Landes, D. (1983). *Revolution in Time: Clocks and the Making of the Modern World*, Cambridge, MA: Harvard University Press.

Landes, D. (1998). *The Wealth and Poverty of Nations: Why Some Are So Rich and Some So Poor*, New York: W. W. Norton & Company.

Lannaccone, L. (1991). "The consequence of religious market structure," *Rationality and Society*, 3: 156–77.

Lawrence, C. (1984). *Medieval Monasticism: Forms of Religious Life in the Western Europe in the Middle Ages*, New York: Longman.

Le Goff, J. (2015). *Must We Divide History into Periods?*, New York: Columbia University Press.

Leicester, H. (1965). *The Historical Background of Chemistry*, New York: John Wiley & Sons.

Lewy, H.; Altmann, A.; and Heinemann, I. (eds.). (1960). *Three Jewish Philosophers: Philo, Saadya Gaon, and Jehuda Halevi*, New York: Meridian Books and The Jewish Publication Society.

Lin, Y. (ed. & trans.). (1943). *The Wisdom of Confucius*, New York: Random House.

Liu, X. (2010). *The Silk Road in World History*, New York: Oxford University Press.

Lumsden, C. and Wilson, E. (1981). *Genes, Mind, and Culture: The Coevolutionary Process*, Cambridge, MA: Harvard University Press.

McAuliffe, J. (ed.). (2006). *Cambridge Companion to the Qur'an*, New York: Cambridge University Press.

McClellan III, J. and Dorn, H. (2006). *Science and Technology in World History: An Introduction*, Baltimore, MD: Johns Hopkins University Press.

McCloskey, D. (2010). *Bourgeois Dignity: Why Economics Can't Explain the Modern World*, Chicago, IL: University of Chicago Press.

McEvedy, C. (2002). *The New Penguin Atlas of Ancient History*, New York: Penguin Books.

Mackenny, R. (1987). *Tradesmen and Traders: The World of Guilds in Venice and Europe, 1250–c. 1650*, Totawa, NJ: Barnes and Noble Books.

Maddison, A. (2007). *Contours of The World Economy, 1–2030 AD: Essays in Macro-Economic History*, New York: Oxford University Press.

Madigan, K. (2015). *Medieval Christianity: A New History*, New Haven, CT: Yale University Press.

Magnusson, R. (2001). *Water Technology in the Middle Ages: Cities, Monasteries, and Waterworks after the Roman Empire*, Baltimore, MD: Johns Hopkins University Press.

Marcus, R. (1990). "From Rome to the Barbarian kingdoms," in J. McManners (ed.) (1990): 63–91.

Marx, K. (1936). *Capital: A Critique of Political Economy*, New York: The Modern Library [Reprint of the edition edited by Friedrich Engels].

Marx, K. (1961). *Capital: A Critical Analysis of Capitalist Production* [in three volumes], Moscow: Foreign Languages Publishing House.

May, H. and Metzger, B. (eds). (1965). *The Oxford Annotated Bible with the Apocrypha. Revised Standard Edition*, New York: Oxford University Press.

Mendelsohn, D. (2016). "How Greek drama saved the city," *New York Review of Books*, LXIII, 11: 59–61.

Mendieta, E. and Vanantwerpen, J. (eds). (2011). *The Power of Religion in the Public Sphere*, New York: Columbia University Press.

Merriman, S. (2009). *Religion and the State: An International Analysis of Roles and Relationships*, Santa Barbara, CA: ABC–CLIO.

Michel, P. (A. Braley, trans.). (1988). *Politics and Religion in Eastern Europe: Catholicism in Hungary, Poland and Czechoslovakia*, Cambridge, MA: Polity Press.

Migdal, J. (1988). *Strong Societies and Weak States: State Capabilities in the Third World*, Princeton, NJ: Princeton University Press.

Moaddel, M. (2005). *Islamic Modernism, Nationalism, and Fundamentalism*, Chicago, IL: The University of Chicago Press.

Mokyr, J. (1990). *The Lever of Riches: Technological Creativity and Economic Progress*, New York: Oxford University Press.

Mokyr, J. (2002). *The Gifts of Athena: Historical Origins of the Knowledge Economy*, Princeton, NJ: Princeton University Press.

Mokyr, J. (2009). *The Enlightened Economy: An Economic History of Britain 1700–1850*, New Haven, CT: Yale University Press.

Moran, B. (2005). *Distilling Knowledge: Alchemy, Chemistry, and the Scientific Revolution*, Cambridge, MA: Harvard University Press.

Morgan, M. (2007). *Lost History: The Enduring Legacy of Muslim Scientists, Thinkers, and Artists*, Washington, DC: National Geographic Society.

Morris, I. (2010). *Why the West Rules–For Now: The Patterns of History, and What They Reveal About the Future*, Toronto: McClelland and Stewart.

Morrison, K. (1969). *Tradition and Authority in the Western Church 300–1140*, Princeton, NJ: Princeton University Press.

Morrison-Low, A. (2007). *Making Scientific Instruments in the Industrial Revolution*, Aldershot, Hampshire, UK: Ashgate.

Mosk, C. (2001). *Japanese Industrial History: Technology, Urbanization, and Economic Growth*, Armonk, NY: M. E. Sharpe [Reprinted by Routledge].

Mosk, C. (2008). *Japanese Economic Development: Markets, Norms, Structures*, New York: Routledge.

Mosk, C. (2011). *Traps Embraced or Escaped: Elites in the Economic Development of Modern Japan and China*, Hackensack, NJ: World Scientific.

Mosk, C. (2013). *Nationalism and Economic Development in Modern Eurasia*, New York: Routledge.

Mwaura, P. (2008). "The role of charismatic Christianity in reshaping the religious scene in Africa: The case of Kenya," in Afe Adogame, Roswith Gerloff, and Klaus Hock (2008): 180–192.

Nahm, M. (ed.). (1947). *Selections from Early Greek Philosophy*, New York: Appleton-Century-Crofts, Inc.

Neal, L. and Williamson, J. (eds). (2014). *The Cambridge History of Capitalism. Volume I. The Rise of Capitalism: From Ancient Origins to 1848*, New York: Cambridge University Press.

Needham, J. (1981). *Science in Traditional China*, Cambridge, MA: Harvard University Press.

Nikhilananda, S. (1956). *The Upanishads: A New Translation*, [in Four Volumes], New York: Harper & Brothers.

Norenzayan, A. (2013). *Big Gods: How Religions Transformed Cooperation and Conflict*, Princeton, NJ: Princeton University Press.

Norris, P. and Inglehart, R. (2004). *Sacred and Secular: Religion and Politics Worldwide*, New York: Cambridge University Press.

O'Donnell, J. (2015). *Pagans: The End of Traditional Religion and the Rise of Christianity*, New York: HarperCollins.

Ogilvie, S. (2000). "The European economy in the eighteenth century," in T. Blanning [ed.] (2000): 91–130.

Ogilvie, S. (2004). "Guilds, efficiency, and social capital: evidence from German proto-industry," *Economic History Review*, LVIII, 2: 286–333.

Ogilvie, S. (2007). "Whatever is, is right? Economic institutions in pre-industrial Europe," *Economic History Review*, 60 (4): 649–684.

Omer, A. and Springs, J. (2013). *Religious Nationalism: A Reference Book*, Santa Barbara, CA: ABC–CLIO.

Paris, P. (ed.). (2009). *Religion and Poverty: Pan-African Perspectives*, Durham: Duke University Press.

Pérez, L. (2008). "Inventing a world of guilds: Silk fabrics in eighteenth-century Lyon," in Epstein S. R. and Maarten Prak (eds). (2008): 232–263.

Peters, F. (1990). *Judaism, Christianity, and Islam: The Classical Texts and Their Interpretation*, Princeton, NJ: Princeton University Press.

Pew Research, Religion and Public Life Project. (2012). "Infographic: The World's Muslims: Unity and Diversity," accessed at www.pewforum.org/2012/08/09/the_worlds_muslims_unity_and_diversity-infographic.

Pickstone, J. (2000). *Ways of Knowing: A New History of Science, Technology and Medicine*, Manchester, UK: Manchester University Press.

Pinker, S. (2011). *The Better Angels of Our Nature: Why Violence Has Declined*, New York: Penguin Books.

Plantinga, A. (2011). *Where the Conflict Really Lies: Science, Religion, & Naturalism*, New York: Oxford University Press.

Pomeranz, K. (2000). *The Great Divergence: China, Europe, and the Making of the Modern World Economy*, Princeton, NJ: Princeton University Press.

Ramadan, T. (2007). *In the Footsteps of the Prophet: Lessons from the Life of Muhammad*, New York: Oxford University Press.

Ramet, P. (ed.). (1989). *Religion and Nationalism in Soviet and Eastern European Politics*, Durham, NC: Duke University Press.

Richardson, G. (2005). "Craft guilds and Christianity in late-medieval England: A rational-choice hypothesis," *Rationality and Society*, 17: 139–189.

Richardson, G. and McBride, M. (2009). "Religion, longevity and cooperation: The case of the craft guild," *Journal of Economic Behavior*, 71: 172–186.

Riley, N. (2013). *'Til Faith Do Us Part: How Interfaith Marriage is Transforming America*, New York: Oxford University Press.

Rogers, C. (Editor in Chief). (2010). *The Oxford Encyclopedia of Medieval Warfare and Military Technology* [in Three Volumes], New York: Oxford University Press.

Römer, T. (R. Guess, trans.). (2015). *The Invention of God*, Cambridge, MA: Harvard University Press.

Ross, W. (ed.). (1955). *Aristotle: Selections*, New York: Charles Scribner's Sons.

Rubin, J. (2010). "Bills of Exchange, interest bans, and impersonal exchange in Islam and Christianity," *Explorations in Economic History*, 47 (2): 213–227.

Russell, B. (1945). *A History of Western Philosophy: And Its Connection with Political and Social Circumstances from the Earliest Times to the Present Day*, New York: Simon and Schuster.

Saliba, G. (2007). *Islamic Science and the Making of the European Renaissance*, Cambridge, MA: The MIT Press.

Saller, R. (2012). "Human capital and economic growth," in Scheidel (2012a): 71–86.

Scheidel, W. (ed.). (2012a). *The Cambridge Companion to the Roman Economy*, New York: Cambridge University Press.

Scheidel, W. (2012b). "Approaching the Roman economy," in Scheidel (2012a): 1–21.

Schumpeter, J. (1939, 1964). *Business Cycles: A Theoretical and Statistical Analysis of the Capitalist Process*, New York: McGraw-Hill.

Shapin, S. (1996). *The Scientific Revolution*, Chicago, IL: University of Chicago Press.

Shoko, T. (2009). "Healing in Hear the Word Ministries Pentecostal Church Zimbabwe," in Westerlund (2009): 43–56.

Smith, A. (E. Cannan, ed.). (1937). *An Inquiry into the Nature and Causes of the Wealth of Nations*, New York: The Modern Library.

Stark, R. (2003). *For the Glory of God: How Monotheism Led to Reformations, Science, Witch-Hunts, and the End of Slavery*, Princeton, NJ: Princeton University Press.

Tar, Z. (1977). *The Frankfurt School: The Critical Theories of Max Horkheimer and Theodor W. Adorno*, New York: John Wiley & Sons.

Taylor, C. (2007). *A Secular Age*, Cambridge, MA: Harvard University Press.

Temin, P. (2013). *The Roman Market Economy*, Princeton, NJ: Princeton University Press.

Tracy, J. (ed.). (1991). *The Political Economy of Merchant Empires*, New York: Cambridge University Press.

Transparency International. (2014). "Corruption Perceptions Index," accessed at www.transparency.org/cpi2013/results.

Trivellato, F. (2008). "Guilds, technology and economic change in early modern Venice," in S. R. Epstein and Maarten Prak (2008): 199–231.

Trivellato, F.; Halevi, L.; Antunes, C. (eds.). (2014). *Religion and Trade: Cross-Cultural Exchanges in World History, 1000–1900*, New York: Oxford University Press.

Tsugitaka, S. (2012). "Slave Traders and Kārimī Merchants during the Mamluk Period: A Comparative Study," downloaded from http://mamluck.uchicago.edu/ Mamluck Studies Review_X-2006.pdf on February 6, 2015.

Turner, A. (2008). "'Not to hurt of trade': Guilds and innovation in horology and precision instrument making," in S.R Epstein and Maarten Prak (2008): 264–287.

Turner, G. (1990). *Scientific Instruments and Experimental Philosophy*, Aldershot, Hampshire, UK: Variorum.

Ukah, A. and Echtler, M. (2009). "Born-again Witches and Videos in Nigeria," in David Westerlund (2009): 73–92.

United Nations High Commissioner for Refugees. (2014). "Refugee Figures," accessed at www.unhcr.org.

Usher, A. (1929). *A History of Mechanical Inventions*, New York: McGraw-Hill Book Company, Inc.

Van der Veer, P. (1998). *Religious Nationalism: Hindus and Muslims in India*, Delhi: Oxford University Press.

Van der Veer, P. and Lehmann, H. (eds). (1999). *Nation and Religion: Perspectives on Europe and Asia*, Princeton, NJ: Princeton University Press.

Van Norden, B. (ed.). (2002a). *Confucius and the Analects: New Essays*, New York: Oxford University Press.

Van Norden, B. (ed.). (2002b). "Introduction," in Van Norden (2002): 3–36.

Van Norden, B. (ed.). (2002c). "Unweaving the 'one thread' of *Analects*," in Bryan Van Norden (2002): 216–236.

Von Reden. (2012). "Money and finance," in Scheidel (2012a): 266–286.

Waley, A. (1939). *Three Ways of Thought in Ancient China*, Garden City, NY: Doubleday Anchor.

Warner, M.; Vanantwerpen, J; Calhoun, C. (eds). (2010). *Varieties of Secularism in a Secular Age*, Cambridge, MA: Harvard University Press.

Weber, M. (1922, 1991). *The Sociology of Religion*, Boston, MA: Beacon Press.

Weber, M. (F. Knight, Trans.). (1923). *General Economic History*, London: George Allen & Unwin Ltd.

Weber, M. (T. Parsons, Trans.) (1958). *The Protestant Ethic and the Spirit of Capitalism*, New York: Charles Scribner's Sons.

Westerlund, D. (ed.). (2009). *Global Pentecostalism: Encounters with Other Religious Traditions*, London: I. B. Tauris.

White, H. (1980) "A heteroskedasticity-consistent covariance matrix and a direct test for heteroskedasticity," Econometrica 48 (4): 817–838.

White Jr., L. (1978). *Medieval Religion and Technology: Collected Essays*, Berkeley, CA: University of California Press.

Whitmarsh, T. (2015). *Battling the Gods: Atheism in the Ancient World*, New York: Alfred A. Knopf.

Wilson, Andrew (2012). "Raw materials and energy," in Scheidel (2012a): 133–155.

Wise, M.; Martin, A. Jr.; Cook, E. (1996). *Dead Sea Scrolls: A New Translation (with Commentary)*, New York: Harper San Francisco.

Wittberg, P. (1994). *The Rise and Fall of Catholic Orders: A Social Movement Perspective*, Albany, NY: The State University of New York Press.

Index